THE KINDNESS
OF STRANGERS

THE KINDNESS OF STRANGERS:
PENNILESS ACROSS AMERICA

MIKE McINTYRE

BERKLEY BOOKS, NEW YORK

THE KINDNESS OF STRANGERS

A Berkley Book / published by arrangement with
the author

PRINTING HISTORY
Berkley trade paperback edition / November 1996

The Putnam Berkley World Wide Web site address is
http://www.berkley.com/berkley

ISBN: 0-425-15455-6

BERKLEY®
Berkley Books are published by The Berkley Publishing Group,
200 Madison Avenue, New York, New York 10016.
BERKLEY and the "B" design
are trademarks belonging to Berkley Publishing Corporation.

PRINTED IN THE UNITED STATES OF AMERICA

10   9   8   7   6   5

THE KINDNESS
OF STRANGERS

ONE

My head throbs from hunger and heat as I wilt on the side of a country road in northern California. The cardboard sign I level at oncoming traffic reads "Eureka," though my latest discovery is that I'm out of water. I don't have two dimes to rub together, let alone a lucky penny. I ate my last meal two nights ago—in a dream.

The summer sun tattooing my face suggests hitchhiking inside a microwave oven. My baseball hat would bring relief, but it stays in my backpack, leaving drivers a clear look at my baby blues. No matter. Nobody stops. And who can fault them? It's 1994. This is America. Land of the free and home of the serial killer.

I stagger around the bend in a futile search for another road that feeds into Highway 101. When I return, someone has taken my place. His dark eyes fix me through strands of greasy, black hair. I don't have the strength to fight, or run.

"You must've just got dropped off," I say, squinting at the stranger. "Where you coming from?"

"Jail."

The man laughs. He doesn't have a tooth in his head.

He says his name is Rudy, and the judge gave him three weeks for unpaid traffic tickets. He says he's heading home to Leggett, about fifty miles north, to check on his gold mine.

"I'm anxious to get back up there," he says. "I just found a big vein supposed to be worth half a million dollars."

Yeah, I know, Rudy's a dreamer. But like they say, without dreams, you got nightmares.

His red day pack is torn and frayed. Papers poke through the busted zipper. I wonder what else is inside.

"Hey, you don't have any food you could spare, do you?" I say. "I haven't eaten in days."

He reaches into his grimy jeans and pulls out two pieces of candy, each wrapped in cellophane.

"It's the only food I got," he says, holding the candy in his palm.

They're frosted gumdrops. One orange, one grape. I eye the sweets as my saliva glands do back flips. I settle on the grape one.

"Go ahead, take 'em both," Rudy says.

I grab the orange one, too.

"Well, I'm gonna walk up the road a bit," he says. "They see two of us here, they won't stop. With two of us, they figure we're gonna pound them into the dirt."

Before he's around the bend, I tear open the wrapper of the orange gumdrop. It's heaven to wedge something between my bellybutton and my tailbone, even if only a lump of sugar. I tell myself I'll save the grape one for later, but I gobble that down, too.

I fish a black felt pen from my pack and lower my sights. I scratch out "Eureka" and write in "Willits." It's only a seventeen-mile ride. But the motoring public blows by me like I'm waving a sign that says "Homicidal Maniac."

I pace circles in the dirt, my knees ready to buckle. If I drop in the road, will somebody stop for me then?

There's a noise behind me and I whirl to see the disheveled figure of Rudy. He's got something in his hand, but it's not candy.

"Hey, I got to thinking up there on the freeway: *He doesn't have any money.*"

Rudy unfolds two one-dollar bills and smoothes them flat against his chest. He irons out every wrinkle, as if the notes were shirt collars bound for church. He extends the money toward me.

I stare at the greenbacks. Two dollars. I know what that will buy. A loaf of bread and a pack of bologna. Or maybe a jar of peanut butter. I won't have to worry about food for three, four days. "In God We Trust," it says. Hallelujah! I'm born again.

"Go on, take it," Rudy says.

I reach for the cash, then pull back.

"I can't," I say. "I'm crossing America without a penny."

Last summer, I drove from my hometown of Tahoe City, California, to New Orleans. I spent much of the trip on U.S. Highway 50. It's called the Loneliest Road in America, and for good reason. I ran ninety across Nevada and could go an hour without seeing another car.

East of Ely, in the middle of the desert, I came upon a young man standing by the roadside. He had his thumb out and held a gas can in his other hand. It was obvious the guy needed help.

I drove right by him.

Someone else will stop for him, I reasoned. Besides, he's not really out of gas. That red can is just a ploy to flag down a car and rob the driver.

I drove on into Utah, however, then Colorado, still thinking about the hitchhiker. Leaving him stranded in the desert didn't bother me as much as how easily I'd reached the decision. I never lifted my foot off the accelerator.

There was a time in this country when you were a jerk if you passed by somebody in need. Now you're a fool for helping. Gangs, drugs, murderers, rapists, thieves, carjackers. Why risk it? I Don't Want to Get Involved has become a national motto.

I flashed on my final destination, New Orleans, the setting for Tennessee Williams's play *A Streetcar Named Desire*. I recalled Blanche's famous line at the end: "Whoever you are—I have always depended on the kindness of strangers."

The kindness of strangers. It sounds so quaint. Does such a trait exist in America anymore?

Closing in on New Orleans, I wondered: Could a person journey coast to coast without any money, relying solely on the goodwill of his fellow Americans? If so, what kind of America would he find? Who would feed him, shelter him, carry him down the road?

The question intrigued me. But I knew it was a question without an answer.

Who would be crazy enough to try such a trip?

"What?" Rudy says. "You can't use two bucks?"

"I appreciate it, but I can't accept money."

Rudy wanders off, shaking his head. I'm not sure I get it either. I set out on this journey three days ago from San Francisco. I'm now actually *west* of where I started. Only three thousand miles to go.

I walked out the door a pilgrim. But today I feel like a refugee from the world of common sense.

TWO

hree weeks earlier.

I'm sitting in my car, parked in a condo complex down the road from my office near San Francisco. It's lunchtime, but the turkey sandwich rests untouched on the passenger seat. I barely notice a doe and her fawn step by the window. It is a golden California day, and I am crying.

I turned thirty-seven this week. I've been a newspaper reporter for a decade. The pay and perks are good. I've traveled all over the world. I live in a nice apartment with a beautiful girlfriend. There are people who love me.

But all of that is little consolation when you know you're a coward.

If I were told I was going to die today, I'd have to say I never took a gamble. I played life too close to the vest. I was never up and I was never down—the perfect shill.

Wiping tears from my eyes, I know it's time to bet or fold. Just this once I want to know what it feels like to shove all my chips in the pot and go for broke.

When I get back to the office, I corner my boss before I lose my nerve.

"I'm a long yo-yo on a short string," I say. "I'm ready to snap."

"Do you need some time?" he says.

"Yeah, all I got left."

I drive up to Lake Tahoe to say good-bye to my family and tell them the logic behind chucking a perfectly good job in the middle of a recession.

It's a spiritual sojourn, I say. I'm making a leap of faith a continent wide. I'll go from the Pacific to the Atlantic without a penny. A cashless journey through the land of the almighty dollar. If I'm offered money, I'll refuse it. If I see a coin in the road, I'll step over it. I'll accept only rides, food, and a place to rest my head. Wait and see, it'll work.

My relatives line up to attack the plan like children going after a piñata.

"I hate being broke and having to scrounge," says my younger brother, Pat, who has struggled financially most of his adult life. "Why would you want to deliberately put yourself in that position?"

"You'll get rousted by the cops," says my dad.

"We'll see how far he gets," says my stepmother.

And this encouraging note from my grandma: "You're going to get *raped* out there."

My final destination is Cape Fear, North Carolina, chosen as a symbol for all the fears I know I'll have to conquer if I'm to go the distance. If I make it to Cape Fear, it will be as a different man from the one who starts the journey.

I'm afraid.

I've been afraid my whole life.

I was born scared.

I grew up afraid of the baby-sitter, the mailman, the birds in the trees, the next-door neighbors' cat.

I'm afraid of the dark. I'm afraid of the ocean. I'm afraid of flying.

I'm afraid of the city and I'm afraid of the wilderness. I'm afraid of crowds and I'm afraid to be alone. I'm afraid of failure and I'm afraid of success.

I'm afraid of fire, lightning, earthquakes.

I'm afraid of snakes. I'm afraid of bats. I'm afraid of bears.

I'm afraid of spontaneous human combustion.

I'm afraid of losing an arm. I'm afraid of losing a leg. I'm afraid of losing my mind.

Yes, and I'm afraid of dying, too. But what really scares the hell out of me is living.

I'm afraid.

I rise early the morning of September 6 and scan the paper. The O. J. Simpson murder trial is the top story. Oliver Stone's movie *Natural Born Killers* is number one at the box office. A third body has been found shot to death on Interstate 80. And two men from the Midwest are on a cross-country killing spree.

I've got great timing.

"Do you think I'll make it?" I ask my girlfriend Anne for the millionth time.

"Yes, I really do," she says.

We met two years ago in Guatemala. I was living in a cabin on the side of a mountain, writing. She had come down after college to learn Spanish. We quickly decided to marry, then canceled after the invitations were ordered. Despite our second thoughts, the relationship has survived and grown stronger. We later moved to Budapest, Hungary, to work for an English-language newspaper. Now San Francisco. We've been apart before, but we both know this time is different.

Anne doesn't delay the inevitable. She hugs me and leaves for work. Before closing the door, she smiles bravely through tears. She has never looked more beautiful. I hear the soft click of her heels crossing the tile floor below. Then the pound of the lobby door swinging shut.

I shave with more care than usual, then shower, letting the hot water run down my body long after I'm clean. I dress slowly. As I pull on my socks and hiking boots, I'm aware of the numbers flipping on my clock radio. I feel like I'm preparing for my execution rather than the adventure of a lifetime. I half expect a warden to appear in my bedroom doorway and say, "It's time."

For my last meal, I walk to Mel's Diner over on Lombard and order the Elvis Scramble. Elvis died on my birthday, and this breakfast seems served up by fate. I don't have an appetite, but when the waitress sets the plate of chorizo, eggs, and refried beans before me, I eat every bite.

Back at my apartment, I write a check to Anne for two months' rent, plus extra for the bills. I hoist the pack my brother lent me onto my back. It weighs about fifty pounds. Funny that a pack without food or cooking utensils can be so heavy. I may starve, but at least my corpse will be clad in clean underwear.

I take a last look around my home, then gently close the door. I slide the key back under. Ready or not.

Outside, I see two women in BMWs arrive simultaneously at the last parking space on the street. Neither will budge. One lays on the horn and won't let up. The other screams, "Fucking bitch!" I walk on, happy in knowing I'm not the only idiot in the village.

I've walked down this street hundreds of times, but today it feels new. I pass the Chinese laundry that overstarches my shirts for ninety-nine cents, the trendy cafe that charges me a buck-fifty for a cup of designer coffee, the movie theater where Hollywood mugs me for seven dollars. The marquee reads: CLEAR AND PRESENT DANGER.

I reach the end of the block, then turn back. I forgot something. My bank is on the corner. A bum and his shopping cart are parked in front. I drop my last three dollars and sixty-eight cents in his Styrofoam cup and head for the Golden Gate Bridge.

THREE

Fog glides through the twin towers of the Golden Gate Bridge like a spirit. My head spins as I lean over the rail and watch a ball of spit hit the water. I look back at the city I'm leaving and see my neighborhood. *It's not too late to change your mind,* I tell myself. *Yes, it is,* replies an inner voice.

The walkway is thick with tourists. I reach back out of reflex to check for my wallet. For the first time in memory, there is only the feel of a denim pocket flat against my ass.

I make the visitor center parking lot on the other side of the bridge and drop my pack near the freeway on ramp. My plan is to travel through rural America, sticking to two-lane roads. It will be more interesting, I figure, and safer. But I must first get out of the Bay Area, and that means heading north on an eight-laner.

Except for a few local rides in high school and college, I've never been a hitchhiker. I know the baggage that mode of transportation carries. I won't thumb rides on this trip. I'll write signs indicating where I want to go. It's a subtle difference, but I like to think of what I'm doing as carpooling.

I get the first sign from my pack and display it to vehicles pulling back onto Highway 101. My destination: "America."

Drivers mouth the word through windshields, then smile with recognition. Tour bus riders laugh and nudge fellow passengers. One man in a car with Tennessee plates hoots halfway to Memphis. I'm glad my sign is getting kudos, but I'd prefer a lift.

Three women ride by on bicycles. "It's a bit vague," one says. "I'm keeping my options open," I call back.

A young man with a serious look wanders up and stares. He speaks with a German accent. "Where is this 'America'?"

Indeed.

"Hop in, partner."

The man looks to be in his fifties, his beer belly wedged behind the wheel of an American beater a block long. Girlie tattoos cover his arms. Is he a kind stranger, or just kind of strange? I hope for the best and slide in.

"You hear about them two guys killing their way 'cross the country?" he says.

"No," I lie, nervous about this fellow's choice for an ice-breaker.

"One's twenty-three and the other's sixteen. They steal a car, kill the people, and when it runs out of gas, they take another car and kill again." He pulls the lighter from the dash and holds it to the end of a cigarette. "It's a sad world. I'm kinda glad my time is almost up. It's gonna get worse before it gets better."

His name's Art, and he's on his way home to Santa Rosa, an hour up the road. He had his eyes checked this morning in the city and had to pull over because his pupils were dilated. He blinks and squints, trying to keep his land yacht between the white lines. We pass my old office. No regrets, yet.

Art was career Navy, then dumped his last dollar into a sea-food restaurant. He went bust after opening another. His wife took off when her mother died and left her some money. That was six years ago. Art's not sure where she is. He's lost track of the kids, too. These days, he shares an apartment with a waiter and tends bar when he can. He hasn't worked in eight months.

"They won't hire anyone over fifty," he says.

He dials in a classic rock station. Led Zeppelin's "What Is and What Should Never Be" blares through cracked speakers. The cloth ceiling lining falls on my head.

"Do you think I'm crazy, Art?" I say, after telling him my story.

"Hell, no!" he yells, like he's angry. "I envy you!"

Art drops me at a gas station at his exit.

"Hell," he says, "maybe you'll find Utopia out there and won't want to come back."

I consult the AAA road atlas I packed. Ukiah is another sixty miles north. A book I read lists it as one of the one hundred best towns in America. I wonder if "best" relates to "kind" as I write "Ukiah" on a sheet of yellow paper and tape it to my piece of cardboard.

A driver stops on the on ramp. "I'm only going to Healdsburg," he says through the passenger window, "but that'll get you fifteen miles closer to Ukiah."

I cram my pack into the backseat of his tiny import. The guy says he's going to see a friend in Healdsburg. He's a large man, with a rough complexion and an unnatural orange tint to his hair. I try to make eye contact, but he doesn't look at me. He shifts into fifth, and I tense as his hand brushes my leg.

"You really should see the Russian River," he says. "I ought to show you my favorite place."

I tell him I was at the Russian River a couple of months ago—with my girlfriend. He drops the subject.

The man drives by the first of two exits for Healdsburg.

"Where are you turning off?" I say.

"Oh, I guess I should drop you downtown. I'll take you back. I've got time."

He takes the second exit. My gut tells me to get out here, but I know the odds of catching a ride are better at the on ramp in town. We cross the overpass and head south.

We coast down the off ramp at the central exit. Healdsburg is left under the freeway. The man rolls through the stop sign and continues straight.

Before I can protest, he says, "I'll show you the river in case you get stuck here and want a place to camp."

He rounds a blind curve. A yellow sign warns, "Not a Through Road." There's a gravel pit on the left, fields to the right. I feel all sense of control seep out of me. For the first time in my life, I think I know what it's like to be a woman. The man drives on.

The road dead-ends at the river. The man turns the car around, then cuts the engine. A van is parked to my right, next to an embankment. I can't see inside the tinted windows. I watch the man out of the corner of my eye and wait for his buddy to emerge from the van with a knife, or worse.

"This is a good place to get your dick sucked," the man says.

The remark ricochets off the windshield, then hangs in the air like some kind of verbal graffiti. Blood pounds against my eardrums. The day outside looks like a movie. If I can only stand in the sun, the rest of this might vanish. My fingers grip the door handle, but I can't bring myself to open it. I can't even breathe.

Finally, the white noise is broken by the sound of the engine. We're moving again. The man says something about the trees, how good they smell. Yes, I agree, inhaling deeply.

He drops me by the freeway and asks how long I plan to be on the road. I tell him about two months.

"Well, have a good trip."

I'm too unnerved to get in another stranger's car today, so I let my shaky legs carry me into town. There's a farmers' market in the city parking lot. Free samples, I figure. I make several passes down the line of produce stands, smiling and nodding at the vendors, but nobody shoves food in my face.

A clerk at the Chamber of Commerce hands me a list of lodging options in the area. Accommodations fall in the categories of "expensive," "moderate," and "budget." For some reason, there's no category called "free." The sheet gives the name and address of a private campground, however, and I ask for directions.

I walk the six miles to the campground, not knowing if the owner will let me spend the night. The country road winds through the Alexander Valley, part of Sonoma County's famed wine region. Neat rows of grapevines stretch out to the mountains. A sagging wire fence is all that keeps me from the clusters of plump, juicy fruit. It's been eight hours since the Elvis Scramble, but I'm not yet desperate enough to commit trespassing and petty theft. I walk on, my stomach cursing my conscience.

A sign at the campground entrance tells me a campsite costs five dollars. Another sign hanging from the nearby trailer tells me the man to see about a deep discount is named Chief. I knock on the aluminum siding. A large Indian appears in the doorway. Chief, I presume.

"I'm Mike McIntyre. I wonder if I could stay here, and I'll do some work for you in return."

Chief gives me a long glance from behind the screen door. "For how long?"

"Just for tonight."

"Pick yourself out a spot."

I say thanks and ask what he needs done.

"I can't think of anything right at the moment. Go ahead and spend the night."

The campground sits on what was once a Wappo Indian reservation. "Everyone left to go work for the white man, and the government took it away from us," Chief says. Now he works for the white man who bought his boyhood home from the government. He's petitioning Congress to return the land to his tribe.

He was a big city cop before he tired of the politics and corruption and turned in his badge. His old lieutenant, now with the police department in another city, wants Chief to quit the campground and join the force. But Chief won't hear it.

"I like it out here," he says. "When I wanna take a piss, I just walk outside and take one. You can't piss in the city."

It's the day after Labor Day weekend, so the campground is mostly empty. I unroll my sleeping bag beneath an oak tree. I didn't bring a tent. My lack of shelter might be the excuse wary strangers need to invite me into their homes. Especially when it rains.

I sit on the picnic table and write in my journal. I look up to see the empty barbecue taunting me. A man a few sites over grills chicken. The family across the path cooks steaks. Long after nightfall, I sit in the dark, listening to the belches and sighs of happy campers. Then I go to bed hungry for the first time since I was a kid.

The next day, a trucker carries me to the Ukiah exit. I walk the mile from the freeway into town, passing every fast food chain in existence. I get the shakes when I wait too long between meals. But I'm all shook out. What's left is a headache that could split an atom.

I study the downtown restaurants like a robber casing banks. I know my next move. But where? When? I circle the block three times. When I screw up enough courage, I slip through a doorway. Inside, I find a cafe still under construction. Stupid! I stammer my rehearsed offer to work for food, just the same. "Sorry," the owner says. Her look tells me that in a span of twenty-four hours, I've turned into one pathetic dude.

A woman and two men chat on the sidewalk. The woman glances over the shoulder of one of the guys and flashes me a smile. She looks like a girl I went to high school with twenty years ago. She sat behind me in biology class, blowing lightly on my neck and whispering, "I love you." Or perhaps it was the overhead fan, and her muttering, "I loathe school."

I turn the corner and imagine her chasing after me, gushing, "Is that really you?" I tell her it is, and everything else. She must get back to work, but I absolutely can't leave town until we've caught up. She hands me her house key and jots down her address. "The refrigerator's full," she says. "Help yourself to anything."

I think I'm entering the early stages of dementia.

I wander the streets and end up in the city park. Three bums occupy the bench near the drinking fountain. They swig from a jug of red wine as an Elvis Presley tape plays on their boombox. "Dave! Dave! Dave!" one of them bellows. "I'm fucking drunk! Dave!" The one on the end leans over and vomits to "Don't Be Cruel."

I scan the park and zoom in on three women eating sack lunches. I stake out a spot between them and the garbage can. On closer look, I see that one of them eats from plastic tableware. That means leftovers, not trash. Another one is fat. She didn't get that way counting calories. Sure enough, she gobbles every bite, then devours a candy bar. The third one, though, looks promising. She's skinny. There's half a sandwich still in her hand, and she's definitely slowing down. From this angle, it appears to be avocado and Jack, with sprouts, on a fresh croissant. It's got my name on it, I know it. It won't be in the can long enough to be called garbage. But wait! She's getting a second wind. She polishes off the whole thing. As a final insult, she licks her fingers.

Before I left San Francisco, my good friend Bruce gave me nine energy bars for the trip. I put them in the bottom of my pack, next to my winter gloves. My goal was for all nine snacks to arrive with me at Cape Fear. That would mean an abundance of kind strangers. But here it is only day two, and I'm ripping open the wrapper of a wild berry energy bar. It tastes like sawdust. It tastes great. I swallow the last bite, then slump against my pack in defeat.

I sense that my luck isn't about to change here, so I head for the highway, running the gauntlet of fast food restaurants. A shabby fellow overtakes me on the sidewalk and ducks into the shrubs bordering a shopping mall parking lot. He reaches down and comes up with something yellow in each hand. My eyes bulge. I know what they are, but I can't quite believe it.

"What are those?"

"Pears!" the man says.

"They okay to eat?" I ask excitedly, wading into the bushes.

"They're good! This is the Pear Tree Shopping Center." He points to a sign overhead. And so it is.

The ground is covered with ripe pears. I rinse one off with my water bottle and bite into the fruit. Sweet, sticky juice dribbles down my chin. Incredible! I finish off the pear and eat another, and another. I store a few more ripe ones in my pack for later, plus a firm one that should be ready to eat in a couple of days.

A balding schoolteacher drives me to Lake Mendocino, nine miles north of Ukiah. Bob hitched around the country in the sixties, so this ride is a trip down memory lane for him.

"I admire you for what you're doing," he says. "Americans are too comfortable. We forget. It's humbling to know that all you have is in that backpack."

I wait for Bob to invite me to stay at his place tonight, but he doesn't. Instead, he hands me a small bag of sunflower seeds that's already been opened. "There's your dinner," he says, chuckling. When I hop down from the pickup, I behold the seeds and wonder: *Is the bag half empty, or half full?*

The visitor center in Ukiah told me there was free camping at the lake. But when I reach the registration booth at the campground run by the federal government, the woman inside says, "That'll be twelve dollars, please." I tell her there must be a mistake. No mistake, she tells me. Free camping was phased out in the eighties.

The sun is setting. I don't want to hitchhike in the dark. There's nowhere to go, anyway. I ask the woman if I could pick up trash in return for a campsite. She radios the ranger. I repeat my request to Ranger Laura when she arrives in her truck. She doubts it, she says, but she'll run it by her supervisor. She radios him, and he says he's got to check with his boss. I see my tax dollars hard at work. Finally, word comes back from on high. "You've got a deal," Ranger Laura says, handing me a plastic bag.

I can't believe the crap people leave behind for their fellow campers. My bag soon swells with gum wrappers, plastic tableware, beer cans, soiled toilet paper, spent condoms.

Ranger Laura pulls up forty-five minutes later. "I think that's enough, Mike."

I toss the trash in the back of her pickup.

"Have a good night," she says. Then: "Do you have food and everything?"

"Actually, no."

"So you're just relying on the kindness of strangers?"

"Exactly."

She holds a bag of carrots out to me. I take two. They look like bars of gold.

The sunflower seeds and carrots don't satisfy. I wake the next day hungry enough to swallow my tongue. My hip is sore from the rocks pushing up through my thin sleeping pad. My neck has more knots than a tree.

I get to my feet and feel light enough to blow away. The surging ache in my head threatens to pop my eyes from their sockets. The muscles in my jaw clench involuntarily.

I hike the two miles back out to the freeway on ramp. The sun is a monster. A helicopter circles above the lake. It's been up there all morning. After a while, I see the county coroner's wagon drive by, and I know somebody's summer vacation has been cut short. I almost envy him. I really do.

Four hours pass. No one looks tempted to stop. The idea that has been lurking in the wings now takes center stage in my fevered mind and delivers its impassioned, one-word soliloquy: *Quit.*

I decide to hoof it back to town. I'll call Anne at work and have her wire me money. I'll hop a Greyhound back to the city.

Tonight, I'll be parked in my couch, watching "Jeopardy," a beer in my hand. I'll deal with the shame on a full stomach and a good night's sleep.

Then I hear my stepmother's voice: *We'll see how far he gets.*

I flush with embarrassment and self-loathing. It's true. I'm a quitter.

I've been a quitter all my life. I quit Little League. I quit the Boy Scouts. I quit so many colleges, I can't remember them. I quit a construction job in Saudi Arabia after six months. I quit the Navy's Officer Candidate School after two weeks. I quit my position as a congressional staffer after one day. I've quit many a good woman. And if there were a club for quitters, I'd quit that, too.

We'll see how far he gets.

It's funny, the places we finally decide to make a stand. Take here, for example. A freeway on ramp in northern California. Why here? Why now? This journey has yet to make sense. It may never make sense. But one thing's for certain: If I turn back, I'm no better than road kill. The mileposts may only mark a fool's progress, but I intend to see Cape Fear, or die trying. I can't quit. I simply can't quit this trip.

And I know I have no right to ask, but I beg you, America, please don't quit me.

FOUR

A Toyota pickup with a camper shell pulls over, and I have to squint to make sure it's not a mirage. I hoist my pack onto one shoulder and will my legs to carry me swiftly to the truck before the driver changes his mind. The cab is littered with McDonald's bags, burger wrappers, coffee cups, stir sticks, and hash brown containers. The guy, Randy is his name, was down near Los Angeles, checking on some property in the desert. He's heading home to Humboldt County.

"I've got a small nursery up there," says Randy, who has red hair and a wispy mustache. "I make seventy-five dollars a week off it at the farmers' market. My wife's got a good job. I used to grow pot, but I got busted, so I can't do that anymore."

Humboldt County is famous for two things: giant redwood trees and some of the finest marijuana to have ever graced a bong. The growers were mostly hippies, content to make a quiet living. Then pot hit six thousand dollars a pound, and everybody got in on the act, even redneck ranchers and grandmothers. A cult of greed descended on a region long known for its counter-culture values. Volkswagen buses were traded in for Jeep Cherokees. Grocers openly sold the number one cash crop at checkout stands. The government answered with Operation Green Sweep, a crackdown with whirlybirds, paramilitary troops, and German shepherds. A neighbor snitched on Randy. He got ninety days, plus probation. But the feds never found the fifty grand buried on his land.

"I didn't even have to do my time," he says. "I got a work furlough 'cause I showed the court the business license for my nursery. They thought I had a regular job, like everybody else. They didn't even come out and check. They're so stupid."

The freeway turns into a two-lane highway and winds through a river canyon. Sunlight radiates through tree limbs and glints off the hood. The air smells clean. I tell Randy how great it is up here.

"No, it's not!" he snaps. "It's fucked up! Politicians have ruined it. Everybody used to grow pot, but pot's linked to hippies, and politicians hate hippies. One of every seven people in prison is in for pot. They don't care if it's less harmful than tobacco and alcohol. They don't care if it's the best medicine known to man. They don't care if it can make good clothing. This country's so fucked up. They know there's a revolution coming, so they gotta keep all the young people locked up. If there's a club for revolutionaries, I'm gonna join.'' He catches his breath. ''I'm an angry man, I guess you can tell.''

He pulls off at the McDonald's in a small lumber town, and my stomach growls with anticipation. But at the drive-thru intercom, Randy barks, ''Gimme a large vanilla milkshake,'' and reaches for his wallet. There's a long, sad moment before he turns to me and says, ''Do you want something? Do you want a hamburger?'' I say, great, and sit a little higher in the seat. Randy leans over to the squawk box and says, ''And gimme two cheeseburgers and a glass of water.''

Randy sets the bag of burgers on the seat between us and pulls back onto the highway. The bag just sits there, like a third passenger. I know one of those burgers is mine, but I don't want to be rude. Finally, Randy reaches in and tosses a burger on my lap. ''There you go,'' he says. ''It isn't much.''

Oh, but it is. At long last, meat! I take small bites and chew long after the food has been broken down into mush. Randy harps more on the government. I nod a lot, and say ''yeah'' and ''hmm'' and ''it's insane.'' But I'm not hearing much. I'm transfixed by the burger wrapper in my hands. I study the yellow and red sheet of paper, carefully reading every word of it, as if it were literature.

We reach Garberville, in southern Humboldt, late in the afternoon. Randy has to go west, so he stops to let me out. Dark clouds roll over the ridge. I know what's coming.

''Does your nursery have a roof on it?''

''Yeah,'' Randy says cautiously.

''Do you think I could crash there tonight?''

''It's way out in the woods.''

''How far?''

''Twenty-six, twenty-seven miles.''

I take that as a ''no'' and thank Randy for the burger and the ride. I get out of the truck and almost step in a cardboard box sitting in the dirt. It's funny how quickly perceptions can change. Three days ago, I would have said the box at my feet contained

spoiled produce. Now, all I see is food. Sure, that rotten tomato
and shriveled celery aren't fit for pigs. But the head of cauliflower looks like it might be edible—after some salvage work. I
carry the vegetable to a gas station and hose off an army of ants.
The black fungus won't wash away, though, so I crack open the
head and eat it inside out. All in all, a tasty snack.

Things are looking up.

I ask a local merchant if there's a safe place I can lay out my
sleeping bag tonight. He tells me the nearby Humboldt Redwood
State Park has 155,000 acres. "It's probably illegal, though," he
adds.

"Yeah, but is it safe? I mean, are there wild animals out
there?"

"We have some bears, and there are some mountain lions."

Enough said.

I walk down the main drag. A woman with hairy legs appears
from behind my pack and says, "Hi, do you need any help finding anything?"

I ask if she knows a spot to camp.

She says, "The best thing is to make friends with somebody."
I'm about to say, "Do you want to be my friend?" but she skips
ahead. "I'm in a hurry now," she calls back. "I've got to coach
a soccer game, but I'll look for you later." I know that's the last
I'll see of her.

It hasn't rained since spring, but the sky doesn't look like it
has forgotten how. I spot an outdoor restaurant with covered
picnic tables and figure I can sit out there tonight after it closes.
At least I'd stay dry. I walk on, hoping for something better.

I hit the edge of town and turn back. A man stops me. He's
in his fifties, wearing jeans and a baseball cap that reads, "Beef."

"You look like you need some directions."

"No, not really. I'm just kind of wandering."

"How far you wandering?"

"All the way to the Atlantic Ocean," I say. Then I add, "Without a penny."

A smile fills his face. "Say no more. Follow me."

Next thing I know, I'm standing in the studio of the local radio station, KMUD. The man, Roger, is a rancher who hosts a talk show twice a month called "Life in the Country." He's in a bind. One of tonight's guests has canceled. Could I pinch hit? I tell Roger I'm always happy to do my part for public radio.

"I'm gonna have you on the air with a local fire fighter who's just back from fighting two fires in the Tahoe National Forest," he says. "We'll have sort of an over-the-back-fence talk."

I'm still reeling from the sudden turn of events when I see what appears to be a man dressed as a woman stroll across the parking lot and enter the studio. His long blond hair is held in place by a white bow, and he's wearing a pink tank top and red lipstick. Beard stubble pokes through caked makeup. What really gives him away are his arms. They're the size of howitzers. I'm six-foot-four, and we stand eye to eye. He grips my hand and pumps it hard. He says his name is Diana. He's tonight's other guest.

"Roger, I'd like to keep the conversation more on fire fighting," Diana says, "rather than the cowboy logger turned cowgirl logger."

"Okey-dokey."

In the few minutes before we go on the air, I learn that Diana used to be called Dennis, and he's not what he seems. He really is a she. The sex change—"gender reassignment," in the parlance of transsexuals—was done years ago. All that remains is some electrolysis. Diana tells me that's the worst part, but I can't imagine anything more painful than losing the family jewels.

The three of us squeeze into the tiny sound booth. As Roger greets his listeners, I steal glances at Diana. I've never met a transsexual, not that I know of, anyway. Fatigue, anxiety, and hunger combine with the surrealism of the moment to leave me giddy. I fear I may laugh like a hyena. I consider gagging myself with a handful of foam from the soundproof wall. But Roger asks the first question, and I settle down. Though penniless, I am, after all, a professional.

Roger proves an able interviewer. He pulls my whole story from me, and then some. Callers ask about my travels to thirty-five countries, most of them as a journalist. I tell them how I went skiing in Bosnia during the war. How I witnessed the return of the condor to the Colombian Andes. How I found Romanian orphans living in the sewers of Bucharest. I hear myself talking and think, *How could you quit such a fascinating job?* But one thing I've always found frustrating about being a reporter: You're never able to fully enter the world of your subjects. When your notepad fills up, they go back to their lives, and you return to your hotel to order room service and watch TV. On this trek, there won't be an expense account standing between me and a fuller version of the truth.

By the end of the show, KMUD listeners have concluded that my trip is nothing short of a pilgrimage, a spiritual journey. I'm heartened by their enthusiasm, as I sometimes think of this adventure in similar terms. Then again, it's an easy audience. This is Humboldt County, where welfare recipients are called gurus. I'll have to wait to see how my enlightened poverty trip plays in Peoria.

Diana hasn't said boo. With Roger's encouragement, I've hogged the whole hour. It's too bad. There's a lot I'd like to have learned about her.

So it's a pleasant surprise when Garberville's only transsexual fire fighter leans over and says, "Mike, if you don't have any other plans, I'd like to take you to dinner."

We go to an Italian-Mexican restaurant where a football game plays on a giant video screen. Roger and the producer, Mitch, join us at the table. There's also Linda, from nearby Redway, and her eight-year-old daughter, Iona. Linda heard me on the radio and rushed to town to buy me dinner. Now that Diana's springing, Linda insists I spend the night at her house. I happily accept, with one regret: I'll never know how Diana intended our evening to end.

I'm glad to see I still know how to read a menu. I order lasagna, garlic bread, and the salad bar. That ache camped out in my head the last three days will soon be folding its tent.

In her previous life as a man, Diana was known as a fearless fire fighter and one of the region's top loggers. As a woman, not much has changed.

"I dropped a tree the other day that was seven-foot-four at the butt," she says. "I'm still a redneck, I'm just a little different now."

Diana's taco salad arrives, and she takes a bite, smearing her red lipstick. "I've always been maternal. My crew called me Mom, even before I was a woman."

Linda asks how her family reacted to her sex change. Diana's relatives have raised cattle in the area for several generations.

"My dad said it'd be easier if I was dead," she says softly. "With ranchers, you always want to breed up. You want your next calf to be better than the last. He looked at me and figured that I was a throwback."

The table falls silent.

"People come up to me now and say, 'Hey, I like to wear dresses sometimes.' And I say, '*Eeoo*, how weird.' They think I'm gay. I'm not. I've known I was this way since I was four. The thing is, when you go through your inner change, I can't see it. When I go through my change, it's there for everybody to see."

Diana spent last winter in the San Francisco area, in group counseling with other recent transsexuals. She worked a construction job to pay the bills. One day, she was remodeling the kitchen of a wealthy family's house. The couple saw how well she got along with their kids and invited her to move in as the nanny. She became the auntie for the whole upper-crust block, a real-life Mrs. Doubtfire, and no one was ever the wiser, not even her employers. On nights off, she went out with her six-foot-eight boyfriend.

"I could wear heels everywhere," she says.

We all erupt with laughter.

The check arrives, and Diana snaps it up with her sausage fingers. I've planned this journey in my mind for a year, but I never came close to imagining who would be buying my first dinner.

I look at Diana and think, *Kindness is strange, but never long a stranger.*

FIVE

I load my pack into Linda's minivan, and we head for her house. She stops at the supermarket in Redway and asks if I want anything. I'm too shy to say, so she fills a plastic bag with trail mix. Perfect. At the checkout, we see Diana come in and grab a cart. She waves. The whole scene now seems normal.

Linda is forty-two and twice divorced. Besides Iona, she has two other daughters: Fauna, aged ten, and Sequoia, sixteen. Iona and Fauna split time between Linda and their father, who lives in the same neighborhood. They attend one of Humboldt's many self-styled alternative schools. Sequoia, who studies dance, lives with Linda's first husband, in Santa Cruz. Linda and her second ex founded two hugely successful mail-order record companies, specializing in children's and world music. They've just been bought out by a Hollywood entertainment conglomerate. Linda is a rich hippie.

She grew up poor in San Francisco, the only child of an Irish merchant seaman and a Swedish maid. Her mother was an alcoholic who died in an insane asylum. When Linda last saw her, she was strapped in a straitjacket, her head shaved for electro-shock therapy. She swore at Linda in Swedish, blaming her daughter for her wretched life.

Ashamed of her background, Linda compensated by entering the glamorous world of high fashion. She became the buyer for an upscale San Francisco department store. A blond woman with stunning Scandinavian features, she was squired about town by wealthy men. When that lifestyle rang hollow, Linda dropped out to study herbal medicine. She arrived in Redway in the seventies, part of the second back-to-earth wave of hippies to invade Humboldt County. She delved into yoga, astrology, Eastern religions, quantum physics, and Indian mysticism. She set about repairing her soul.

Linda owns one of the area's original hippie mansions, a two-story octagonal structure built with scraps of redwood left behind by logging companies. A skylight in the shape of a pyramid crowns the roof. The house is circled by wooden decks. The trees are so close you can reach out and touch them. It is a most unconventional home. Forty African drums fill a corner of the living room. There is no TV, no curtains in the windows, and the girls call their mother Linda.

After the girls have gone to bed, I sit with Linda on a wicker sofa, gazing out the picture window into the dark forest. The house is still. Linda says she is inspired by my journey. After a decade as a cynical journalist, I've developed a pretty accurate bullshit meter. Nothing registers on it now. Linda seems to possess an inner calm, an unshakable sense of her place in the universe. I feel like a sham in comparison. I want what she has. I confess to her that I am not brave and wise. I'm a frightened boy in the body of a man. I'm afraid of the dark, the wind in the trees, the animals in the forest.

Linda smiles kindly. "When I first came here, I lived in a cabin I found out I shared with raccoons and skunks and bats. They'd all nestled away in there. I snipped pot for a living, ten dollars an hour. I did it at night by lantern. The bats swooped all around me, and I worried. But I learned that they weren't going to hurt me. They'd fly past and swirl around in these same patterns. After a while, I saw that they recognized me. They knew who I was.

"An Indian taught me something I'll never forget. He said, 'We don't have a word for loneliness in my language.' I said, 'Why, because you're always surrounded by uncles and aunts and grandparents?' He said, 'No. It's because we think of nature as our kin, so we are never alone.'

"I thought, 'How great. When you realize that the bears and the bats and the trees are all your relatives, you can never be lonely.' "

Linda looks at me and says in a solemn tone, "Reverence. You can't repair your soul until you have reverence. Don't be afraid of the dark, Mike. Don't be afraid of nature."

We talk late into the night, then Linda shows me to the guest room. A bed! With flannel sheets, no less. I drift toward sleep, feeling safe and warm and profoundly grateful. Diana bought me dinner, but Linda gave me food for thought. And sometimes that's the best meal of all.

In the morning I shave and shower, washing my hair with Linda's Irish moss shampoo. The shower is made of stone and stands in a corner of the greenhouse, butting up against a wall of glass. I bathe, naked to the world, or at least to my cousins, the redwoods.

Linda fixes French toast, with honey in the batter, as I eat sliced cantaloupe and sip grapefruit juice. Fauna and Iona turn cartwheels across the hardwood floor. I've never been a comfortable guest, even in good friends' houses. But I feel totally at ease in this stranger's home. My stomach churns, but not from hunger. I must soon leave, and I know the uncertainty of the road is about to resume.

Linda hands me the bag of trail mix, along with a mutzu apple and two lemon zucchinis from her organic garden. The load adds a good seven pounds to my pack, but it's weight I'll gladly carry.

She and the girls drive me back down to the highway in Garberville. I thank Linda and tell her that if the rest of my trip goes a tenth as well as it has here, it will be a great journey.

"Well, if you settle for ten percent, that's what you'll get," she says. "On your journey, don't compromise your vision. You're on a vision quest. You're an archetype. You represent middle America, who just got fed up and wants to discover the real America. Maybe America is now spelled with a small *a,* and you're out trying to find the capital-*A* America."

Linda leans over and hugs me, and gives my cheek a kiss. I say good-bye to the girls and step out of the van. I'm standing in the same spot where I found the cauliflower yesterday.

"Remember," Linda says through the open window, "don't compromise your vision."

SIX

I compromise my vision in Arcata, California.

A guy with a goatee offers me shelter and I quickly accept. His name's Stitch, and he's come to this coastal college town to play a gig with a band called Freeland. He says I can crash with him at the apartment of a friend of a friend of the lead guitarist's. I stand through four hours of jazz-blues-funk, applauding wildly at Stitch's ponderous bass solos. After the last set, he lingers with a pair of Freeland groupies. I hover at the edge. Stitch doesn't know me now, and who can blame him? I wander off to sleep in the city park, just inside the tree line, too scared to go any further into the woods. The sweeping headlights of passing cars keep me up most of the night. Serves me right.

At dawn, I walk out to Highway 299. I'm finally aimed east. A man of about fifty, with baggy ethnic pants and a drum the shape of a TV picture tube, walks up and introduces himself as

Brother Tom. He hitchhiked his way through the sixties and seventies, but now restores houses and cares for his two teenaged
daughters. He's returning to his roots this weekend, thumbing to
a music festival in the mountains. As car after car ignore my sign
and his thumb, Brother Tom lays out the Zen of hitchhiking.

"See all those cars passing you? Don't worry about them.
They're not your ride. Your ride's comin'."

My ride turns out to be a small camper truck. The driver hops
out to open the back, and Brother Tom gives her a hug. "Mike,
I want you to meet my beautiful sister Mo." She's twenty, in
cutoffs, with long brown hair and ample breasts barely contained
by her bikini top, and from the way Brother Tom holds her, I'd
say they weren't siblings.

Mo's an engineering student at the college in Arcata, but this
semester she's working and living on an organic farm up the
road. She should be in the fields this morning, but Brother Tom
talks her into catching the concert with him. We stop by the farm,
so Mo can get her sleeping bag. She asks if the rules of my
journey permit me to accept food. No, I tell her, I'm a breathar-
ian. She sees I'm kidding and fills a paper sack with organic
tomatoes, zucchini, and melons.

I lay in the back of the truck and talk to Mo and Brother Tom
through the sliding window. Mo says as long as she's skipping
work, she'd like to climb Mt. Shasta. But that's more than fourteen thousand feet of mountain, and Brother Tom's wearing slip-
pers. A bit farther on, Mo decides what she really wants to do
is go see a friend up in Ashland, Oregon. Brother Tom takes a
pass; he can't miss the all-percussion group that kicks off at
midnight. I wish Mo would ask me.

She looks at me in the rearview mirror. "You're welcome to
come with me," she says, smiling.

"That'd be great, if you don't think I'd drag you down."

Brother Tom says, "Mike, you're not dragging anything.
Maybe you were, but you're in an up-tempo mode now." He

bangs on his drum and adds, "This is a most harmonious harmony we're having here."

"I'd love the company," Mo says. "Then tomorrow you can look at your map and see which way you'll go across Oregon."

We drop Brother Tom in Weaverville, and drive north on Highway 3. The road winds for two hours through the sawtooth peaks of the Trinity Alps and deposits us in Yreka, just south of the Oregon border. Mo shares her tofu and pita bread with me. I've never had tofu, and I don't know if I ever will again, but right now it tastes swell.

Rain greets us at the state line. This would unnerve me if I didn't have a place lined up for the night. But I'm staying with Mo and her friend, so it can rain cats and dogs and elephants, for all I care. How wonderful, I think, to come penniless into a strange town on a stormy night and be free of anxiety. Mo's friend is a cook. Maybe we'll drop by his restaurant for a meal on the house. Maybe there will be a few beers in the deal. Then I hear Mo's voice interrupting my reverie.

"I'll probably have to wing it like you tonight," she says. "I'll want to visit with Matt, but he's got a small place, and I know his girlfriend won't want me to stay over."

My heart races. This can't be happening. Not two nights in a row. But it is. Mo's parking in downtown Ashland. She's opening the back to her camper. I'm grabbing my pack and my bag of vegetables. It's pouring. The butterflies in my stomach feel like pigeons.

"Stay dry," Mo says.

I nod and swallow hard.

Ashland is renowned for its annual Shakespeare festival, drawing tourists from around the world. Years ago, I was the theater columnist for the *Washington Post*. I always dreamed of going to Ashland. Now that I'm here, I can't even buy a playbill.

A woman with a teardrop tattoo under her right eye tells me there's a free meal in the park. I follow her to a gazebo, where

Ashland's homeless have gathered to feast on barbecued chicken, burgers, and vegetarian egg rolls. They are mostly a band of futon-hopping hippie urchins, who live on faith and psychedelics.

I talk to a guy my age named Sumi. He says he hurt his back and lost his landscaping business. The room he rents eats up his disability check. There's nothing left for food. I tell him about Guatemala, how gringos can live down there comfortably on a fraction of what it costs in the States. After his third trip through the beggar's banquet, Sumi swears he's moving to Guatemala. He thanks me over and over. He'd like to let me sleep on his floor, he says, but his place is too small. He's sorry. That's okay, I say, though I'm more sorry than he is. I give him my bag of produce, keeping only a honeydew melon.

I want to rush to a pay phone and call Anne collect, but can't. I told myself I wouldn't call home until I get close to the end. The slightest bit of concern or doubt in her voice will be all I need to chicken out. I don't want to be like a high wire artist who looks down and sees he's working without a net.

Diners dressed in the rugged, yet tony attire of the Northwest upwardly mobile emerge from trendy restaurants, carrying wide umbrellas. I inspect the storefronts, trying to look at once fascinating and needy, hoping a local citizen will stop and say, "Hey, I bet you'd be a great houseguest." But I am invisible. After midnight, I resign myself to another dreaded inevitability of this journey.

The police arrest people who camp in the park. If I want to sleep tonight, I must do it in the Rogue River National Forest, about a mile above town. A fellow vagabond tells me to look for a gate that blocks a dirt road. The cops won't bother me beyond there.

Yeah, but what else will?

My umbrella won't cover me and my pack, so I pull a plastic bag over my pack and walk up a narrow road that leads past spacious houses spread over a wooded hillside. Each porch, lighted and dry, is a picture of despair. The last street lamp fades behind me. I hear the creek, falling from the reservoir on my left, but can't see it. The road bends, and I find myself in total darkness. My pace slows, until finally I stop walking, unable to take another step.

I haven't always been afraid of bears. I only got scared when my friend, the Sawman, let it slip on a backpacking trip that the lumbering beasts are faster than any human. That was eleven years ago, and I haven't slept in the woods since. I know that this fear is irrational. I know that, statistically, I am in greater danger asleep in my city apartment. But my intellect has always had its ass kicked by my imagination.

Tonight can be different. I have a choice. I can step into the blackness, deal with the fear, and get some rest. Or I can turn back to town and sit up all night, a lamppost as my baby-sitter.

I turn back.

Suddenly there is a shadowy figure before me. "How far to the gate?" I blurt, partly startled, but mostly ashamed to be seen walking *away* from the forest with a backpack.

"Are you going to sleep up here?" the man says.

I can make out a rain hat and glasses, but I can't see his face. I figure he must live in one of the big houses down the road. Maybe he'll take pity on me and let me sleep on his porch. "Yes," I answer tentatively.

"Do you have a tent?" he says.

"No."

"Do you have a tarp?"

"No."

"You don't have a tent or a tarp, and you're going to sleep out in the rain?"

"I have a plastic poncho and a space blanket. I figured I'd put my sleeping bag between the two."

"Well, I'll show you a flat spot I know of."

I follow the man around the bend, further into the black night.

"Where were you headed just now?" I say.

"On a hike."

"In the pitch dark?"

"I'm having a little talk with myself."

He turns abruptly up a steep mountainside. I stop on the road.

"Hurry," he says. "If the police see us, they'll arrest us. It's fire season, and no one's allowed on the watershed."

I turn on my flashlight, but the man commands me to turn it off. I start up the mountain, groping at roots in the wet ground. My pack catches a branch and I stumble backward, bracing myself against a boulder. I hike up the hill, slipping and sliding, raindrops pelting my face. We stop about two hundred yards up. I bend over and suck in the damp air. It is only now, deep in the dark forest, I realize that my guide is not a member of the landed gentry.

"You live up here, don't you?"

"Yeah, for four years. But I live way up there, where they can't find me. The place I'm going to show you is where I first thought of living, but it's too close to the trail."

He tells me to walk about thirty yards to my right. I wish I could see his eyes. But there is only a voice in the dark, and I decide to trust it.

"Back in there is a flat spot," he says. "Some bums were camping out there. There should be some old plastic. I don't know if it's still waterproof or not. If you're not too sleepy, use your flashlight and look around for some string. What you want to do is tie one end of your space blanket between two trees, and somehow stake the other end of it to the ground. You'll get a little wet, but it's better than sleeping in the rain."

I reach for the man's hand.

"I'm Mike," I say.

"Randy."

His hand is smooth and cold. He lets go, then vanishes into the night.

I feel my way through the trees, tripping over dead branches. Invisible limbs brush my cheeks. There is a loud humming noise.

It is the sound of my heart pounding in my ears. I can't find the flat spot, but force myself to stumble farther into the woods.

The dim beam from my flashlight finally falls on a narrow clearing. A mound of something I can't make out is heaped in the middle.

"Anyone there?" I call.

I edge closer and find a soggy sleeping bag, a ripped tent, and a tattered piece of plastic. A dirty T-shirt hangs from a tree. Empty beer and whisky bottles litter the ground. The tent is useless, but bits of nylon rope are tied to its corners. I lean my pack against a tree and quickly get to work.

Rain trickles down my neck as I tie one end of my space blanket to a pair of branches about a yard apart. I anchor the other end to the ground with rocks and beer bottles. I hear a sudden crash behind me. I reel and point my flashlight like a gun.

"Who's there!"

But it's just my pack, tipped over from the tree.

I lay my poncho on the ground beneath the lean-to, then unroll my sleeping bag and climb in. After a few minutes, I'm aware of a crackling noise in the forest. It sounds like branches and twigs snapping underfoot. It gets louder. Someone or something is creeping into my camp. If it's a bear, I know I'm supposed to play dead. I lie still, not even breathing, but I fear my thumping heart will shake the ground and betray my location. The crunching sound draws nearer. I lean out from under my shelter and poke a hole in the dark with my flashlight.

"Hey!" I shout.

I sweep the flashlight back and forth across the trees. Nothing. But the sound is still there, right by my left ear. Whatever is making it is almost on top of me. I strain to listen. I close my eyes. I listen harder.

It's suddenly clear. It's the rain tapping on my space blanket. The drops hit different sizes of folds in the foil and create a symphony of scary sounds—twigs crunching, branches snapping, trees uprooting from the ground. I let out a deep breath. I lie back and listen to my lean-to. My relief is soon replaced by more anxiety. If it sounds this real, I wonder, then how will I know the real thing when it comes for me?

Then I hear Linda's soothing voice: *Don't be afraid of the dark. Don't be afraid of nature. Reverence.*

I repeat the phrase over an over in my mind, like a mantra, until at last I make peace with the black night and slip away into slumber.

In the morning, I feel like a he-man. I may not yet be one with nature, but at least I'm no longer afraid to spend the night at her house.

SEVEN

My ride drops me on the outskirts of Klamath Falls, Oregon. It's only an hour east of Ashland but looks like another planet. Trees, hippies, and marijuana have been replaced by steers, cowboys, and chewing tobacco. I get the idea that folks in these parts can go a long time without mentioning their karma or their wounded inner child.

Citizens in four-wheel-drive pickups scowl at me from underneath the brims of cowboy hats. One youth leans over the steering wheel, as if trying to touch me through the windshield, and flips me the bird. I smile and wave. In the interests of harmony and personal safety, I put away my sign and walk ten miles around the city to pick up Highway 140. I draw a new sign for Lakeview, a hundred miles east, my frozen fingers rigid around the felt pen.

A couple in their thirties stops for me in a Ford pickup. "Hop in back," the man says. "We're going to Lakeview to get some hay." The woman calls out the window, "Holler if you get cold.'' We get up to speed and the wind chill makes it feel like I'm riding in Siberia. I'm glad when the rain comes and the couple stops to let me in the cab.

Brad and Ellen were both married before and support six kids between them. Brad, who has a droopy black mustache and a black cowboy hat, works in a lumber mill. Ellen, whose thick makeup covers a worn but kind face, is a waitress. They hold hands, Brad alternating his other hand between the wheel and a coffee cup that fills with his tobacco juice. They've endured some hard knocks but remain as optimistic about the future as high school sweethearts.

"If I work swing shift this year, I'll make almost ten dollars an hour," Brad says.

It's four in the afternoon when the sun makes its first appearance of the day. The sky glows with a rainbow so perfect it could be anchored by *two* pots of gold. A hawk surfs the currents high above. A billboard in the shape of a cowboy marks the city limits of Lakeview, at more than four thousand feet, the ''Tallest Town in Oregon.'' Brad drops me at the town's single blinking light.

"It'll take you a while to get out of here," he says. "When you do get out, be careful. Beyond here is the high desert. There's nothing but sage, coyotes, and rattlesnakes. If you have to bed down in the brush, watch where you sleep. There's rattlesnakes everywhere.''

Lakeview is a misnomer. There's no lake and there's no view. It's a mill town, on its way to becoming a ghost town. A faded white *L* brands the dull brown hill above.

I use the bathroom at the gas station. The attendant says it's going to drop to twenty tonight. With civic pride, he adds that it once snowed here on the Fourth of July. I almost ask him if I can sleep in the men's room. It smells like piss, but at least it's warm. Then I figure that would be only slightly better than snoozing with the snakes. I know I can do better.

I wander the quiet streets until I find myself standing before the Catholic church. I remember that it's Sunday.

I had no religious training as a child, and I've never been a churchgoer, except for weddings and funerals. I'm not a believer, nor am I an atheist. I can't even claim to be an agnostic. On the question of God, I remain passionately noncommittal—a heretic in all camps. I actually consider myself to be a spiritual fellow, in a small *s* kind of way, but organized religion scares the bejeezus out of me. Even the sight of stained glass sends a shiver down my spine. So it is most curious that I'm now knocking on the rectory door, about to ask the padre if the Lord's house could spare a pew for the night.

There's no answer.

A housepainter working nearby thinks the priest might be at the parish hall, a few blocks away. He offers to drive me over, and I set my pack atop a pile of paint buckets and ladders in the back of his truck. No one's at the parish hall, either. The painter, whose name is Mike, asks if I'm looking for a place to stay, and I tell him yes. He drives me to the Church of Nazarene and waits in the truck.

"Is the priest here?" I ask the old man who answers the door.

"We don't have a priest, we have a pastor," he says. "There's a church service now. He'll be through in a few minutes."

I walk back out to the truck. Mike notes the weather and asks if I have a coat. A light one, I tell him.

"I've got an old coat I can give you," he says. "I live nearby."

I wait in the truck as Mike rummages through his garage, which is cluttered with the tools of his trade. A tricycle sits on the front lawn. I hear a woman's voice call out from inside the house. "It's nothing, honey, I'll be back in a few minutes," Mike says, shutting the garage door. He hands me a bulky green Army-style jacket splattered with white paint.

"It's not much to look at, but it'll keep you warm. If nothing else, you can use it to sleep on."

"It's perfect," I say. "Thanks a lot."

Mike swings me back by the church. He says if things don't

work out to come to his house, and he'll think of something. I sense a moral quandary churning within him. I think he'd like to do more, maybe invite me home to dinner, offer me his couch. But there is the owner of the tricycle to think of, the woman at the kitchen door. How do you balance compassion with responsibility? At what price trust?

I set my pack and new coat on the church steps. The service ends, and a few parishioners file out, clutching Bibles. They all wear smiles. They want to know who I am, where I'm from, where I'm going. A young man with a cat at his feet extends his hand. One of his eyes droops horribly down and to the side. He speaks in a hypermonotone.

"My name's Michael. I've been a Christian since 1971. I was born March 11, 1971. I have a receding hairline, see? I've always wanted to look young because I'm never going to die because I have Jesus Christ in my life. I got hit by a drunk driver. I was walking down the road and he hit me from behind. I didn't break a bone—"

"Take your cat and go home, Michael." The voice is booming but jovial. I look up to see the huge presence of Pastor Larry. He has a beard and rosy cheeks. His expansive girth makes the wooden cross hanging from his neck point out. He smiles kindly at me.

"My name is Mike McIntyre," I start in. "I'm from San Francisco, and I'm on my way to the East Coast. I wonder if I could sleep in your church tonight?"

"I can't let people sleep here, that's a board decision." But as soon as it's out of his mouth, he adds, "Come in."

It's a simple church. Folding chairs. No stained glass. Pastor Larry says he doesn't know where I'll sleep, and I say the floor will do fine.

"I've got to be perfectly honest with you," I say. "I put myself in this position. I'm on a sort of spiritual journey." I tell him about my penniless itinerary.

He offers to get me a motel room. I wouldn't have to touch

any money. It would be paid for with a voucher. I'm tempted by the vision of a bed and sheets and a shower, but I tell Pastor Larry to save the funds for the truly needy. He then offers to call a family that takes people in from time to time. That's great, I say, that's what this trip is about. There's no answer, so he calls a second family. The line's busy.

I ask Pastor Larry if he's originally from Lakeview.

"No, I grew up in Phoenix and southern California. I was a biker. I was in a gang. Then one day the Lord told me that if I remained a biker, I was going to die. I saw the light at the end of a double-barreled shotgun. A guy from a rival gang aimed at my chest and pulled the trigger. It just made a noise, and I figured it must've been blanks. After we won the fight, one of our guys put the gun in the air and squeezed the trigger. His arm about blew off from the recoil. I knew then what the Lord was saying. I've been a Christian for fourteen years and a pastor here for eleven. I still ride bikes. I sometimes witness to the bikers. It's fun."

He tries the number again. I hear a man's voice on the other end say, "Send him on over." Pastor Larry suggests the man come get me. He hangs up and says, "Tim's a little, how shall I put this? Tim's a little rough. But he's a good man. He's fallen for the Lord hard."

A minute later, I hear an approaching clamor, children yelling excitedly. Tim blows into Pastor Larry's office, his three daughters hanging from him, as if he were a jungle gym.

"Is this the fellow?" Tim says. "Is this the millionaire? Ha, ha, ha!"

He's about thirty, with short-cropped hair and bent glasses. He wears sweats and a dirty white T-shirt. The tail of his flannel shirt is ripped and hangs down the side of his leg. I feel conspicuous in my handmade Italian sweater, new Levi's, and Hi-Tec hiking boots.

Tim dropped out of high school to work in a northern California lumber mill. When he got laid off, he moved his family to Lakeview. The closest job he could find was 150 miles south in the Nevada desert. He repaired mining equipment and slept in a tent, returning home once every ten days. He recently got hired on at a Lakeview lumber mill, where he works six days a week, from four in the morning until eight at night.

He and his family live around the corner from the church in a two-story duplex. They used to sublet one side, but had to evict the tenants because they trashed the place. Tim and his wife, Diane, don't plan to rent it again, though it's obvious they can use the money. They want to keep the unit open for people who need emergency shelter. Tim calls it their ministry.

"Just showing up at church on Sunday and putting a few shekels in the plate isn't enough," he says. "If you're gonna be a Christian, be a Christian."

Tim gives me a tour of tonight's quarters, as Julia, Charlotte, and Kristina scamper about the vacant duplex. Stuffed plastic garbage bags sit like beanbag chairs on the bare floor. Wind whistles through the busted doorjamb. Paint peels from grimy walls. The curtains are torn and stained. Upstairs in the bathroom, the toilet has overflowed repeatedly, leaving the floor as soggy as quicksand, the tub ready to sink into the living room.

"It's not the Ritz," Tim says with a chuckle.

But I tell him how I slept last night in the rain, and how right now this dry refuge looks as good as any five-star hotel.

Tim invites me to Sunday supper, and we all walk next door, Julia leading me by the hand. "Mom, our guest is coming!" she calls. We hit the door just in time to see Diane sweep a pile of dirt and scraps from under the dinner table and hide it behind the kitchen wall. She sets the broom against the counter and smiles shyly.

Tim's home looks like a tornado blew in, made itself something to eat, and blew back out.

"The place is kind of messy," he apologizes. "The kids live here."

A shirtless boy, Philip, is already at the table, eating a slice of white bread. Diane sets a bowl of beans and potatoes in the middle of the table and sits down. Tim picks up a Bible and reads Psalm 75: "Unto thee, O God, do we give thanks. . . ." When he's finished he turns the casserole toward me and I scoop some into a plastic bowl, Tim cracking about how they broke out the china for me.

"People have found out that poor people's food is the best food," he says. "Nobody but poor people ate beans and potatoes, now a lot of people do." He looks at Diane and says, "Honey, we have some fruit, don't we?" Diane gets up and after a few minutes returns with a bowl of sliced apples and oranges. As I serve myself, I get a bad feeling that the kids won't be finding any fruit in their lunch bags tomorrow at school.

There is but one picture on the wall, a sagging poster depicting two small boys in overalls, one asking the other, "Been farming long?" Tim takes in his humble surroundings and laughs.

"In our church, we have these three-on-three nights, where two couples go to a third couple's house for dinner," he says, pushing his busted glasses back up the bridge of his nose. "Wait'll they come to our house."

I say, "Hey, you're doing a great thing here. You've got your family intact. Do you know how many families aren't eating together tonight?"

Tim says he knows he's blessed. He asks me my story, and I tell him. It doesn't seem to matter to him that my poverty is self-imposed and temporary.

"It sounds like you're searching for something," he says.

"I am."

He steps away from the table and comes back. "This is what I found when I was searching for something," he says, handing me a pamphlet entitled "Four Spiritual Laws." It's a fire and brimstone tract, not exactly what I'm looking for, but I thank him just the same. He asks if I own a Bible and I tell him no. He gives me a Gideon's, the cover of which bears tooth marks, as if somebody had tried to swallow salvation.

"Thanks," I say.

But Tim's not through giving. He wants me to have his tent, the one he slept in when he worked in the desert. I appreciate the offer, I say, but I can't accept it. He insists. He never uses it, he says, it just sits in the garage. Even if that's true, I know he could sell it. I regret telling him about last night. Tim won't give up. It seems there's no way I'm leaving without his tent. Finally, I agree to take it, knowing it's probably one of his family's more valuable possessions.

In the morning, I stop by the post office on my way out of town. Before I left home, I bought a stack of stamped envelopes and postcards. I jot a note to Anne or another friend or relative every day. That way, they'll know where to start looking if something goes wrong. Pastor Larry comes in as I'm walking out the door. He's bundled up in a parka, and he mock shivers when I tell him I'm heading farther north.

"How are you fixed for food?" he says.

"Going day to day."

He offers to bring me a sack of canned goods from the church food bank. Great, but I can't carry more than a can or two, I tell him. I wait on the sidewalk, and Pastor Larry returns on his Honda Gold Wing motorcycle. He wears black shades and a black helmet, and I can see how he was once a bad-ass biker. But now he's Santa Claus with an early Christmas stocking.

"I couldn't make up my mind," he says, pulling cans from a paper sack. Tuna, sardines, pork and beans, two tins of lunch loaf, a sleeve of soda crackers, plastic utensils, and a can opener. He packs the bag and hands it over.

"Let me ask you something," I say. "What do you think about what I'm doing—the ethics of it?"

"I think it's wonderful. Look, you're not making any demands on anybody. You tell people what you're doing, and they either help you or they don't." He looks over at my pack. "Do you have any way to protect yourself?"

"How do you mean?"

"What if someone tries to take your pack?"

"You mean, if somebody pulls a gun on me?"

"Or if there are three of them. You know, some of these cowboys out here have some funny ideas about outsiders."

"I won't get in a truck with three cowboys."

"Well, if you get in a situation," advises the gang member turned preacher, "tell them *sensei* told you to take a journey. Most everyone knows *sensei* is a karate teacher."

Pastor Larry bows his head and offers a bikeside prayer for my safety. I thank him for everything and head for the edge of town. As I walk down the road, I see a new shape to the shadow I cast, the tent strapped to my pack. I walk on, wondering how it is that the people who have the least to give are often the ones who give the most.

EIGHT

The Road to Cape Fear turns north out of Lakeview and bisects that wasteland known as southeastern Oregon. I stand on the shoulder of Highway 395, in sight of the occasional car that stops to fill up at the last gas station for a hundred miles. The sun shines, but it acts like it's got a faulty thermostat. I must remind myself that technically it's still summer. A pair of gloves is in my pack, but if I put them on in September, what will I have to look forward to wearing next month in the Midwest? Finally, a new, red, four-door Chevy pickup hauling a horse trailer pulls up to the pump and the driver waves me over.

"You're the first hitchhiker I've picked up in fifteen years," the man says, flashing a smile that reveals a mouthful of white capped teeth.

"Well, until this trip, I hadn't hitchhiked in fifteen years," I say. "So I guess that makes us even."

Jerry is driving home to Boise, Idaho. At forty-seven, he owns a company that manufactures steel chemical tanks, some as big as a merry-go-round. He spends three months a year on the road—from California to Nebraska—testing his clients' tanks, certifying that they meet federal guidelines. He hauls his testing equipment in the horse trailer. A cellular phone, laptop computer, and fax machine ride in the backseat of the pickup. He's returning from a job in Klamath Falls. On longer trips, he flies his own plane.

The view through the window looks like a black eye. A gust of wind buffets the truck as we whisk by Lake Abert, a dark alkaline pool that reflects the clouds racing overhead. A purple bluff to the west jumps up two thousand feet from the desert floor and keeps us company for the next half hour. The rest of the land is covered with sagebrush.

"The person who finds a use for sage will be a billionaire," Jerry says.

Jerry exudes the ease and confidence of a self-made man, but also displays immense gratitude. He is a man who made a U-turn in life and is now aimed down the right road, mindful of the perils of detours. Waiting for him at home are his third wife and their two young daughters. The couple tried without luck for years to have a baby. Then, middle-aged and with no time to wade through the public adoption system, they turned to private sources. Jerry's girls are now five years and seven months old. He used to work sixteen-hour days, but now he's home for dinner each night. When he's out of town, he calls his eldest daughter every day—as much for his own good as for hers.

"It's my second chance at a family," he says.

Jerry's second wife was the girl who grew up next door to him in southern California. They were married fourteen years, but never had kids. She was an alcoholic, in and out of rehab. Jerry wouldn't quit his wife, attending countless AA meetings with her. Then when he was laid up in the hospital with a broken neck, his wife left him.

Jerry's first marriage was a disaster that lasted five years. Those were the days of the Bad Jerry. He was a drinker, a carouser, and, at times, a scoundrel. The couple had two boys, but Jerry was a negligent father. When the relationship headed south for good, Jerry's wife and kids were living with another man by the name of Stevens. Jerry kicked down his front door one day and threatened to kill him.

"I used to have a bad temper," Jerry says.

Jerry's wife married her boyfriend and disappeared. She never forgave Jerry for his years of straying. She changed the boys' last name and wouldn't tell them where their father lived. After he moved to Idaho and turned his life around, Jerry tried in vain for years to find his sons. Whenever business took him to California, he pored through phone books, dialing every Stevens listed.

"But you know how many Stevens there are?" he says.

Then eight years ago on Thanksgiving, Jerry was summoned from the table by a phone call. It was Tommy, his youngest son, who had tracked his father down on his own.

"We were both bawling on the phone," Jerry says.

Tommy, then seventeen, moved to Idaho to live with Jerry and his current wife. But after four months, he grew restless and returned to California. Jerry understood; his son had another life, but he told Tommy to remember that he would always be there for him.

A short time later, when Jerry was in California, he called his eldest son, Billy, and asked if he wanted to meet. Billy said he had to work on his car. When Jerry called the next day, Billy said his car was still broken. Jerry offered to come get him. Billy said he'd have to call him back. He never did.

Jerry's sons are now grown men, not much younger than me. Jerry lives with the hard fact that despite best intentions, some things can't be fixed. Still, he tries. He got an 800 number so

Billy and Tommy can call him anytime, from anywhere. It never rings.

We pull into a truck stop in Burns, Oregon. Burns isn't exactly the middle of nowhere, but it's right on the edge.

"Want some lunch?" Jerry says.

I already told him about my journey. I remind him I'm penniless.

"I'll buy you lunch. It's no big deal."

The offer comes just in time, as the beans I ate at Tim and Diane's last night have long since worn off, and my head feels light enough to float away like a helium balloon. We slide into a booth and I order a double cheeseburger, fries, and a Coke. Jerry finishes his sandwich and lingers over a second glass of iced tea, then a third.

He isn't a Bible thumper, and he doesn't ask my beliefs, but he feels compelled to share where he stands on matters of faith.

"It's not good enough being a good person. Your heart's gotta be in the right place. I've always been a Christian, but I was on the fence. Now I say no to my temptations."

"What are your temptations?" I say.

Jerry blushes. "Women," he says with a chuckle. His smile quickly fades. "If I say yes to my temptations, I know all my treasures will be here on earth, rather than for eternity. Do you know how long eternity is?"

We drive east from Burns on Highway 20, climbing over Stinking Water Pass, then Drinking Water Pass. Magpies greet us on the other side of the summit as the high desert gives way to a broad basin. A sign tells me I'm now in the Mountain Time Zone, and I think of how far I've come, and how far I've got to go. We're suddenly over the Snake River and into Idaho. It's been my longest and favorite ride of the trip, and I'm sorry it's about to end. I'd like to go home with Jerry, meet his wife, play with his little girls. But I know that won't happen. Jerry has already lost one family. He's not about to risk losing another.

The rush hour traffic of the greater Boise area is unsettling after the solitude of rural Oregon. I steal nervous glances at the digital clock on the dashboard. It will soon be dark, and I'll be standing on the side of yet another unfamiliar road.

"So, do you know which way you want to head?" Jerry asks.

"I don't know, I'll have to look at my map in the morning. Do you know a place I can pitch my tent tonight?"

"How about I get you a room at the Comfort Inn? Wouldn't you rather have a bed and a shower?"

"Wow, I'd really appreciate that," I say, my throat catching with gratitude. "You know, before this trip, it was always hard for me to accept anything from anyone. I always tried to be the giver. I'd do favors knowing I'd never ask for anything in return. I never wanted to take anything because I never wanted to feel like I owed anything. I think I used it as a shield, as a way of keeping people at a distance. But now I've put myself in a position where I have to accept favors daily, yet I know I'll never be able to repay people. It feels funny."

"Mike, on this trip, keep in mind that when people give you something, there's a reason for it. They have their own motivations for helping you."

Jerry parks in front of the motel office. He pays for the room with a credit card and gives me the key. I consider asking him what his motivation is for helping me. But it's soon clear.

He pulls a business card from his wallet. On the back, he writes down his 800 number—the one he got for his sons, the one that never rings.

Jerry's eyes are moist when he hands me the card.

"If you need something out there and you can't get a-hold of your dad, call me."

NINE

I get Jerry's money's worth at the Comfort Inn. In the morning, I hit the free Continental breakfast in the lobby, loading up on bagels, cream cheese, sweet rolls, and orange juice. I haul my booty, along with a complimentary copy of *USA Today,* back to my room, where I gorge out in front of "Good Morning America." After a long soak in the tub and a shower, I pack the extra soap and shampoo samples, then watch the movie *Malcolm X* on HBO until check-out time.

I walk down a commercial boulevard out of Boise, heading for open spaces. A large, balding man stops for me in a Nissan Sentra. He says he used to be an attorney in Boise but now lives in Hawaii. He flew over for his high school reunion. His wife stayed in the Islands.

"Have you had your lunch yet?" he says.

"No."

"Neither have I. I know a nice little restaurant on the road that leads out of town. I'll buy you lunch, then you'll be on your way."

The sudden offer raises my suspicions. Besides, I'm not even hungry. But a penniless traveler never knows when he'll next eat, so I reluctantly agree.

We both order the special of the day, chicken fried steak. Something about the man pushes my uh-oh button. He won't look me in the eye. He doesn't ask me any personal questions, not even where I'm from. And for a guy who lives in Hawaii, he looks awfully pale.

He says he stopped picking up hitchhikers after a friend was killed by one several years ago. He recently resumed giving rides because he likes to help people. He says the president of a local college is a close friend. It's as if he's trying to convince me of something, put me at ease.

The man says he's been moving some boxes out of storage, but it's been difficult because he recently suffered whiplash in a car wreck. He mentions the beautiful home in Boise he is house-sitting. I sense this is all leading up to a request for help, with an offer of a night's shelter in return. I rehearse my polite refusal in my mind.

"Do you want some pie?" the man says.

"Oh, no thanks. I'm stuffed."

"Well, I'll drive you out to the stoplight. It'll be easier for you to get a ride out there."

I recall the guy in California who drove me down the dead-end road. I may be paranoid, but there's no way I'm getting back into this man's car.

"That's okay. You've done enough."

"It's no trouble."

"No, really, thanks. I'll just walk out that way."

"It's no trouble at all."

"I'd like to walk, really. I need to work off my lunch."

"Well, all right," he finally says.

I retrieve my pack from the man's car and thank him for the meal. It's broad daylight and we're in a crowded parking lot, but I'm afraid of him. I can't get away fast enough.

When I was a kid growing up in California, there was a string of murders attributed to a man called the Zodiac Killer. After each death, he claimed responsibility in a card or letter that bore astrological symbols. He once mailed a card to the news media from a post office near my home at Lake Tahoe. I worried about the Zodiac Killer a lot. He was never caught. Years later, one expert claimed that the notorious murderer was a real estate agent living in northern California. But today, part of me is convinced that the Zodiac Killer is a retired attorney from Boise, Idaho.

Walking down the street, I keep turning around, expecting to find him following me. I imagine him turning up further along the Road to Cape Fear. Will he be my last ride?

I chastise myself. I'm to blame for this fright. I got too greedy. It was stupid to accept lunch from a stranger who triggered my mistrust. I must be more careful. For the rest of the trip, I vow to listen to my instincts before my stomach.

TEN

A junior high school on the edge of Boise is letting out when I drop my pack in the dirt. I draw a sign for a place called Murphy, a dot on the map in southwestern Idaho. I don't know what's there, but it's away from the city. Kids cruising in cars read my destination and bust loose laughing. I guess Murphy is where all the geeks live.

An old Jeep Wagoneer stops to pick me up. The driver, Sue, must weigh close to 250 pounds. Her fifty-five-year-old mother Edie rides shotgun. Sue's little girl Katie, an adorable child with blond hair and blue eyes, stands on the floorboard, as my pack and I now take up the whole backseat. Sue's other daughter, Laura, age eleven, is sprawled across her grandmother's lap. She wears a protective helmet. Her body is as limp as linguine.

"Murphy!" Edie says in a voice like gravel. "Boy, you sure are a brave soul. There's nothing but desert out there."

I tell her I'm avoiding the freeways and traveling through small towns.

"There isn't even a town there. Murphy!" Then, in the next breath: "Well, you want to have supper with us?"

The offer comes sooner than the one extended by the man earlier today. Yet Edie's weathered face and simple ways convey a raw honesty. I'm not even hungry, but I'm suddenly smitten with this crusty woman. I quickly accept.

Sue turns into a tract housing development set among dull brown hills void of trees. From Edie's appearance—she's dressed in baggy sweats and a dirty T-shirt—I expect her place to be a dump. But when we pull into the driveway, I see that hers is the tidiest house on the street. The modest box with while aluminum siding is bordered by a neatly trimmed lawn. Concord grapes hang from a lattice arbor out back. Edie has just been to the farmers' market, where she sold ten dollars' worth of grapes, which I gather for her is no small sum. When I use the bathroom, I notice the tub is spotless. Decorative baskets adorn the kitchen wall. A collection of antique spoons hangs from a cabinet in the living room.

Edie invites me to run a load of wash. The laundry room is a sight more welcome than the kitchen table, as my jeans and shirt can probably stand on the side of the road and hitchhike by themselves.

As Edie fixes dinner, Laura watches her from the kitchen table. She bounces in her chair, a sock dangling from her mouth.

Edie moves fast in the kitchen, a habit from her early years as a restaurant worker. She peels and mashes potatoes, and boils a pot of water for corn on the cob. Chicken roasts in the oven. I offer to help, but she says sit tight.

Sue parks her ample behind in an easy chair in the front room. She plunges her hand into a bag of potato chips and swigs from a two-liter bottle of 7-Up. Her son Kyle, aged three, slaps her knee. His short-cropped hair is offset by a ponytail.

"I'm gonna go see Daddy," he whines.

"No, you're not gonna be seein' Daddy."

Sue is married to a man down in Texas. A few days ago, she gathered up Kyle and Katie and left him. For good, she says.

"I'd like to beat my husband's face in, make it all bloody, and leave him to die in the street," she says, grinning wickedly.

Sue never married Laura's father, a neighborhood boy who got her pregnant when she was fifteen. One day, when Laura was a baby, Sue fell asleep in another room while listening to loud music. She didn't hear her daughter entering the earliest stage of sudden infant death syndrome. When she awoke and saw she wasn't breathing; she phoned her mother, who worked as an orderly at a hospital. Edie rushed home and performed CPR on Laura. She saved her life, but she had already lost much of her brain.

Through the years, Sue proved a careless mother, leaving Laura with anybody. Edie hired a lawyer and sued for custody of her granddaughter. She went to school and got a license to care for the severely handicapped. The state now pays Edie to care for Laura at home, a cheaper and better alternative to putting her in an institution.

Edie sets a plate heaped with food in front of me, and I thank her.

"We don't have much, but we don't mind sharing what we have," she says. "I know what it's like to be hungry. There've been times when I've been down to my last ten cents, but people have always helped me."

She asks if I want regular bread or homemade bread.

"I bet your bread is lots better," I say.

"I think so. We grew up making our own bread. We thought store-bought bread was like candy. When we had store-bought bread, we thought we'd died and went to heaven."

I saw off a slice from the dense loaf. To economize, Edie substitutes Karo syrup for sugar and boiled potato water for milk. It's delicious.

Edie cuts kernels from an ear of corn and mashes them in a bowl. She spoon-feeds the mush to Laura, who hums as she chews. Sue fixes herself a plate and goes back into the living room to watch Oprah on TV.

"She used to be beautiful, this girl," Edie says. "I don't know what happened to her."

Sue has more problems than an expanding waistline and a bad marriage. She's currently on parole, the result of a conviction for dealing cocaine. Edie kept Kyle and Katie while Sue served five months in jail.

I hear a door open down the hall. Edie's thirty-year-old son Jay appears in the kitchen doorway. He wears a black cowboy hat, snakeskin cowboy boots, and a belt buckle as big as a dish. He struts through the kitchen like he's just come in off the range. Without barely a howdy-do, he pours himself a cup of coffee and retreats to his bedroom.

Jay has an ex-wife and two kids. She tired of supporting him and kicked him out. He moved back home, where he mooches cigarettes and gas money off Edie. He busted up her Wagoneer four-wheeling in the desert. He's supposed to be out looking for a job to earn the sixteen hundred dollars it cost Edie to fix the Jeep, but he spends most days in his room smoking cigarettes and drinking coffee.

"He thinks the world owes him a living," Edie says.

Jay and Sue each draw four hundred dollars a month from their father's disability pension. Sue tells me with glee that the sum jumps to nine hundred a month as soon as her dad dies of lung cancer.

Edie was married to the kids' father, a hardware salesman, for five years. They were living in Arkansas when he ran out on them. Edie spent her last twenty dollars on a motel room and a baby-sitter, and that night she found a job in a local pizza parlor.

"I've always been able to work, and I've always been able to feed my kids," she says.

There was no alimony, and her ex-husband was a deadbeat dad, welching on child support. Edie managed by holding down two jobs. She avoided the welfare roles and never took a penny of public assistance. She also never remarried, nor got involved with another man. She remains self-sufficient to this day.

Edie invites me to stay over. "You don't wanna be out on that road at night," she says.

I tell her I'm happy to pitch my tent in her backyard.

"Or you can stay in here," she says. "We won't bother you."

"Thanks, I really appreciate it."

"Well, you look clean-cut," she says. "You don't look like one of those killers."

Edie wipes Laura's face with a wash rag. She pours some orange liquid in a tube and gently squirts it down her throat. Even with the medicine, Laura suffers two to three grand mal seizures a day, thus the need for her helmet. She can't talk, but Edie says they communicate fine. She is a tireless advocate for her well-being. When doctors told her Laura couldn't walk because her brain fails to connect with her muscles, Edie refused to listen. She carried her granddaughter to specialist after specialist until she found one that saw Laura lacked certain bones in her feet. She will soon undergo an operation that should allow her to walk. Edie also fought to mainstream Laura into the local school system. She now attends classes with normal eleven-year-olds.

"Okay, Grandma's gonna give you a bath now, Laura," Edie says.

I offer to do the dishes, but Edie insists I make myself at home in the front room. She bathes Laura and puts her in brown pajamas with feet. Sleepers Laura's size come only in brown, she says. They sit on the sofa next to me. Edie polishes a silver spoon she bought at a garage sale and watches a documentary about ancient Siam on the Discovery Channel. I almost tell her I've been to Thailand, but I don't want to sound boastful. It suddenly occurs to me how odd it is to be staying in the house of a total stranger. But a moment later I think maybe this is the way it's supposed to be. Maybe what's really unnatural is the great lengths we take to avoid one another.

After the show, I fold my clothes from the dryer. Edie added fabric softener to the wash, so my shirt smells fresh and clean. She moves Laura to her favorite chair at the kitchen table. She makes a pot of coffee and has a smoke. It's the first time I've seen her doing nothing since we met four hours ago.

"I admire what you're doing," she says. "I wish I would've

done that when I was your age. I coulda gone to that big concert back East.''

''Woodstock?'' I say.

''Yeah. And I didn't go. I coulda been part of something that was almost historic. There were four carloads of kids that went from here. I coulda got a baby-sitter and went, but I didn't. I could kick myself now. When you get to be my age, you'll be able to look back and say, 'I did this.' '' She sips her coffee and says wistfully, ''Boy, you're taking me back now.''

I ask Edie what her dream is. She says that because she's three-quarters Crow Indian, she was able to obtain a 120-acre parcel on a mountainous reservation in Montana. One day she'd like to sell her house and move there with Laura.

''I wanna build a log cabin, and I wanna get a horse for her. That's my plan.'' She looks adoringly at her granddaughter. ''I love her. She's special. The doctors said she wouldn't live past five, but here she is. As long as God gives me the strength, I'm gonna take care of her. I really believe God made her this way so I could have her.''

For such a decent and caring woman, I'm surprised to learn that Edie had a terrible childhood. Her mother was an alcoholic, murdered at age sixty-five by the last in a long line of drifters she picked up in bars.

''She was always drunk, bringing home strange men,'' Edie says. ''As old as I am, I can still see these scary old men standing over me when I was little. We roamed around the country that way. She'd lock me in a motel room for two or three days,'til she got off her drunk. Sometimes, the police knocked the door down and took me to orphanages. One time we were in Mexicali. She was with this guy and they had a fight. The police came and took us all to jail. They put us in this cell with other people. There was water up to my ankles. The toilet was stopped up and overflowing. There was a mattress on the floor, and when I laid down it was sopping wet. I'll never forget that, boy. When I had kids, I made a promise to myself that they'd never see that kind of life, and they never have.''

Edie sets out a sleeping bag for me. She says good-night and takes Laura back to her bedroom. Sue lounges in the easy chair. She wears a nightgown that could be mistaken for a tent. She fiddles with the cap on a bottle of sleeping pills. She says she was out until three in the morning. I see the giant hickey on her neck and imagine the rest. She has to get up early tomorrow to make a call. One day a year, the city of Boise takes applications for subsidized housing. Appointments are granted over the phone between 7:30 and 8:00. Now that she's leaving her husband, an affordable apartment is critical to Sue and her kids. She pops a couple of pills, washing them down with 7-Up. She lumbers toward the guest room, ushering Katie and Kyle along with her. Kyle takes his time.

"Git to bed!'' she says. "I'm gonna kick your ass.''

"Got your alarm set?'' I call after her.

"I don't need an alarm. These guys are my alarm.''

I think Sue a fool for taking a chance on such an important call. Then I decide I'm more concerned about it than she is.

Jay emerges from his room, this time wearing a $150 cowboy shirt designed by the country-western singer Garth Brooks. He opens the front door to let in a bubbly blond woman named Stacey, who has apparently just tapped on his window. Stacey is married, but I gather she spends more time with Jay than with her husband. I watch TV while they play slap-and-tickle at the kitchen table. They are joined by Ricky, a young man from the neighborhood who enters through the back door. The trio smokes and jokes, nobody uttering an intelligent remark. I keep hearing them say, "Eleven.'' Something happens at eleven, I don't know what. But it's only ten. I wish they'd just leave, so I can go to sleep. Finally at the appointed hour, they head out.

I'm too long for the couch, so I unroll the sleeping bag on the floor and flip out the lights. A half hour later, Jay and his friends are back. I feign sleep. They lollygag in the kitchen, louder than before. I hear them count their money out on the table. They have $2.90 among them. They take turns calling the local Denny's, trying to learn who's working. I guess one of their friends gives them food. They leave again, and at last I'm able to sleep.

In the middle of the night, I'm awakened by the creak of the front door. It's Jay and Stacey. They giggle as they tip-toe into Jay's room and shut the door. I hear another door open down the hall, then footsteps.

"Jay, this is the last time!" Edie growls. "I'm tired of this. You wanna fool around, you do it on your own time!"

"Back off and fuck off!" Jay yells from the other side of the door.

I wince in the dark.

When I come out of the shower in the morning, Edie has breakfast on the table. Fried eggs, potatoes, sausage patties, and toast—my fourth meal in the last twenty-four hours. She feeds Laura, then dresses her for school. I do the dishes over much protest from Edie and help Kyle put on his shoes. It's well past eight when Sue shuffles groggily from her room to resume her position next to the chips and soda. Maybe she'll get that apartment next year.

Edie fixes me a bag full of grapes from her backyard, prunes, and a loaf of her homemade bread. When I leave, Sue is trying to get through to the housing office, complaining that it hurts her fingers to push the buttons. Jay is still asleep in his room with Stacey.

"He and I are gonna have a talk," Edie tells me in the driveway. "He goes and picks up these floozies in the bar and brings 'em back home. He thinks this is his private playground. I don't do that in my house, and I don't want him doing that in my house."

I guess it's a story as old as Cain, but I've never been able to figure how good people can produce rotten kids. I ache for Edie. She deserves better than Jay and Sue. They can't see in a lifetime what I know in a day: Their mother is a saint. I think of Laura and how lucky she is to have Edie. And I think of myself, and how fortunate I've been to know her, if only for a short while.

"I wanna give you a good luck piece," she says. "My friend gave me two of 'em, and I wanna share one with you."

She holds out a Canadian dollar, polished to a shine. When she presses the coin into my palm and closes my hand around it with her rough fingers, I feel an emotion that can only be described as love.

"Carry this with you and you'll never be broke," she says.

For the first time since I met her, Edie's creased and kind face hints at a smile.

ELEVEN

I walk down the road, my fingers turning the coin in my pocket. The money is foreign, so I'm still penniless, but I suddenly feel wealthy. I realize that this is no longer my trip alone. If I fail to reach Cape Fear, I'll let down a growing number of people who find hope in this journey.

Two young men with dirt bikes in the bed of their pickup drive me to Murphy, the seat of Owyhee County. The region was named for the Hawaiian natives brought over in the early 1800s to trap beaver. A large group of the Hawaiians were sent into the Snake River Valley, never to return, presumably killed by Indians. Owyhee is Idaho's largest county—the combined size of Connecticut, Delaware, and Rhode Island—yet has only one person per square mile. When my ride drops me in Murphy, it looks like the census takers may have padded that figure.

None of the town's alleged fifty citizens are in view. The only sound in this dust-blown land is the drone of hot air colliding with more hot air, and the flap of an orange windsock perched above an empty airstrip.

A woman in the sheriff's office says I can camp on the lawn in front of the jail. After closing time, I get my first look at the tent Tim and Diane gave me. It's navy blue and pitches into the shape of a dome. The inside is filled with dirt from Tim's days at the Nevada mine, and my head and feet touch the corners when I lie down—but it's home.

I tear off a hunk of Edie's homemade bread and break out the bag of trail mix Linda bought me back in northern California. I lie on my back and gaze at the stars through the mesh top of the tent. When I roll over to go to sleep, a coyote in the desert bids me good-night.

In the morning I shampoo my hair and shave in the sink of the bathroom in the courthouse. When I'm home, I shave only three times a week, due to a combination of sensitive skin and general laziness. But on this trip, I try to shave daily, so as to put my best face forward to would-be benefactors. My logic proves correct this day. The fellow who stops for me says he never gives strangers rides, but I look different.

"I think people still respond to decency," he says. "I think that's what you struck in me."

Don, a local hay grower, is driving fifty miles east to Mountain Home to get a tire fixed. That will put me at Interstate 84, but I see on my map there's a two-laner that heads out from there across the gut of Idaho. Don asks where I'm from, then lets me know how poorly folks from my home state are regarded in these parts. A Californian is lower than a snake's belly. The very term "Californian" is synonymous with that local swear word *environmentalist*. There is mounting resentment against Californians who cash out and invade the intermountain states, bringing with them such twisted liberal notions as conservation and imposing them on the natives. Most recently, irrigation in the area was suspended—threatening to bankrupt many a farmer—while environmentalists fought for the rights of a new species of snail discovered in a reservoir.

"It's gettin' to be where a guy who wants to live off the land and raise a family can't do it anymore," Don says.

As if on cue, we pass a spray-painted plea on the blacktop: "Don't Californicate Idaho!"

Don doesn't hold my birthplace against me. He even offers me a can of soda resting on the seat.

"But what are you going to drink?" I say.

"Oh, I'll be by a Pepsi machine before you will," he laughs.

He stops at a truck stop in Mountain Home to let me out. Before he drives off, he says, "You know, these days people all think we're masters of our own destiny. I couldn't go out and do what you're doing if I thought like that. I hope you know you couldn't do what you're doing unless there's someone looking over you."

I wish I shared Don's blind faith. Life would be that much simpler. But in a way he's right. While I worry about dying—and even conjure grisly scenarios involving my demise on the Road to Cape Fear—I simultaneously believe that on this journey I am immune to death. Perhaps it is no more than a neat mental trick that allows me to hop into cars with total strangers. Or maybe it is proof positive that I am not an atheist.

For the second time today, I am picked up by the first car that comes along. Casey, a recent college graduate, buys me a hot dog at a convenience store, but he isn't much for conversation. It's a silent two-hundred-mile shot across the state to Idaho Falls. We blow by the Craters of the Moon National Monument and Arco, the first nuclear-powered city in America. About all Casey has to say is that the Mormon Church is a cult. Like Utah, southern Idaho has a heavy Mormon population. Casey says you're either with them or against them. So when we reach Idaho Falls, I'm surprised when he drops me in the parking lot of the Mormon temple.

Everyone in my girlfriend Anne's immediate family is a practicing Mormon, except for Anne. As long as I'm here, I figure I'll have my picture snapped in front of the temple and give it to Anne's mom when I get home. A couple of women volunteers from the visitors' center see me standing in front of the temple with a camera and they come outside. They are both wearing dresses that almost reach the sidewalk. One of them asks if I want my picture taken in front of the temple and I say yes.

"Where are the men?" she says to the other woman. "See if one of them can take his picture."

I wonder why a man is needed, and so must the other woman, who says, "Well, I can take his picture."

The women invite me into the visitors' center, where I lean my pack against the wall. My eyes dart to a table with some cake and punch, but it's not that easy. I'm first handed off to one of the men. The guy looks about dead. You could put a fist in the space between the knot of his tie and his shriveled neck. He speaks in a thin-lipped monotone, yet he's as subtle as a jackhammer.

"Have you ever considered missionary studies?"

He leads me around the room, stopping in front of pictures of places inside the temple I'm not allowed to see because I'm not a member. In one picture, a whirlpool tank is supported by the statues of twelve oxen. This is where Mormon ancestors who lived before the founding of the church are belatedly baptized. Another picture shows the Sealing Room, where couples are married not until death do they part, but for all eternity. There's also a picture of the childhood home of Joseph Smith, founder of the religion. The story goes that God revealed the *Book of Mormon* through a stack of gold plates Smith found buried in a New York mountain. That was in 1827, but the plates were somehow lost. This is what troubles me about organized religions: The crucial evidence is always missing.

The man hands me a pencil and asks me to fill out a card. I don't know why, but I actually put down my real name and address. Now some missionary in San Francisco won't rest until he personally places a copy of the *Book of Mormon* in my hands.

At least now I get cake and punch.

The volunteers ask what I'm up to and I tell them. Surely, one of them will seize the opportunity to drag a sinner home and show him the appeal of the wholesome Mormon life. But no offer is extended. They already know where I live. I'm already in the factory, somewhere down the assembly line. I leave the temple, marveling at the efficiency of the salvation industry.

I hike through town along the Snake River. There's a wooden raft anchored to the bank, and I consider playing Huck Finn for the night. But it's out in the open, leaving me an easy target for cops and robbers. I continue along the shore until I come to a private campground.

"Are you the manager?" I say to the teenaged girl inside the office.

"No, I just work here, but I'm pretty important."

I offer my labor in return for a campsite.

"Oh, I couldn't decide *that*," the girl says.

"I thought you said you were important," I tease.

"The owner's gotta decide that. She'll be in after five."

"What do you think she'll say?"

"Probably no."

I return to the office a half hour later, and I'm greeted by a woman with a warm, friendly smile. But when I run my pitch by her, the smile melts faster than a snowball in August. I see myself sleeping out on that raft yet.

"I've got hired men who do all my work, and they're through for the day," she says.

I tell her I'm passing through and I don't even need a whole spot. A patch of grass will do.

"Well, I hate to see you be without a place to stay," she says. "Why don't you take one of those tent sites over there."

As it turns out, the woman is a recent transplant from northern California. She is from the Alexander Valley, the very place where Chief let me camp on the first night of my journey.

There's a play area in the back of the campground. I spot a pair of swings and I sit in one. The rubber and canvas seat cradling my behind feels familiar, yet it's been at least twenty-five years since I've sat in a swing. When I was a little boy, the first poem I remember my mother reading to me was called "The Swing." It was in a book of children's literature she kept by her bed, and I often begged her to read it to me. I was enthralled with the image of flight. Of all the toys in the playground, the swing was my favorite. It was magical. And now I ask myself how I ever let a quarter century pass without sitting in a swing. If I had not embarked on this journey, would the swing have been lost to me forever? I give the ground a shove with my foot and start swinging. It all comes back. The muscles don't forget. I pull hard on the links of chain and climb higher. I throw my head back and look down at the ground. You're never alone on a swing. A swing swings back. Together you make music. There is the creak of the bolts, the scrape of your shoes dragging in the dirt. I pull harder, climb higher. I see the sun setting over where I've been, the moon coming up over where I'm going. I scoot to the edge of the seat. Soaring ever higher, I wonder: Do I still remember . . . how to jump?

TWELVE

I make West Yellowstone, Montana, by noon the next day. I was last here in 1988, covering the devastating forest fire in the national park for my newspaper. It's odd how the profane is never far from the beautiful. With its phalanx of souvenir shops and burger stands, West Yellowstone is a blight on the land worse than the charred remains of the famous park across the state line in Wyoming.

I figure kindness may be a rare commodity in a town that needs to sell so many T-shirts. I stay only long enough to hear one joke. A local citizen asks if I know the difference between a black bear and a grizzly. I don't.

"If you climb a tree and the bear climbs after you, it's a black bear," the man says. "A grizzly just knocks the tree down."

With this unsettling image in my mind, I press farther north into Montana.

The Big Sky State is enjoying an Indian summer, with temperatures in the eighties. My ride drops me in Bozeman, a rustic college town of sun-splashed brick buildings, cozy bookstores, and inviting cafes. It is a town I'd like to linger in—if I had any money. I promise myself I won't settle for a campsite tonight. But I am pacing the main drag well past dark on a Friday night and a kind stranger has yet to approach me.

I stand outside a coffeehouse called the Leaf and Bean. A band has launched into its first set. The place is empty. Two young women sitting behind a cash box inside the front door gesture at me to come in. They point at the cash box, as if to say, "We really need the money."

A sign in the window reads, "Please Don't Stand in the Doorway." A third woman inside now walks briskly toward me. She must be the owner or manager, coming to shoo me away.

"Are you going to come in and see the show?"

"I don't think so," I say, taking a step down the sidewalk.

"Because you don't have any money?"

"Yeah," I smile with embarrassment.

"Come in," she says, grabbing me by the arm.

The band's name is Fear Politik. They are quite loud, so I can't hear what the woman says to her employees when we walk by the cash box. I just smile and give the women a thumbs-up. It is only when Fear Politik takes a break that I can hear again and learn that my sponsor does not work at the coffeehouse.

"I tell them that if someone is standing at the window, the only reason that they don't come in is that they don't have any money," she says. "If they let people in early for free, it encourages other people to come in."

She gives her name as Barbara. She says she is a folk singer. She is forty and has the air of a Bohemian. A green beret sits atop her black hair, which is streaked with gray. She is extremely hyper, at times ready to fly off her stool. She speaks in a rapid New England accent.

"Do you need a place to stay?"

"That'd be great."

"You're not Ted Bundy, are you?"

"No," I say, reminding her that the infamous serial killer was executed several years ago.

Barbara talks nonstop. At one point she catches her breath and says, "Enough about me, what about me?" and babbles on. I strain to keep up. But with the heavy-duty decibels of Fear Politik assaulting my ears, Barbara may as well be whispering her life story to me in Albanian.

I piece together the tragic tale during the next break. Barbara is one of eleven children from a Catholic family in New Hampshire. One of her brothers was killed in a car crash. She married a carpenter and had two daughters. He left five years ago, refusing to pay alimony or child support. Lena, aged seventeen, lives in Connecticut with her father's sister. Alicia, fourteen, lives with Barbara in Bozeman. After her divorce, Barbara worked as a nanny in Maine. There she met a laborer turned musician from Minnesota. After a three-week courtship, they married. The new husband turned brutal and abusive, once dragging Barbara by the hair down a dirt road. She wouldn't leave; he finally did. While she was driving to Connecticut to visit Lena, Barbara's car was rear-ended. She injured her head and now suffers seizures. She later hurt her back while trying to lift a woman in a wheelchair. While laid up, she taught herself to play guitar and wrote some songs. She is almost as broke as me. To make the rent recently, she pawned her treasured Guild guitar for seven hundred dollars. She now plays a borrowed guitar. She moved to Bozeman nine months ago to help her younger sister, Colleen, who was recovering from a car accident of her own. Barbara plans to record a CD with Colleen.

After Fear Politik wraps up its last set, Barbara heaps praise on the young nihilists. We walk down the wide streets of Bozeman, past spacious houses with wraparound porches. Barbara confides that she recently fell and hit her head. She warns me that she has dizzy spells. She may pass out on the walk home. I should be ready to catch her.

Barbara has worn me out. I'm spent. The pack on my back feels like an anvil. All I want to do is fall into bed. Now Barbara is telling me she's lost. We cut circles in the dark until we arrive at a corner she thinks looks familiar.

She and her daughter live in the converted basement of a house. The room is cluttered with mismatched thrift store furniture. There is a fish tank with no fish. Barbara's five-month-old Australian shepherd Maya has further trashed the place in her absence, knocking over a plant and crapping on the floor. It is past midnight, but Alicia is not home. She sleeps in the apartment's single bedroom. Barbara sleeps in a twin bed against the wall in the living room. A mattress lies on the floor beneath the kitchen counter. The pillow is covered with a Dick Tracy pillowcase. This is my bed for the night.

I unroll my sleeping bag and crawl in. Barbara asks if I'd mind if she plays the guitar. I tell her not at all, as anything will be an improvement over her incessant chatter. She sings a song she wrote called ''Sunset Park.'' It's about her abusive second husband. Her voice is pleasant though unremarkable. I fall asleep as Maya chews on my foot through my sleeping bag. My last thought is of waking up in a storm of duck feathers.

In the middle of the night, I hear Barbara at the front door.

''There's a famous man here,'' she whispers. ''He's traveling across the country with no money.''

''Mom, I'm tired,'' Alicia says. ''I'm going to bed.''

*   *   *

When I wake in the morning, Barbara has already showered. The bathroom is pitch dark, with no light bulb or window. I unscrew the bare bulb from the living room ceiling and put it in the bathroom. A plastic garbage bag serves as the shower curtain. When I'm getting dressed, I hear Alicia talking to two girlfriends in the living room.

"I'm about to meet the famous guy."

I can practically see her rolling her eyes through the door.

I come out to meet the teenagers. Amber is all arms and legs; she wears bowling shoes. Cindy is a butterball with braces. Alicia is sad and beautiful. A goofy country song that mentions Elvis and Shakespeare in the same verse plays on the radio. The girls dance around the room.

They leave after the song, Barbara failing in her mission to get her daughter to eat, not that there is much in the way of food. I finished Edie's bread yesterday in West Yellowstone and now feel woozy. I've been reluctant to eat the canned goods Pastor Larry gave me, as I'll need them should the trip turn sour. Barbara labors in the kitchen to fix me a pair of apple pancakes. It is an agonizingly slow process interrupted often by her ongoing commentary. She also does not own a spatula. When she finally sets my breakfast before me, the pancakes are a pathetic pile of pieces. They taste like sand, but they fill the hole in my stomach.

Barbara's sister Colleen comes over. She is younger than Barbara by nine months.

"I warmed the womb for her," Barbara says.

Colleen is six feet tall and four months pregnant. Unlike her sister, she is as mellow as a dose of Valium, with a voice full of whisky and cigarettes. She came west to Montana sixteen years ago with an all-girl rock band and never left.

"This is Michael, he's traveling across the country with no money," Barbara says.

Colleen stage whispers behind her hand, "Barb, a stranger. A *stranger*, Barb."

"I asked him last night if he was Ted Bundy and he said no. Look at him. He's so sweet."

"Barb, serial killers are all nice guys."

"He didn't kill me all night long. And if I was gonna get killed, I'd want him to do it," Barbara says, smiling at me.

Colleen begs Barbara to go get coffee with her. She gave up caffeine when she got pregnant, but today has an unshakable java jones. She will pay Barbara to come and even offers to buy me a cup. Barbara agrees on the condition that Colleen sing a song with her. I listen politely through another rendition of "Sunset Park."

We climb into Colleen's beat-up Subaru station wagon. I smell a strong gas leak, which I think would harm Colleen and her unborn baby more than caffeine. The coffee shop is scrapped in favor of the doctor's office. Colleen has a risky pregnancy. At thirty-nine, she is on the old side to be having her first child. Also, she severed an artery in her thigh during the car accident. She must go daily to the doctor's office for an injection that thins her blood and prevents clotting.

While Colleen gets her shot, Barbara tells me I should spend the weekend. I'm only twelve days into the trip, but it feels like it's been twelve months. Though rewarding, this journey is like a twenty-four-hour-a-day job. I'm zapped. Barbara's is not the ideal sanctuary, but I need a place to regroup, free from the draining questions of where I'm going to sleep and how I'm going to eat.

Colleen drives us to her place, a tidy house on the other side of Bozeman. An Indian medicine wheel adorned with blue feathers hangs from the living room wall. Colleen uses the bathroom and comes back out with her hair in a ponytail and her face streaked with rouge as thick as war paint. I chop celery and Colleen fixes a bowl of tuna and makes me two sandwiches.

Her husband Mark comes home for lunch. He is a finisher at a guitar factory outside of town. His hands are orange from staining a custom guitar for Bob Dylan. Mark is nine years younger than Colleen. He's a fan of the conservative talk show host Rush Limbaugh, and he takes the inevitable swipe at my penniless journey. But once he learns that I don't accept money, Mark is intrigued by my mission and allows me a guilt-free free lunch.

The doorbell rings. It's a German named Hans, a carpet cleaner who has come to give Mark and Colleen an estimate. When he is not cleaning carpets, Hans is a devoted member of the Montana-based doomsday cult the Church Universal Triumphant. He also plays guitar. He mentions in passing that the pawnshop sold Barbara's Guild guitar.

"My guitar has been sold?" Barbara says.

Hans nods.

"Oh no!" Barbara shrieks. She bolts out the door, holding her hands to her mouth. She stops at the sidewalk and turns back. "Oh no! My beautiful, beautiful guitar has been sold!" She runs down the street and disappears around the corner.

"She's gone," I say.

"She'll be back," Colleen says. "This is what you call a flight of drama."

Barbara returns in five minutes, the owner of a new personality.

"I decided it's okay," she says, all smiles. "Someone else can enjoy my beautiful guitar now."

When we get back to her place, Barbara confesses the obvious. She is a manic-depressive.

She sits in the yard playing her borrowed guitar while I write in my journal at the kitchen table.

Barbara comes back inside as the sun starts to set.

"I was thinking about your trip. It makes me sad because I was thinking about all the people who haven't had twelve days of kindness in their whole life. People tell me I'm the unluckiest person in the world, but I feel so blessed. I have appreciation. I have gifts. I should be a homeless person. I should be starving. I should be in an institution. I live for all those people who don't have the will to live."

I'm relieved when Mark and Colleen pick me up to go watch a video at their house. Barbara stays home in case her friend Paul drops by. He is a student from Belgium who came to the university to study bugs. Some nights when he finishes in the lab, he sleeps at Barbara's on the mattress with the Dick Tracy pillowcase. Barbara says Paul is jealous of me because of my trip. I have freedom, while he must meet family expectations and become a cookie-cutter-perfect Belgian scientist. He would love to trade places with me. I know the feeling. Some days I'd rather be a Belgian scientist. Barbara has flipped for Paul. He is half her age and due to return to Belgium in two days.

"You better pick a new obsession, Barb," Colleen says.

When I get back to Barbara's, Paul is sitting on her bed, petting Maya. He strikes me as a shy little boy with a blond goatee. Before long, he announces he must leave. Barbara walks him outside. I get into bed. They are standing in the driveway a long time, doing what awkward lovers do in the dark.

In the morning, Barbara comes out of Alicia's room and asks where Paul is. After I dozed off, he apparently came back in and slept in Barbara's bed. Alicia spent the night at a friend's, so Barbara slept in her room.

"I don't know," I say.

Barbara slumps on the couch, fidgeting with a pillow on her lap.

"He told me he doesn't want to say good-bye," she says, frowning. "This is his way of saying good-bye. He wants me to hate him."

I reassure Barbara that Paul will say good-bye before he flies home. As soon as the words leave my mouth, he whisks through the front door carrying a grocery bag full of milk, juice, and pancake mix. He sets the bag on the counter and leaves again without breaking stride. Barbara looks at the meaning of the interlude from every negative angle.

"I don't think you should analyze things so much," I say.

She says men have abandoned her all her life. When she was a little girl, her father would lock her outside. Her first husband left her. Several times, her second husband packed his bags and set them by the door for her to see before he finally left for real. Now Paul.

I tell her she should recognize the pattern so she won't repeat it.

"I've had forty years of trauma and abuse," she says. "It's all I know."

Barbara has a million plans for a career in music, but I doubt she will ever play the guitar as well as she plays the victim. She is paralyzed, unable to act on any of her dreams, anxiously awaiting her next dose of despair. I fear that when I leave tomorrow, she will see me as yet another man abandoning her.

She pulls a handful of orange berries off a bush in the yard to toss into the pancake batter. When I point out that they are probably not edible, she cuts up an apple. After my second breakfast of apple pancakes, I wash the dishes.

"Maybe I ought to kidnap you," Barbara says, "like in *Misery*, and have you write my story."

"That would be a federal offense. Besides, it's already been done."

"Only in the movies."

Paul returns yet again. This time he stays while Barbara cooks him some pancakes. Alicia rolls in around noon and flops on her mother's bed.

"I'm gonna have a heart attack," Alicia says dramatically.

She pops up and gets a carton of chocolate ice cream from the freezer. She scoops with a teaspoon into a coffee cup. She keeps missing and picks the ice cream off the counter with her hands and puts it in the cup. She collapses on the couch.

Paul mumbles something and leaves, closing the door behind him. Barbara sits in a round rattan chair held together with duct tape and stares at the door.

Alicia says what I'm thinking.

"He's got a stick up his butt. He's stupid. He's the biggest kiss-up. He's a pussy."

"Ali!" Barbara says. Then she turns calm. "Ali, Colleen thinks you've had sex, but I told her that if you had, you'd tell me."

"Mom, I kissed a boy last night."

"You kissed a boy?" Barbara squeals. "Who? Who?"

"Ryan."

"Ryan?"

"Then I got laid!" Alicia blurts.

"Ali!"

"I got laid. *Laid*—I love that word," Alicia says, spooning ice cream into her mouth.

"Ali, don't talk like that. That kind of talk is not becoming."

"*Coming*," Alicia moans, writhing on the couch. "You said *'Coming'*."

The rattan chair breaks and Barbara crashes to the floor. The chair lands on her head. Together they look like an upturned cup and saucer. Alicia bounces up from the couch and flies out the door.

"I've lost my childhood," she yells to the world.

I can't stay down in the basement alone with Barbara. I grab my journal and walk out. When I come back, it's after five o'clock. The apartment is nearly dark. Barbara stands in the kitchen, a vacant look on her face.

"How you doing?" I say.

"Not good. I was in a coma for four hours."

"What?"

"I'm going through abandonment syndrome. When Paul closed that door in my face, it triggered it. I had flashbacks and went into a coma."

I get a sick feeling, like someone who nearly reaches the end of a long dark tunnel only to find an oncoming train. I know now that it's too late. I've stayed one day too long.

Barbara stirs the pieces of a burned pancake in a skillet with a knife. She says she is making pancakes for my trip. She tells me she is dizzy. She starts to cry. I tell her I'll finish the pancake and I help her to the couch.

"I'm going into shock," she says.

"What do you want me to do?"

"Don't call the hospital! I can't go back to the hospital again!"

She holds her head in her hands and weeps uncontrollably. I'm frightened—for her and for me. Alicia is not home. I haven't seen Colleen since last night. There isn't a phone in the apartment. I could run upstairs, but I'm afraid to leave Barbara alone.

"Have you taken your medication?"

"Yeah," she wails.

She shudders and bawls about how her two husbands abandoned her, how her father locked her outside, how Paul shut the door in her face. She asks for a box of crayons and a pad of paper from the kitchen drawer. She attacks the paper with a crayon, slashing as if she held a knife. A picture of a sleeping woman emerges. She is purple. Barbara fills the rest of the paper with sharp geometric figures, colored red and orange and yellow. When she is finished, she cuts up the picture into heart-shaped pieces and tears them all in two.

"Help me think of other reasons for Paul's behavior," she says.

When I don't answer, she says, "I was gonna get on a bike and then pull in front of a car."

"You don't want to do that."

"It would be less painful," she cries, heading off on another jag. "Part of it would be for the pain. I need to be hit right in the face."

"Do you want me to call Colleen?"

"No! She'll try to commit me. I can't go to the hospital again! I'll lose Ali!"

"You're not going to go to the hospital," I try to soothe her.

"You don't want to. Just relax. Don't think about everything at once."

Barbara wails and weeps and draws, hacking away at the pad. I'm afraid to go and I'm afraid to stay. Five hours pass. Just when I think she is calming down, she loses it again.

I get up and wash the dishes. I scrub the knife that Barbara was using to flip pancakes. It has a melted handle, a triangular blade, and a serrated edge. Barbara catches me looking at the knife and reads my mind.

"Don't worry, Michael, I won't snap and take it out on you. I could never hurt you."

That may be true, I think, but perhaps someone else inside her could.

"God sent you here to save me, Michael. You're a Godsend."

She rocks back and forth, holding herself.

"I don't usually treat my guests this way," she sniffles. "You are seeing me have a total nervous breakdown."

She catches her breath, then bawls, "See what you pay for pancakes?"

THIRTEEN

When I climb the stairs from Barbara's basement apartment the next day, I feel as if I'm emerging from a torture session in a dungeon. I welcome the freedom, but I'm more unsure than ever about what lies ahead. All of the goodwill saved from the early part of the trip has been spent in Bozeman. There's nothing left in reserve. I've lost my edge. I'm fat and weak and vulnerable. The pack on my back feels strange. The sign in my hand feels strange. It's like I'm starting over.

I'm good for only twelve miles, which puts me in Livingston, Montana, a town that could serve as a set for a Hollywood western. The bartender at the Hotel Murray lets me watch "Monday Night Football," even though I can't buy a drink. I help myself to a free slice of happy hour pizza. I'm grateful when the game goes into overtime, delaying the search for a place to sleep.

I bed down on the lawn behind the train museum. But when my eyes adjust to the dark, I see I'm not as hidden as I thought. After a furtive stroll, I lay my bag out on a patch of grass behind the city library. It's bordered by a public parking lot and an apartment building whose tenants keep odd hours. The locomotives in the switching yard shake the ground all night. I'm not sure if I sleep or not. When I notice the time and temperature sign at the bank, it reads 6:38 and 46°. My eyes sting. The Absaroka Mountains looming above town are the color of a bruise.

J. D. and Kristin stop for me at the I-90 eastbound on ramp. J. D., twenty-six, is a ringer for the late rock legend Jim Morrison, with long, curly brown hair, dark shades, and a pretty-boy pout. Kristin, twenty, is a walking wet dream, with bleached blond hair, short jeans cutoffs, and centerfold breasts. Her T-shirt says "Jaegermeister," and I can read every letter.

They have been driving all night from Oregon. They are both originally from Bismarck, North Dakota. J. D.'s mother is driving from Bismarck to meet them tomorrow in Billings, Montana. She has the couple's seven-month-old daughter, Summer, who she has been watching while J. D. and Kristin have been working in Oregon. J. D. says he's a welder. Kristin doesn't say what she is.

We barrel down the freeway, heavy metal blaring on the stereo. J. D. pulls into a truck stop thirty miles west of Billings. While Kristin uses the restroom, he opens an ice chest in the back of the pickup.

"Want a beer?" he says.

It's nine in the morning. I've got an empty stomach. I'm riding through America with a pair of perfect strangers.

"Sure, why not?" I say.

As I gulp from the can, I see the sky reflected in J. D.'s sunglasses, and by the time I reach the bottom, I've got a feeling that anything can happen, and that's just fine.

Back on the road, J. D. reaches between his legs into a second ice chest on the floorboard.

"Want another?" he says. "They're like potato chips, you can't have just one."

"If you're gonna be a bear, might as well be a grizzly," I say, cracking open the new beer.

J. D. opens another for himself and one for Kristin, who rides between us, her sleek legs bent high by the transmission well.

"What are you doing out here?" J. D. says.

"A month ago I went in and told my boss I'd had enough."

"You woke up with one nerve and he was on it," J. D. says, grinning.

"Something like that," I say, and I tell them the rest.

When Kristin hears I'm from San Francisco, she says she was recently in the Bay Area. Some town that starts with the letter *M*, she says. We spend a few miles trying to figure out the name of the place. I give up and ask her what she was doing there.

"Visiting a friend," she says.

"Tell him what you were *really* doing," J. D. says.

"You tell him. You're the one who put me on the plane."

"We were running a scam on some old guy," J. D. says. "Some rich dude who wants to marry her."

"I met him in Vegas," Kristin says.

"That's what she does," J. D. says. "Hustles and dances."

"I was an *escort*," Kristin corrects him. "This guy picked me up in a limo, and two hours later I had fourteen hundred dollars. I didn't even have to fuck him—the first time. Now he wants to marry me. He even wants to adopt my daughter. He had this financial statement printed out on a computer, showed me how I'd be taken care of. But I said, 'No way.' I like my freedom."

"We're scamming him for thousands," J. D. says.

"It's not a scam," Kristin says. "It's money. I only sleep with guys that have money. If you're gonna do this, you might as well go for the high end. Why fuck someone for twenty bucks?''

Kristin ran away from home when she was thirteen. Even at that tender age, she found work as a stripper in a Portland bar. Two years later, she stole a car and returned to Bismark, where she met J. D. They have been traveling together for five years, Kristin turning tricks in every state in the West. Somewhere along the line, I figure, she got breast implants. But there are some things I can't ask a woman, even if she's a whore.

''How's all this set with you, J. D.?'' I say.

''It was hard when we first got together, but it's okay now that I've matured. With her, I'm never broke.''

Kristin drags on a cigarette. J. D. fishes out three more beers. I can see the Billings skyline when he tells me he's really not a welder.

''This summer in Oregon, we were dealing drugs. Dealing 'em and using 'em. Dealing enough to use.''

''What kind of drugs?''

''Crank,'' J. D. says. He grins. ''Yeah, life's always a lot more complicated than it looks. Another reason we're coming over to Billings is she's gotta have an abortion tomorrow.''

''Yeah, one baby's enough,'' Kristin says. ''I wanna be a good mother.''

She pulls out her wallet and shows me pictures of Summer.

''I'm fifteen weeks pregnant. Too late to get an abortion in Oregon. They let you have one up to nineteen weeks in Montana. It's gonna be a two-day procedure.''

While Kristin has her wallet out, J. D. asks her how much money they have.

Kristin counts the bills.

''Three hundred.''

''And we owe my mom two-fifty for the abortion,'' J. D. says. ''That leaves us fifty bucks to play with.''

He looks at me. ''You're welcome to hang with us. We're just gonna go to a bar and make some calls.''

"Well, you know my story. I don't have a penny."

"It doesn't matter to me," J. D. says.

"Sounds good."

J. D. parks in front of a dive called The Lobby. When we hit the door, sunlight washes over a roomful of professional alcoholics. I use the bathroom. When I return, a draft beer is waiting for me on the bar.

"Who should we call?" J. D. says. "Carol?"

"No, I don't wanna call Carol," Kristin says. "She's a bitch. Besides, if we call her, we'll have to see Alex and them."

"Let's call Wanda then."

"Wanda outta jail yet?"

"We'll find out," J. D. says, then walks to the pay phone.

The morning disappears in a blur of beer and shots of tequila. J. D. and Kristin try their luck at the video poker machines. The fifty dollars gets chewed up fast. Kristin moves down the bar, and a man in a cowboy hat chats her up. Kristin leans over the bar, affording the cowboy a better look at what's stuffed inside her T-shirt. The cowboy buys her a drink. Then another. J. D. continues to play the poker machine.

"You got a real lucrative act going here," I say.

"Yeah, I never have to buy her a drink."

Kristin walks by us. She's trailed by the cowboy.

"I'm going to the bathroom," she says.

"Okay," J. D. says without looking up from the screen.

Kristin and the cowboy return five minutes later. There's suddenly money for more beer and video poker. I guess Kristin doesn't always work the high end of the hooker's ladder.

An old man with three teeth in his mouth sits at a table crowded with empty beer cans and a sketch pad. J. D. and Kristin sit down and pay the man twenty bucks to draw their caricatures.

J. D. challenges me to a game of pool. I win. Then I win three more games. Then it's one o'clock, time to go to Wanda's.

We drive down a country road, my hand riding the air outside the window. I'm drunk and the sky looks like a scene from the Bible.

J. D. pulls alongside a prefab house with a couple of junked cars out front. Kristin goes inside.

"You'd never know these guys were millionaires," J. D. says.

Kristin and Wanda come out to the truck. Wanda wears hideous eyeliner and has the torn-up look of a speed addict. She is under house arrest, serving time for a drug bust. She wears an electronic bracelet on her wrist. If she leaves her front yard, the police will know.

"It's gonna take two hours," Kristin says to J. D. "And it's sixty."

Wanda's husband is the one with the methamphetamines, and he's not home.

J. D. pulls a fifty from his wallet.

"If you want," Wanda says, "I'll go in for a quarter and you guys pay forty-five."

J. D. and Kristin agree.

"I better get back in, in case they call," Wanda says, shaking her bracelet.

We drive to another bar on a road fronting the freeway. J. D. and Kristin argue on the way. I can't tell over what because the stereo is cranked to ten. By the time we catch up to Kristin, she is nudged up against another cowboy. J. D. and I take the stools on the other side of Kristin. The cowboy shoots us a glare. J. D. gets up and walks away, chuckling. He is still wearing his sunglasses. Kristin and the cowboy walk toward the bathroom.

There are more games of pool and more beer.

"Man, you're a hard person to get drunk," J. D. says.

When Kristin comes back, she's wearing fresh lipstick. She sits at a table next to the pool table and orders nachos. When she's through eating, I move in and scarf down the leftovers.

"Okay, I want your best game," J. D. says. "Let's play for something."

"I don't have anything to bet," I remind him.

"Yes you do. If you win, I'll give you a bow tie. If I win, you've gotta wear it."

J. D.'s game steps up a notch, and it's likely he's been sandbagging me. That's okay, I've been holding back, too. But now I'm playing out of my head, sinking everything and wishing I had money to bet.

"It's three o'clock," Kristin says as I drop the eight ball for the win.

We pile into the pickup and head back out to Wanda's. J. D. stops at a mini-mart for a six pack of beer and a jar of caffeine pills, which he pops when his supply of speed runs low.

"You wanna do a little crank with us, Mike?" he says.

"Nah, I can't. In my profession we get drug tested." It's true, but I also have no interest in taking methamphetamines.

Kristin says to wait in the car while she goes inside to Wanda's to buy the drugs. J. D. pulls a dollar bill from his wallet and folds it into something that makes me laugh.

"Here's your bow tie," he says. "I'm trying to corrupt your trip."

I put the dollar bill in my pack, knowing I'll give it away later.

Wanda's husband hasn't showed up with the drugs, so we go inside and wait for him. A baby girl bounces in a portable swing in front of the TV. Wanda sits on the couch, spraying Bactine on a cut on her hand then blowing on it. She keeps spraying and blowing, and I think she's going to use up the whole can.

A man appears from out of nowhere. He's wearing a camouflage T-shirt.

"Need to talk to ya," he says to Wanda.

I assume he's her husband, but J. D. says he's not. I sit in a chair, drinking beer. I can't believe how stupid I am, waiting in a house full of strangers for a drug delivery.

Kristin fidgets and says she can't wait any longer. We get up to leave.

"I don't know what could've happened," Wanda says. "It

usually only takes him two hours. Try calling me at four-thirty or quarter to five.''

She turns to me. "So, do you want some money?''

Wanda knows I'm traveling penniless. "No, I can't," I remind her.

"I've always wanted to say that!" she cackles. "Well, at least I can give you some food.''

She hands me an apple and a piece of freshly baked peach cobbler wrapped in a napkin. I eat the food on the ride back into Billings.

J. D. says to Kristin, "How 'bout we say our adioses to Mike and get us a motel room?''

So this is it. Next thing I know, I'm getting dropped in the middle of downtown Billings by a prostitute and her boyfriend. It's cold and the sky is gray and Billings looks hard and mean, and it is only after J. D. and Kristin pull away that I realize I've left my sweater in the back of their pickup.

The heavy afternoon hangover is on its way. I stumble down the street, searching for whatever it is that's supposed to happen next.

FOURTEEN

I find the Montana Rescue Mission where I figured it would be—on the other side of the tracks. The houseman looks like a biker, equipped with ponytail and beard. He tells me to attend chapel at seven, eat dinner, then check back and he'll see about finding me a bed.

I sink into the last vacant chair of the shelter's TV room. The men around me are dirty and damaged. One guy is missing an arm, another a leg. The fellow by the door mumbles to himself and clutches a colostomy bag.

The man next to me gets up and Al takes his place. Al is sixty-seven and looks like Bob Hope. He worked thirty years as a waiter in New York City. He remembers every meal served, every tip received. He never married. He roams the country, staying in homeless shelters when broke, cheap motels when flush. He is eventually heading for a VA hospital in Tennessee, where there is a doctor who is supposed to be able to fix his eyes. Al is going blind. He lives on his monthly Social Security check of $596. The next check arrives in ten days.

"I may stay longer than ten days, let the money accumulate," Al says. "It's a hundred thirty-nine a week. But if I stay an extra week, it'll almost be two hundred. See?"

The houseman announces over the speaker that it's time for chapel and everybody shuffles out. I walk downstairs, pack on my back, for what I think is the chapel.

"Sir, where are you going?"

It's the houseman.

"To the chapel."

"This is the chapel," he sneers, rapping on a sign I missed. "See? Right here on this door where it says 'Chapel.' "

The guy is a smart-ass and a thug, but I hold my tongue because I'm too tired to argue and I've yet to get a bed.

The preacher wears jeans and the coat of a blue suit. He's a cross between a third-rate televangelist and a bad stand-up comic. He paces in front of the pews, arms flailing, talking rapidly about his former life as a drug user, alcohol abuser, and chaser of wild women. He moved to Los Angeles, where one day he found a pile of human feces on the seat of his car. Shortly thereafter, he found God.

Dinner is meatballs and noodles, salad, and powdered milk. There are also a few stale cakes donated by a local bakery. A shelter worker walks down the line, randomly asking men to blow into a Breathalyzer. Two guys don't pass the test, and the worker orders them out of the shelter. They protest, but the preacher is there to help drag them away. I suddenly realize that if I'm asked to blow, I'm out of a meal and a bed. I guess I don't look as drunk as I feel because the man with the Breathalyzer skips me.

I can't check in until all the regulars have, so I wait in the TV room. I lean on my pack, too exhausted and hung over to focus on the tube. Al plops down next to me.

"Don't let me interrupt you if you're watching a program," he says.

Before I can answer, the retired waiter is off on another restaurant-related reverie.

"I had a second breakfast today at a little place near here. It was good. Eggs, sausage, potatoes, toast, coffee. Three-ten. Tipped her fifty cents."

Al elaborates on the break down of his finances, but it's all noise. I unzip a pocket on my pack and pull out the bow tie J. D. gave me.

"Here, have a bow tie," I say, handing Al the folded dollar.

"Isn't that something," he says, handing it back.

"No, that's for you. It's my last dollar. I don't need it."

"What?"

"I don't need money."

"You need it for some things, I'm sure."

"No, you take it."

As I'd hoped, Al is up and out the door with the dollar. But he returns all too soon. He carries a few loose cigarettes he bought at the corner liquor store. He gestures to a grubby man talking on the phone.

"I met that guy outside and I told him the story of how I came into the dollar," Al says conspiratorially. "I was gonna give him a few cigarettes. Now I see he's on the phone, so I know he's got someone. Even if it's just a friend, he's got someone. So I don't know now. I don't know if I'll give him the cigarettes or not."

I can barely hold my head up. Al sounds like he's talking through a tin can pressed against my ear.

"See? He's on the phone. That tells me he's got someone. He told me outside he didn't have anyone. I'm not gonna give him the cigarettes.''

The man with the Breathalyzer strides into the TV room. He stands in front of an Indian slumped in a chair. The Indian is passed out. The man with the Breathalyzer shakes the Indian awake. He pokes the tube into his mouth.

"Blow hard.''

The Indian blows.

The worker reads the contraption. He squats down so he's in the Indian's face.

"What's your name?''

"Kelley,'' the Indian says.

"That your first or last name?''

"Last.''

"What's your first name?''

"Johnny.''

"Johnny, you're intoxicated. You can't stay here tonight. Get your things and leave.''

The worker walks away and the Indian falls back asleep.

"See, look at him on the phone,'' Al is saying. "He's got someone.''

The Breathalyzer man returns and wakes the Indian.

"Johnny, get your shoes on and leave. You can't stay here tonight.''

"You know what?'' Al says. "I'm gonna give him those cigarettes after all.''

The houseman calls me into his office. He reads me a list of questions, marking my answers on a form attached to a clipboard.

"I'm gonna put your address as the mission.''

"Fine.''

"How long you lived here?''

"I've been in Montana five days.''

"Any drug or alcohol problems?''

"Nope," I say, trying my best to look sober.

An old whiskered man enters the office. "My mattress has been pissed on," he says.

"Ernie, all those beds been pissed on." The houseman turns to me and asks his last question. "Do you consider yourself homeless?"

I have to think on this one. I know I've got a home I can go back to any time I want. I also know that at least part of the reason I'm standing here relates to my work as a writer. But at this moment, I don't feel any more special than old Ernie here and his pissed-on mattress.

"Tonight, yes," I say.

A bed costs three dollars or four hours of work in the morning. I consider myself lucky to be assigned to the laundry detail. The houseman hands me my bed number and I go upstairs.

The dorm room is wall-to-wall bunks. The beds are covered with funky patch quilts. I find my bunk, a top one. The mattress is ripped and sunken and yellow. An empty soda can and two hair-clogged razors are stuffed underneath. I wonder if Ernie wants to trade.

"Whattaya gonna do with that pack?" someone calls out from the sea of bunks.

"I don't know." It dawns on me that my pack is worth more than the combined possessions of my bunkmates.

Flabby men with tallowy legs and stained underwear step from the communal showers. A few guys read atop their bunks. One bearded man with greasy hair and a moronic look stares at me while picking his feet. There are no windows. The smell is awful.

I leave my pack and shoes on the floor and climb into my bunk. I must curl up in a ball to keep my feet from kicking the head of the guy to my south, and my head from touching the feet of the guy to my north.

"Lights out!" the houseman barks over the intercom.

I fall asleep to a symphony of wheezes, coughs, snores, and farts.

*   *   *

The morning pancakes are burnt. Even so, they taste better than Barbara's. I sit across from the only woman in the cafeteria. She sleeps in her car and eats at the shelter. She has a black eye.

''As soon as my old man's outta jail, we're gonna go to Florida,'' she says.

I ask why her boyfriend is in jail. She makes a fist and presses it to her black eye.

I report to laundry duty and learn that I've been reclassified. The supervisor, Jimmy, hands me a push broom. I guide it up and down between the rows of bunks. Jimmy whistles a lonesome cowboy tune.

When I finish sweeping, Jimmy rolls out a bucket and mop. He tells me to change the water every two rows, and don't let anybody track my work up. He comes out from the laundry room every so often to reposition a fan that blows dry the spots I've already mopped.

The man with one leg I saw in the TV room sits on the dorm floor, scraping gunk off the trim with a putty knife. When I get to him, I mop over the tiles where his leg is supposed to be, and remind myself to go back later for the rest.

A skinny tattooed man brings my mopping operation to a halt in row six. He takes his time getting dressed. I don't want him muddying my good work. He puts on every article of clothing he owns—five layers and two pairs of gloves. He transforms from Spider Man into the Incredible Hulk.

Jimmy chases the man out and I finish mopping. I empty the trash and sweep the stairway. Jimmy hands me a Brillo pad. He says to wipe up the tar stains tracked in by the homeless men who have day jobs as construction grunts. This is the hard part—harder than mopping—but I hunt down every bit of tar. I figure Jimmy is the type to check.

I finish at 9:30, two hours ahead of schedule. Jimmy compliments my work. He says I'm always welcome on his detail. I tell him I'm heading east. Still, it's nice to know I've got something to fall back on.

It's cold and rainy when I hit the street. I think a moment, then walk back through the mission door. As they say, there's no place like home.

FIFTEEN

I leave the shelter the next morning, intent on getting out of Montana by day's end. I've always wanted to see Mt. Rushmore. All the places I've been, I don't know why I've never been there. There have been times when I actually got in a car and headed in that direction. But I always got sidetracked. I figure today is the day.

I walk east out of Billings along the interstate. My sign is not out because the freeway splits a few miles ahead. There's not much of a shoulder and the cars blowing past almost topple me down the embankment. An old pickup with a camper shell stops ahead of me in the middle of the road.

"Where yew goin'?" an old man says when I reach the window. He's as annoyed as he is curious.

"South Dakota. Where are you headed?"

"Albuquerque!"

I throw my pack in back and climb in. Wyoming wasn't in my travel plans, but I can get out a bit farther south and cut over to Mt. Rushmore.

Lester is sixty-three. His white hair and mustache pokes out in every direction. His black horn-rimmed bifocals rest on a red nose with little hairs sprouting out like a strawberry. He's been up visiting his grown step-granddaughter over near Helena. He worked on her house a bit, then went backpacking for nine days in the Beartooth Wilderness, sleeping under a piece of plastic.

He comes from a family of thirteen kids in southern Missouri. He pronounces it "Misery."

Lester asks what's up and I tell him.

"Yer not that feller I read about in the Bozeman paper, are yew?"

Before I left Barbara's, she took me down to the local paper and told the editor I'd make a good human interest story. I was surprised when a reporter interviewed me for two hours, and amused when I saw my picture splashed across the front page the next day.

"Yep," I say.

"Well, I'll be dipped in shit."

Lester points to a loaf of homemade bread resting on the seat.

"Tear me off a hunk of that bread, will yew. I gotta git rid of this heartburn. Have yerself a piece, then take the rest with yew. I'll contribute that much to your trip."

Lester is a backgammon fanatic. He's on the road much of the year, traveling to tournaments from California to New Mexico. Before that, he laid sewer lines in Albuquerque.

"I spent forty-one years in a ditch. I been buried, hit on the head by a backhoe bucket, cursed at by drivers, invited a few to step outta their cars—none of 'em ever got out. I've had a full life."

The freeway bends south toward Wyoming, and I can see a dusting of snow on the Bighorn Mountains in the distance. The willow trees are turning from green to yellow, with some already a burnt orange. Antelope galore graze on both sides of the interstate.

Lester pulls in to a rest stop.

"This is a good place to piss. I gotta piss out this coffee. When yew get to be my age, yew don't buy coffee and beer, yew just rent it for a while."

Back on the road, Lester says, "If yew make it as far as Casper with me, I'll buy yew lunch. And to show yew my heart's in the right place, I'll let yew order anything on the menu—long's it's not more'n thirty-five cents.''

He grins.

Casper, Wyoming, is nearly three hundred miles away. If I ride that far, I'll next be heading east through Nebraska, and I can kiss Mt. Rushmore off for yet another time. Still, my gut says stick with Lester. Unlike Mt. Rushmore, my itinerary is not carved in stone.

We cross the state line and gas up in Sheridan, Wyoming. I slide into the driver's seat. I haven't driven a car in three weeks, and the old truck's steering wheel feels squirrely in my hands. But I'm glad to be helping out.

Lester doesn't have any kids. He was married for thirty-one years.

"I got a divorce last April. Got tired of the ass-chewin'. Cost me a hundred fifty thousand dollars, and it was worth it!''

He turns to me.

"Yew married?''

"Nope.''

"Good! Keep it that way. I saw no point to it in the end.''

"Why were you with her thirty-one years then?''

"I don't know!'' Lester says, shaking his head. "Her first husband couldn't keep a job, so she threw him out. Then I work every day and I git thirty-one years of ass-chewin' for my thanks. It didn't matter what I said, I was wrong. Even when I didn't say a thing, I was wrong.''

Before he got divorced, Lester bought a mobile home under a friend's name so his wife couldn't get at it during the settlement.

"I told the feller that if I go and kick the bucket, sell the trailer and throw a party.''

The trees disappear and the sheep have eaten the grass down to the dirt. Lester says it hasn't rained since spring, except for "the fifth of Jew-lie.'' The interstate stretches out across the land like a ribbon wrapped around an unwanted gift.

Lester tells me he was supposed to be back in Albuquerque three days ago, but the fishing was too good in Montana.

"I'll wait a couple days, then call my girlfriend," he says. "Yew don't wanna spoil 'em."

"How long you been with your girlfriend?"

"Been seein' her about fifteen years."

"But I thought you just got divorced."

"I couldn't git any at home. When they shut yew down, no point in arguin'. Just go git it somewheres else."

"How old is your girlfriend?"

"Fifty-two."

"A young one."

"Hell, I got one that's forty I pat on the butt once in a while."

The peaks of the Laramie Range are blanketed with snow when we pull into Casper. Lester guides me to a diner on the truck loop. He flirts with the waitress and jaws with some old-timers about the weather. We both order fried chicken, which comes with lentil soup, salad, fries, and rolls. Lester downs five cups of coffee. He orders a butterscotch sundae and berates me for not doing the same.

I ride with him another sixty miles and get out at a rest stop at the intersection of Highway 20.

"If you could do something different now, what would it be?" I ask Lester.

"Not a thing. Yew are lookin' at the most contented man in the world."

"What's your secret?"

"I guess I make the most of what comes and the least of what goes."

Someone told me at the mission that hitchhiking is illegal in Wyoming. I'm only seventy-five miles west of Nebraska. If the cops give me any problems, I figure I can walk to the state line. But when I clear the first rise in the road, I see I don't have to worry about the law. There's nothing out here but me and the wind.

I don't see a car for a half hour. Then an eighteen-wheeler blows by and just about rips the sign from my hands. The next car isn't for another fifteen minutes. A white Lincoln Continental with a single woman driver. Not a chance. I start looking around for a place to camp in case I get stranded.

I turn around and see the Lincoln stopped on the shoulder a couple hundred yards up the road. I don't think she stopped for me. She's too far away. I keep looking, waiting for her to drive off. After a few minutes, she backs up. I guess she was weighing the odds.

"I never pick up hitchhikers, but you had such a forlorn look on your face," the woman says.

Jennifer is thirty-two. She's a tall, attractive brunette, dressed in a fancy warm-up suit. She's going to Mt. Rushmore.

"What a coincidence. That was my original destination, but I got sidetracked."

"There are no coincidences," Jennifer says.

Riding with Jennifer means a 150-mile detour north into South Dakota—negating half of Lester's ride—but I guess I'm destined to see Mt. Rushmore.

Jennifer is a dentist from Wisconsin. She's been vacationing throughout the West in the rented Lincoln. She was traveling with her boyfriend, a banker from England, but she kicked him out last week because he called her a self-absorbed baby in Big Sur.

Within five minutes, Jennifer tells me she graduated from college in two and a half years, flies her own plane, owns a Mercedes, lectures around the world, sits on the boards of several associations, and treats the Amish at night for free. I wouldn't call it bald bragging, but Jennifer's preoccupation with her accomplishments is off-putting. By the time she concludes her verbal resume, I'm feeling sympathetic toward the English banker.

I flip through one of Jennifer's tour books, reading aloud about Mt. Rushmore. It's open at night. "And it's free," I say.

"Hey, even you can afford that," Jennifer says.

It's pitch dark when we cross into South Dakota and drive up into the Black Hills. A tacky tourist town clogged with souvenir shops announces the entrance to the monument. I don't know why, but I pictured Mt. Rushmore as being out in the middle of nowhere. We drive around a curve and then, boom, there it is. Washington, Jefferson, Lincoln, and Roosevelt—all lit up like the Fourth of July.

Jennifer parks the car and walks up a path. I almost have to run to keep up. We walk down into the amphitheater. I gaze up at the magnificent faces. Finally, after all these years. What a spectacular sight.

"Ready?" Jennifer says as she turns to leave.

We drive down the hill toward Rapid City. Jennifer plans to see the Badlands in the morning. I see lights in the distance. The city is bigger than I thought. My stomach churns. I remember how Mo dropped me back in Ashland, Oregon, after I thought I had a place to stay. I decide to take the initiative.

"So, what's your plan here?" I say.

"I'm going to get a motel, have some dinner, then crash out," Jennifer says. There is an agonizingly long pause before she adds, "I can get two rooms if you're uncomfortable."

I exhale with relief. "One's fine," I say.

We stop at a coffee shop. Jennifer special orders steamed vegetables and rice. She offers to buy me dinner, but I'm still full from the lunch Lester bought me.

"Just water for me," I tell the waitress. "I'm on a liquid diet."

"Are you the Invisible Man?" the waitress says.

She is twenty but looks twelve. She's giggly and blond.

"Nope, who's that?"

"You didn't see that movie?"

"I haven't seen a movie in a while."

"What's the last movie you saw?"

"I can't remember."

"Did you see *Natural Born Killers*?"

The question jars me. I flash on what might be waiting for me out on the road.

"Yeah, that was the one," I say quietly.

I want off this subject.

"So what do people do in Rapid City?"

"There's a meat packing plant. The Coke plant. If you make seven dollars an hour here, that's a good job. My dad's been out of work two months."

I ask the waitress to tell me more about her hometown.

"Gangs have moved in."

"Gangs?"

"Yeah, but they're not real ones. They don't kill anyone. There's about one person a year here that gets killed. That's not much."

"Unless you're the one person who gets killed."

"Yeah," she giggles.

When she returns later with Jennifer's change, she says to me, "Well, I hope you make it to where you're going."

She is cute and friendly, and for just a moment I'm convinced she's the devil.

Jennifer checks us into a roadside motel. The room has two beds. I've stayed in the homes of people I didn't know, but something about sleeping in a motel room with a stranger strikes me as odd. If Jennifer thinks so, she doesn't let on. She comes out of the bathroom dressed in silk pajamas and gets into her bed. The last thing I see before closing my eyes is her—reading a textbook. I fall asleep to the squeak of her highlighting pen.

It's still dark when I hear Jennifer come out of the shower in the morning.

"I'm going to leave in about ten minutes," she says.

I quickly shower and shave and load my pack in the Lincoln. Jennifer stops at a supermarket and buys us some fruit and orange juice. We drive an hour east and enter the Badlands National Park. It's otherworldly, a place I could explore for days. But Jennifer zips through the park like she's in a race. I ride another hour east with her then decide I've got to get off the interstate and slow down. I see a tiny spot on the map called Murdo. I ask to be let out there.

Jennifer has been a machine. We've spent the last twenty-four hours together, but she has revealed nothing of herself that is personal, real. I can't leave without taking one crack at her armor.

"What's your biggest fear in the world?" I say.

"I don't have any fears."

SIXTEEN

It is Homecoming Day in Murdo, South Dakota. The street and storefronts are whitewashed with messages: "Go Rebels!" and "Crush the Chieftains!" The noon whistle blows and the sidewalks fill with parents and children, some dads lifting infants onto their shoulders. A woman tells me the parade will be over in two minutes. It takes that long because it circles the block twice. The last parade was in June, when Murdo celebrated the paving of Main Street. The town's other roads are still dirt. I take in the scene, the grain bins and water tower in the distance, and realize I've crossed over from the Wild West into the Heartland of America—plains, pickups, and prayers.

The homecoming king and queen ride past and wave. They look at once young and old. At seventeen, they can already see the balance of their lives stretched out before them, as predictable as the prairie. The postmaster leans in the doorway of the post office and watches for the umpteenth time. Kids rush into the street with plastic bags, snatching up sweets tossed from the floats. A politician in a convertible throws the most and the best candy. Some things are the same everywhere.

I sit on a bench to write a letter to Anne. A woman stops to talk with me. Doris is sixty-six. She has a friendly smile and the nasal twang of the Midwest.

''You know, you get out in these rural areas and you see we're the glue of America,'' she says.

Doris grew up in western Minnesota. She went to college at South Dakota State because tuition was only thirty-four dollars a quarter, including room and board. She met her husband there. They have five grown children. Their youngest son has cerebral palsy and lives in a senior citizens' apartment complex in Rapid City. The rest of their kids are married and live on farms.

Before long, Doris has invited me to come spend the night at her house.

''I looked at your nice backpack; that tells me you've got a mission,'' she says, like it's all the reason she needs to bring a perfect stranger home without consulting her husband.

I finish my letter and catch up with Doris at the Uptown Market, where they are handing out free hot dogs. We each eat a hot dog, then drive out to her daughter's place, a modern log cabin set in the middle of a six-thousand-acre cattle ranch. Linda and her husband Larry raise up five hundred head of beef cattle a year from calves. Last winter it got so cold, they had to catch the calves as they dropped from their mothers so they wouldn't freeze. Piles of rolled hay dot the landscape. Linda's son and daughter ride bikes near the barn. Linda teaches her kids in a makeshift classroom in the home.

Larry ambles up. He's a lanky galoot, with salt-and-pepper hair and a bright smile gleaming under a beat-up brown cowboy hat. He gets right to it.

''I got a feeling our paths aren't going to cross too many more times,'' he says. ''So I'm going to tell you the one thing that has given me the most joy in my life, and that's the son of God, Jesus Christ, who died on the cross for my sins.''

Before I have to respond, Doris's husband Pete drives up in a Mack truck loaded with corn. He backs up to the grain bin. Larry cranks up a tractor, which powers an auger that carries the kernels up and deposits them in the bin.

Larry tells me that if I ever pass through again, I'm welcome to stay.

"We'll polish a nail for you," he says.

"He means we'll have a bed for you," Linda says.

I ride back into Murdo in the truck with Pete. His hands are black as coal and his teeth are packed with bits of raw corn. We park the truck on a dirt road and walk to the firehouse. The volunteer firemen are hosting a pancake and sausage dinner. Doris is already there. Larry and Linda soon show up, as well as the rest of the town. It's a roomful of honest faces, folks who aren't ashamed to tell a stranger how they get down on their praying bones every night.

A man mentions to Pete that his cistern is about dry. Most folks outside of town aren't hooked up to Murdo's water line. Pete is sixty-eight and semiretired—the "semi" part meaning he now works six days a week instead of seven—but he still hauls spring water to his neighbors. It's two dollars for a thousand gallons and a buck-fifty a mile. Water rarely crosses my mind when I'm home, but it strikes me that it has been a recurring theme of this journey. I'm always drinking it, looking for it, or thinking about it. Now here I am, the guest of a water man.

Pete and I bounce along a dusty road into a pink sunset. Pheasants fly up from the culvert as we rumble by. Tiny shoots of winter wheat poke through the ground. They'll soon be covered with snow, not to be harvested until next summer.

Pete plucks a pamphlet called "The Way to Life" from the dash and hands it to me.

"A lot of people go through life and never know the meaning of life," he says. "It's not enough to believe and do good deeds. You've got to receive Jesus Christ as your own personal savior."

I ask him when he knew for certain. He says it was when he got married. Then something catches his eye out the window.

"Sometimes traumatic things move people to Christ, sometimes away. I'll tell you a story. See over there?" He points to a stand of cottonwoods and a few grain bins near the White River. "That was my house. I was five, my brother Eddie was six, and we had a younger brother who was four. Our dad told us to go open the gate and let the cows down. We got up to the top of the hill and opened the gate, and the bottom just dropped out of the sky. It rained thirteen inches in a half hour. That's a lot of water. I got out of there. I just ran straight down the hill. I knew where home was. By the time I got to the fence, I crawled through and the water was up to my neck. My brother Eddie stayed with my younger brother. Nicky, that was his name. We had company at the house and he was real bashful, so he came with us. He was real little and he shouldn't have been there. I was little too. The water came up and Eddie showed him how to grab hold of the fence and let the water move you down. But he let go and washed down into the river and the river carried him away. And to this day, we've never found him. That was in 1932. Ever since, I've wondered why God took my little brother, yet spared me."

Pete and Doris live eight miles west of Murdo, at the end of a road on the edge of the prairie. The first thing I notice is the poster hanging on the dining room wall. It's the same one that Tim and Diane had back in Lakeview, Oregon—two little boys in overalls, one saying, "Been farming long?" I left the Bible Tim gave me at the shelter in Bozeman because my pack was getting too heavy. Now here comes Pete, a volunteer Gideon, handing me a pocket-sized copy of the New Testament. I guess I'm fated to finish this journey with a Bible in my pack.

The kitchen counters are covered with gallon jugs of spring water. More plastic bottles line the floor. The three of us sit around drinking glasses of water late into the night. Doris marries up the partial empties as we drink, so Pete can have bottles to fill on his next trip to the spring. Doris washes the glasses in a plastic tub and saves the water to flush the toilet. I feel guilty taking a two-minute shower. I really feel bad when I learn how Pete bathes: Doris plugs the tub when she showers, then Pete jumps in and washes up in the gray water.

I sleep soundly upstairs in a pine-paneled room with two windows looking out onto the rolling plains. The sun wakes me in the morning, rising over a purple horizon. When I go downstairs, Doris is cracking fresh wheat for pancakes. The pancakes are wafer thin and melt in my mouth. Doris fries me an egg to go with them.

My plan is to head south today into Nebraska. But Doris is high on the South Dakota state capital, Pierre, about sixty miles north. She offers to drive me. Then Pete says I should just stay and explore around here another day. I give him no argument.

The town where Pete and Doris live is called Okaton, which means "See Far" in the Lakota Sioux language. It sits on a ridge— the ridge being about ten feet higher than the rest of the ground— and you can in fact see a hundred miles farther into the Midwest. The population is nineteen, counting cats and dogs. The post office is so small, you have to step outside to lick a stamp.

The main highway used to run through Okaton, but the interstate turned it into a ghost town. The blacktop is crumbled and potholed. All that remains of a Texaco sign are the *X, A,* and *C.* A faded red grain elevator, its top torn off by a tornado, marks the middle of town. The old one-room schoolhouse sinks into the earth, its window frames twisted and sagging. Houses long abandoned have no paint left to peel. There are a few rusty trailers, some idle farm equipment. The only sign of life is an antiques store that caters to the occasional tourist who wanders in off the freeway. An American flag flaps in the wind, and Christian music blares to no one but me and the wasps.

Pete doesn't get in from hauling water until almost eleven. Doris cooks us a couple of frozen pizzas. I do the dishes, mindful not to rinse as thoroughly as I would at home. I go upstairs after midnight. Pete stays up to prepare for the Sunday school lesson he must give in the morning. The boombox on the kitchen counter is tuned to a Christian radio station. A large vegetable spoon serves as the antenna.

I break out my khaki pants in the morning and press them on the kitchen table with an iron Pete and Doris got as a wedding gift in 1951. We drive two miles to the Evangelical Free Church, a white clapboard building with nine rows of wooden pews. A sign on the wall notes that last Sunday's attendance was thirty-three. The all-time high was sixty-five. The congregation sings several hymns, then the pastor asks for prayer requests. Doris says the church should "pray for this young man who's hitch-hiking across the United States." The pastor fits me in between a church member who is sick in the hospital and a fellow who recently died. He then launches into his sermon, titled "Money Matters."

"Do you know where you're at financially?" the pastor says.

Yes, I sure do, I say to myself.

Doris leaves after the service to start supper. After Sunday school, Pete and I walk toward Okaton.

"We'll hitchhike," Pete says.

Pete's brother Ed stops for us. He's sixty-nine now, but all I can see is a six-year-old boy helplessly watching a swollen river carry away his little brother.

Linda and Larry and their kids are already at the house when we get there. I remind Larry that our paths have crossed three times now, and he smiles. Another of Pete and Doris's daughters, Judy, and her family arrive from their farm down near the Nebraska line. They came to pick up a pair of goats they rented for the summer to the local antiques store's petting zoo. Judy and her husband Keith are my age and already have seven children. Keith used to be a preacher in the area. But he couldn't support his family on the five hundred dollars a month his church could afford to pay him. They moved south, where Keith now shears sheep.

"It was a venture of faith," says Keith, a full-bearded man. "We prayed for a big house with a lot of water and a porch. And the Lord gave us a big house, a lot of water, and *three* porches."

Doris's two eldest granddaughters help her in the kitchen. Before long, they've prepared a feast of pot roast, meatloaf, mashed potatoes and gravy, salad, green beans, homemade bread, and fresh honey. Sixteen of us squeeze around the dining room table like it's Thanksgiving. But this is no holiday or special occasion. It's just life in the Midwest.

I realize that it is only 1:30 in the afternoon.

"Is this the normal dinner hour in South Dakota?" I say.

"This is a little late," Linda says.

"Suppertime for me is anywhere between breakfast and midnight," Pete says.

If I were home now, I'd be watching a football game on TV with a beer in my hand. It doesn't take a genius to see whose life is richer.

Larry regales the table with tales of his accident-prone brother-in-law, Wes, whom he recently visited. In the span of one week, Wes had the misfortune of falling off a motorcycle, getting kicked by a horse, and suffering a rope burn. But the real news, Larry says, is that Wes taught him a new way to castrate horses.

"He doesn't cut the cord with a knife," Larry says between mouthfuls of pot roast and potatoes. He picks up a sugar spoon from the table and strokes the handle. "He just runs his thumbnail up and down that cord until it breaks," he says, demonstrating on the spoon.

"I used to know some shepherds that did it with their teeth," Pete says.

"I knew that one was coming," says Keith, the sheep shearer. "There's a reason God gave us hands. If I did that, I don't know what'd happen."

"You'd have something new in your beard!" Larry cracks, and the table bursts into laughter.

As I wash the dishes, I listen to a household of three generations content to just be together. Doris is right—the glue of
America.

Throughout this journey, kind strangers have been telling me
how brave I am to be crossing the country with no money. They
can't imagine doing what I'm doing. The truth is, I can't imagine
doing what they're doing. Pete and Doris have been married
forty-three years. That takes a kind of commitment I've never
been able to fathom, much less display. While I've been roaming,
searching for life, they've stayed put and built a life. As I pack
to leave, I am filled with envy and regret. It is only a rhetorical
question when I ask myself who's the braver?

SEVENTEEN

Keith and Judy invite me to spend the night down their way,
and nine of us pile into their van. Keith drives, while Judy
breast-feeds three-month-old Theresa. There are no seat belts or
air bags, just a pair of well-worn Bibles on the dash. Fifteen-
year-old Beth sits in the second seat, holding Levi, five, and
Kevin, two. I sit in the third seat with Dalen, thirteen, and Joy,
eleven. Keith and Judy's oldest, Steven, aged seventeen, stayed
at home. Riding in the far back are the two goats, bleating in my
ear like they were being tortured.

Keith pulls into the gas station where Jennifer dropped me off
two days ago. He takes orders for ice cream. Everyone wants a
drumstick.

"Mike?" he says.

"None for me, thanks."

"You sure? It's on the house."

I love ice cream, and I haven't had any in three weeks. I want
to say yes, but can't.

"Yeah, I'm stuffed from dinner still."

Keith pays for the gas and returns from the minimart with a cardboard box heaped with drumsticks. He passes them out.

"Dad, there's one extra," Levi says, noting the lone drumstick resting in the box on the floorboard.

"Yeah, I miscounted," Keith says. "Sure you don't want one, Mike?"

"Well, as long as you've got one extra," I say.

Keith passes back the drumstick with a smile.

We drive into the black night. None of the kids fights or argues, and after a while even the goats settle down. Just one big, happy farm family.

Keith turns off the interstate and heads south on a two-lane highway. After an hour we make a series of turns down gravel roads, passing fields of corn and wheat that are unseen in the dark.

"The thing that keeps people out here in these rural areas of America is their love of independence," Keith says. "But it's a big gamble. The farmer and the ranchers are dependent on economics decided by multitudes of middlemen. If people out here were looking for a steady paycheck, they'd have moved to the city a long time ago."

Keith turns down a bumpy road and pulls in front of a ramshackle building barely standing in a clearing of trees.

"This isn't a show house like Larry and Linda's," Judy says. "It's more of a heap hole."

"No, it looks great," I say.

The house got trashed by an angry hired hand, and the owner now rents it to Keith's family for a hundred dollars a month. An unpainted wall leads up the staircase. The dining room table is laden with junk. Unfolded laundry is piled on two sofas in the living room.

It's ten o'clock on a Sunday night, but there are still chores to be done. I wander out with Dalen to the dilapidated red barn. A rooster lords over a couple dozen hens laying eggs. Kittens scamper in the rafters. Rabbits rattle their cages. Ducks and geese mosey about the hay-strewn floor. Dalen sits on an upturned plastic bucket, milking the goats. A kitten sticks its head in the tin pail and gets squirted in the face.

Outside in the corral, Keith pours grain into troughs for his three horses. He feeds and waters his twelve border collies. Keith wears the belt buckle he won at the county fair when he and one of the dogs combined as cow herding champs. He walks off into the pasture to collect the cows to milk.

"Boss! Boss!" he yells.

I stand by the windmill that drives the well pump and gaze up into the sky. The Milky Way stretches out across the night like an endless spool of cotton.

Keith and I take off our shoes and leave them on the sun porch. The soles are caked with green manure.

"That's our smog," Keith says. "But our smog is biodegradable."

One of the sofas has been cleared for me and some bedding left out. I fall asleep, feeling content and grateful.

It is still pitch dark when I hear a racket the next morning in the kitchen. I figure it must be Judy, up to fix her brood breakfast. But when I walk in, I find Beth tending four skillets, two for eggs and two for pancakes. Her younger sister Joy is setting a table the size of a barn door. Keith, Steven, and Dalen are already out milking the cows. Judy is getting the little ones up. I can only marvel at the family's teamwork.

We all hold hands as Keith offers the blessing. There is bacon to go with the eggs, homemade chokecherry syrup for the pancakes, fruit cocktail, and whipped cream. I wash it all down with fresh cow's milk poured from a gallon-sized glass jar.

Keith and his two oldest sons are scheduled to shear sheep at a nearby ranch. Keith invites me to come along. The younger kids stay behind with Judy for home schooling.

Keith, Steven, Dalen, and I cram into the cab of a beat-up

pickup and bounce along a gravel road. Two collies ride in back. Ours is the only vehicle in sight.

"This is rush hour in South Dakota," Keith says.

Suddenly, I hear a *tha-whack!* I look out to see a meadowlark wrapped around the sideview mirror, its neck broken.

"That's our state bird," Keith says.

"No, Dad, that's Nebraska's," Steven says.

"Oh, you're right. The pheasant is our state bird."

The rancher Keith has contracted with greets us in overalls. He has twelve hundred lambs to shear. Unlike ewes, which get clipped again and again, lambs are sheared only once, when they're six months old. They live another sixty days before they're butchered, their hides becoming winter coats and car seat covers.

Six shearers set up in the barn. Motors dangling by chains from the rafters drive clippers as sharp as razors. Each man keeps track of the lambs he shears with a number counter hanging by his work station. Keith is good for 150 head a day. Steven can shear 100. This is Dalen's first time with a pair of clippers in his hand, and no one knows what to expect of him.

The pay is $1.40 per lamb. Good shearers like Keith can earn more than two hundred dollars in a day. It's a lot of money in these parts, but the work is far from steady. It's rarely more than a few days in a row, and never in the same place.

Keith's collies herd the lambs single file from a pen into a chute. The shearers pull the lambs out by their legs through doorways in the chute. Dalen accidentally lets two out and gets bowled over by the frightened animals.

"Dalen, I know you're good, but one at a time, son," Keith says.

Keith is a pro. He squeezes a leg of a lamb between his knees and holds the animal's face to his chest. He works fast, making long, smooth cuts from crown to tail, careful not to nick the lamb's private parts. The wool falls away and the animal looks like a peeled orange. The whole process takes about two minutes.

The shearer at the end doesn't fare as well. He cuts his left thumb with the clippers and bleeds badly. He puts on a glove, but the blood soon soaks through the leather. The man keeps working, however, as there is no telling when the next day's wages will come.

As wool gathers on the plywood floor, a man sweeps it into a pile with a push broom. He feeds the wool into a hydraulic press, which forces it into a burlap sack seven feet long. Each lamb donates four to five pounds of wool.

Steven holds his own. But by midmorning, Dalen is still struggling with his first lamb. He can't keep it still. His strokes are short and choppy, and the animal bleeds from numerous nicks. Truly a sacrificial lamb.

But with Keith's coaching, Dalen catches on.

"Stretch that leg out," Keith says. "Keep it flat. Nice long strokes. That's it."

By noon, I've seen a way of life passed on, from father to son, here in the heartland.

Judy and the little ones show up to drive me out to the highway. She drops me at a wide spot in the road called Wewela. She hands me a plastic bag with sandwiches, two chicken and two honey.

"Eat the chicken sandwiches first, so they don't go bad," she says.

She also gives me two stamped postcards. She wants me to use one to let her know how my trip turned out. I'm supposed to send the other one tomorrow, telling her who picked me up and where I stayed.

"I'll be worried 'til I hear from you," Judy says before driving off.

Wewela consists of one building, the post office, and it's closed. I sit on the steps and eat one of the chicken sandwiches. I draw a sign for Ainsworth, a town thirty miles south in Nebraska that intersects with a highway that will take me east.

I stand on the side of the road. The only sound I hear is a jillion invisible grasshoppers. A half hour passes before I see a car. It's going in the wrong direction. I get the feeling I may be mailing that first card to Judy from the post office here in Wewela.

I figure it's time to get reacquainted with my pack. I hoist it onto my back and walk down the center line of the empty blacktop. After a mile, I climb a short rise and cross into Nebraska.

My seventh state. I hope it's a lucky one.

EIGHTEEN

I hear a car coming behind me, so I turn and hold out my sign. The four-door sedan pulls to the shoulder, but when I reach the window, I figure I must be seeing a mirage: two sweet little old ladies, dressed in their Sunday finest.

"I know you're not supposed to pick up hitchhikers, but it's so far between towns out here, you feel bad passing a person," the driver says.

I don't know whether to kiss the old biddies or scold them for stopping. This is the kind of thing you hear about all the time on the eleven o'clock news—a pair of senior citizens mugged by a drifter. I've been amazed on this trip by the stubborn capacity of Americans to help a stranger, even when it seems to run contrary to their own best interests. I think of all the families who take me in. I arrive with nothing but my pack, while they expose their homes, their possessions, their children. As scared as I am to trust them, they must be doubly afraid to trust me. Then again, what might truly frighten them is the idea of not trusting anybody. It's like this woman has just told me—she'd rather risk her life than feel bad about passing a stranger on the side of the road. As I slide into the backseat, I realize she would have stopped for the guy with the gas can I left stranded last year in the Nevada desert.

Vi and Helen are sisters. They grew up in Wewela, but now live farther north in Winner. Vi is driving Helen to an appointment with an eye doctor down in Ainsworth, Nebraska. They don't have an eye doctor in their part of South Dakota.

We pass through Springview, Nebraska, a tiny town with a cemetery shaded by ash trees.

"That's where our folks are buried," Helen says. "They paid for a section with six plots," Vi says. "But they were told one of 'em was already buried, someone from the eighteen hundreds. There's no record or marker or anything."

"Dad always said he wanted to be buried there," Helen says.

They drop me at the junction of Highway 20. As I pull my pack from the car, I look at Vi. We speak at the same time.

"Be careful."

There is plenty of traffic, but rides are harder to come by in Nebraska. Still, everybody waves, real friendly. It must be a compromise. They know they're not stopping for you, yet they can't just ignore you like drivers do in California. That would be rude.

It takes most of the afternoon to move sixty miles east. Today's kind stranger turns out to be the town of O'Neill, Nebraska. It has a free campground. There is no shower, but there is a sink I can stick my head under in the morning. The parking lot is full of big rigs with combines on their trailers. They belong to workers from Oklahoma who have migrated north to harvest the corn. I pitch my tent and go for a walk.

The town is named for General John O'Neill, a native of Ireland who served in the American Civil War. He later encouraged Irish immigrants fleeing the potato famine to settle in this fertile region. Owing to its founder's heritage, O'Neill is called the Shamrock City. Green four-leaf clovers dot the sidewalks. Businesses with names like Shamrock Realty, Dougherty's Pub, and Luck o' the Irish Drugs line the main drag.

Despite its charming nickname, something is slightly menacing about O'Neill. An abundance of homeowners feel the need to post ''No Trespassing'' signs in their yards. Youths cruise the streets in flatulent muscle cars. One kid revs his engine at a stoplight and stalls.

I hear the squawk of a public address system in the distance.

''Second and eight,'' the announcer says.

I follow the cheers, past the town water tower, to the high school. The junior varsity football team is playing Ainsworth. It's a Monday night and the stands are packed. The grass is thick and the fall air cool. Men wearing baseball caps with ads for farm equipment mill about the concession stand. Everyone looks serious, except for the children playing tag beneath the bleachers. The game is a rout by halftime, O'Neill leading 20-0, and I walk off in search of real Monday night football.

Signs posted on the school fence note that the area is a ''Drug Free Zone,'' and penalties are doubled for those found guilty. It's dark, and I pass fresh-faced teenagers heading for the gate. I have a sudden fear of being falsely accused of something terrible. Then I get this crazy notion that a bad cop is going to plant drugs on me. I walk back to town in the middle of the street so everyone can see me.

I find a place called Tom's Tavern and take a seat at the end of the bar. Three TVs are tuned to the game. A couple and their young children shoot pool behind me. When the bartender sets a napkin in front of me, I ask her if I can just watch the game. No problem, she says.

The two men closest to me play liar's dice, slamming the leather cups down hard on the bar. One drinks beer, the other whisky.

''Alice, can I get that last one I asked for?'' Whisky says to the bartender. She brings him another drink. He drains it and calls down to the bartender, ''Alice, can I get that last one I asked for?''

A hard-looking woman named Vicki sits down next to Beer

and Whisky, and Beer tries to get her to roll dice, but she says she's not a gambler. Whisky gets up to relieve himself.

"Is it true he's the best lover in town?" Beer says to Vicki.

"I have no idea," Vicki says. "I find that men who talk a lot don't usually have much to say."

Whisky returns to the bar and says, "Alice, can I get that last one I asked for?"

Vicki leaves when Beer won't stop pestering her to play dice. During a time-out in the football game, there's a news update about the people fleeing Cuba on rafts. A character at the other end of the bar says, "What's the Cuban national anthem?" He pauses, then sings, "Row, row, row your boat...." It brings yuks all around.

Denver scores and somebody throws a greasy baseball hat at the mirror behind the cash register. Another fellow named Pee Wee borrows the bar phone to dial a woman he calls Boobs.

"I got a hard-on and nowhere to put it!" he yells into the phone with a fool's grin. Boobs must have hung up because Pee Wee sets the receiver back on the cradle. "Hell, I ain't shy," he says to the bar.

Buffalo running back Thurman Thomas makes a miraculous run from the Denver twenty-yard line. He breaks several tackles, hurdles over downed linemen, and tip-toes along the sideline into the end zone. I can't remember ever seeing such an incredible play.

Whisky whoops. During the slow-motion replay, he says, "Run, nigger! Run! Run, nigger! Run! Good nigger. Good nigger."

I cringe. I haven't heard that kind of talk this whole trip. It is truly hateful. I get up to leave. As I head for the door, Whisky rattles the ice cubes in his glass and says, "Alice, can I get that last one I asked for?"

I walked back to the campground in the dark, filled with un-ease and dread. I fear that the only luck I'll find in the Shamrock

City is bad. I half expect my pack to be gone when I return to my tent. I'm relieved to find it untouched. Still, it was stupid of me to leave it unguarded. If I lost all my belongings, where would I be then? I have to ask myself if it was a subconscious attempt to sabotage my journey. Do I lack the faith to go the distance? I don't know the answer.

I shine my flashlight on my road atlas. The country will soon be more crowded. Vi and Helen told me that people aren't as friendly east of the Missouri River, like it's some sort of proven fact everybody knows. I hope they are wrong.

Near as I can tell, I'm almost exactly halfway to Cape Fear. But am I halfway through my journey? I think of the old joke about the long-distance swimmer who swims halfway across the Atlantic Ocean, decides he can't make it, and swims back. It doesn't seem so funny now. I'm overwhelmed by a sudden sense of displacement. I've heard it said that hell exists only here on earth. I think that might be true. For the first time on this journey, I am not afraid of death. I am afraid of something worse: that feeling of total detachment parked in my soul. I'm so lonely in my tent. I know from the map that I am in O'Neill, Nebraska. I also know that I am lost.

NINETEEN

By morning, despair has been dislodged from my mind by the demands of the journey. I've got places to go, people to meet. Malaise can hitch its own ride.

I slept well. The ground beneath my tent was the flattest and softest yet. My only complaint is that I woke with freezing feet. It is late September, and I know there won't be too many more nights I can camp out.

I walk east through O'Neill, my back to traffic. A man in a

pickup with a camper shell pulls over for me before I stop and hold out my sign.

"You gettin' in shape for elk hunting?" he says with a smile.

The man is tanned, wears glasses and a red T-shirt with the sleeves cut off, and I like him instantly.

I consider the role that fate might be playing in this sojourn. I think of all the good people who have stopped for me and wonder what would have happened had they kept going. Who was in the car behind them? A drunk driver? A rapist? A serial killer? I climb in the truck, thinking the Shamrock City may have been lucky for me in a way I'll never know.

Ron is fifty-four but looks twenty years younger. He is driving an hour east today to check on a client. Ron sells the giant center pivots that irrigate corn fields.

"I help make cheap food," he says. "Where else but in America can you get good quality food for practically nothing?"

He grew up down near Lincoln. He was drafted into the Army in 1965. He proved a crack shot in boot camp, scoring a perfect five hundred on the final shooting test. He took bets on himself in the barracks and bought a new Chevy Impala with the winnings. After a tour in Vietnam, he returned to the States and got married. It didn't work out. Ron then drifted around.

We pass a slow truck that is buried under a mountain of hay.

"I traveled the whole continent, every state, and I came right here to Holt County to live," Ron says. "This is the apple of the country."

He remarried in Nebraska. He now has a little daughter he takes fishing. He is also a passionate elk hunter. As he drives, he reaches into his briefcase and hands me a stack of photos. I flip through pictures of him posing proudly among antler racks of elk he has shot in Montana.

We reach the town of Tilden. Ron stops at a greasy spoon called the Hy-Way Cafe.

"You want a sandwich?" he says.

"I don't have any money."

"You already told me that."

The special of the day is baked steak, potato salad, corn on the cob, cottage cheese, and bread—all for $4.25. Ron is right, our food is cheap, not that I have the right to call anything cheap on this trip.

Ron tells me he has a '58 Corvette parked in his garage. A few times a year, he drives it down to Phoenix to visit his three teenaged kids from his first marriage. He drives 110 miles an hour.

"You know what a state trooper does when he sees you going a hundred and ten?" he says.

"Handcuffs you or laughs," I say.

"He laughs. He can't catch you."

Ron says he has been chased only once.

"I knew he was coming for me because a cop will usually flash his lights and give me a thumbs-down, but this one didn't. I pulled a U-ball and when he saw me the second time, I was going a hundred and fifty. Hee-hee."

Ron pays the bill. I get my pack from his truck.

"Well, you're seeing America at the perfect time," he says. "This'll be one of the best years ever in the Midwest. We've had the perfect combination of rain and sun. Here it is September twenty-seventh, and we haven't had our first frost. It's been a long summer."

I know Ron is cocky, and maybe a little arrogant, but I can't help liking the guy. He has the air of a man who knows he's arrived—and where. It's a trait I wish I had.

I envy and admire so many of the people I've met on this trip. I'm grateful for their rides, their food, their shelter. But the kindest act of all is when they merely are themselves. They help me in ways they aren't even aware of. It is always a comfort to meet an honest man, and I am always sad to say good-bye.

I stand at the intersection in Tilden, holding a sign out for Norfolk, the next town down the road. I don't have any plans to visit Norfolk. It's just that I've found my chances of getting a ride are better if I don't get too greedy and try to gobble up a big chunk of the country all at once.

A Buick Skylark drives by and the woman behind the wheel gives me a long glance. She keeps going, then brakes and turns around. There's been some deliberation, so I know I'm safe. Anybody who wanted to harm me would have pulled over right away.

"Where you going?" she calls through the window, like she knows I can't possibly be heading for Norfolk.

"East," I say.

"Well, I'm going to Omaha. I can take you that far."

Omaha is more than a hundred miles away. It will be close to dark when we get there. I don't want to arrive in a city at night with no money. I figure I'll ride with this woman a while, then hop out in whatever little town looks the kindest.

Joan is a short, buxom woman with a husky voice. Long, curly brown hair frames her weathered face and falls from under a battered black hat with a fake pink rose stapled to the front. She looks every minute of her forty-four years, and then some. She also looks like a nice person.

"I know what it's like to be out there," says Joan, who used to thumb rides herself. "My boyfriend says I shouldn't pick up hitchhikers, but I do. I don't want to live in a world where I have to be afraid to help someone."

Joan lives in Burton, Nebraska, nearly two hundred miles in the other direction. She says she is driving to Omaha to play bingo. She also says she has to see a doctor there every two weeks. I wonder why anybody would drive six hours one way every two weeks for a doctor's appointment, but I don't ask.

She is originally from near San Diego. I tell her I'm a fellow Californian. I mention how surprised I was to learn that the big city problems we have out West—gangs and drugs and the like—also exist here in the heartland.

"As an ex–drug addict, I know," Joan says.

"What kind of drugs?"

"Heroin."

"How long you been clean?"

"Three years."

The way she says it, I know it's been a bitch.

Joan became a single mother when she was fourteen. When her son was twelve, she sent him to live with her mother because shooting heroin had become a full-time occupation.

Years later she told her mother, "Mom, I'm a hope-to-die drug addict. I'm gonna die a drug addict. You just gotta accept me the way I am."

Joan's son is now thirty. He lives in Maryland, where he feeds his own addiction—cocaine.

"I thought of saying something to him," Joan says, "but I know the mind of an addict."

Joan plunged into the gutter before she kicked her addiction. She took up prostitution to pay for the drugs. But there was always a line she would not cross. She never became a thief.

"I'd rather sell my body than rip you off," she says. "My girlfriend called me a dope fiend with morals."

Joan was luckier than most. She knew several hookers and addicts who were murdered or died from AIDS. She never shared needles and always insisted her customers wear condoms. As a result, she is HIV-negative.

Her addiction eventually grew into a five-hundred-dollar-a-day habit. Besides turning tricks, she dealt heroin to keep up. She was frequently busted by the police. She got to be on a first-name basis with bail bondsmen up and down the coast of California. Judges always suspended her sentences, until one judge finally gave her ninety days. She pleaded for a drug program instead, but the judge would not relent and Joan served her time. These days, she calls the judge from time to time and lets him know she's still clean.

She moved to Burton for the simple reason that she knew there was no dope there. She came to Nebraska with a girlfriend who also wanted to get clean. But the girlfriend moved back to the city and started using again. Joan was hired as a waitress, her first legitimate job, and found a boyfriend who is drug-free. She tries to lead a quiet life, white-knuckling it on the prairie.

"So now you know why I'm not afraid to pick up hitch-hikers," she says. "I've gone to bed with men I didn't know."

Joan always stays at the same place whenever she travels to see her doctor, a budget motel across the Missouri River from Omaha, in Council Bluffs, Iowa. She says she used to sleep at a campground on the river where campsites cost only $3.50, and she offers to drive me there. I tell her it may as well cost three hundred and fifty because I don't have any money.

"I'll pay for it," she says.

A hooker with a heart of gold.

We hit Omaha at rush hour. It's the first real city I've been in since leaving San Francisco three weeks ago. I feel claustrophobic, and I reach for the dial to turn down the radio so I can concentrate. Then I remember it's not my car, and I'm not driving.

"I don't tell people this, but since you already know I was an addict, I'll tell you," Joan says as we cross the bridge into Iowa. "I have to come down here every two weeks to get my supply of Methadone."

The city is always a risk, she says. That's where the dope is. She doesn't know where exactly, but it wouldn't be hard to find. One time, a year ago, she was in Omaha visiting a friend from the bad old days. The friend mentioned where she could get some heroin. Joan let the image take hold in her mind. How good was the heroin? she heard herself asking her friend. How much did it cost? Twenty a fix, the friend said. Joan shrugged off the offer. If it only cost twenty, it couldn't be that good.

"But then I said yes," she tells me now. "And then I said no."

"Why?" I say.

"I don't know."

Joan gazes out the windshield wistfully. I realize how fragile her sobriety is: Three years is the same as three days. The dragon is never slayed. Every time Joan sees the Omaha skyline, it's like her own journey to Cape Fear. But while I'll stop at the Atlantic Ocean, there is no end to the road she travels. She is forever tested, forever tempted.

Joan can't recall the way to the campground. She turns down several streets and we get lost. We stop at a gas station in Council Bluffs for directions, but the attendant hasn't heard of the place. Joan flips through the phone book. Nothing rings a bell.

It's getting dark. I worry about being dumped in the city. Then it's as if Joan has read my mind.

"Well, the worst thing that'll happen is you stay in my room," she says.

All my anxiety seeps away.

We drive around some more. Joan offers to buy me a hamburger. I decline. I've got food in my pack. Besides, the two bucks she saves on the burger might net her a fortune tonight at the bingo hall.

She finally spots a road that looks familiar. We wend around a municipal golf course until we reach the campground, Friendship Park. Considering it lies in the shadow of Omaha, it is a pleasant looking place, with barbecues and weeping willows lining the bank of the river. Tent sites have jumped to $4.50. Joan pays with a five-dollar bill. She uses the fifty cents change to buy me an orange soda from the pop machine.

Before she leaves, I ask Joan what her dream is.

"I don't know. That's the truth. I've never had one. Like you, you probably knew you wanted to be a journalist. My boyfriend loves cooking. I don't have a dream. Maybe that's my problem."

I think Joan is too hard on herself. I know she has a dream, if only to stay clean so she can dream another day. We do what we have to, and if we're able, we do a little more. Joan has done for me, and I hope I've done for her. Perhaps my journey has helped her say no to her demons for at least one more trip into the city. I don't know.

As she drives away from the campground and disappears from my view, all I can do is hope that she makes the right turns.

TWENTY

I circle the campground, looking for the softest patch of grass. Somebody has fashioned a pathetic tube tent out of a piece of green plastic. The guy sits in his beat-up car, watching a black-and-white TV plugged into a campground outlet. I'm sure there's a sad story in this, but I don't want to hear it. I pitch my tent on the other side of a trailer.

Before long, a retired couple comes out of the trailer. They are from Skokie, Illinois, near Chicago. Mel looks like a professor, with glasses and white hair. Judie is plump and chatty. She walks over to my picnic table to visit. Mel hangs back by the trailer. When he hears me tell Judie I'm hitchhiking east, he urges me to stay at least fifty miles south of Chicago.

"Parts of it are *eee-vil!*" he calls over dramatically, hands cupped around his mouth. Then the mosquitoes chase him back inside.

I ask Judie if they are originally from Chicago. Mel is, she says. She was born in Austria. Eager for conversation, I tell her I passed through Austria last year on my way to Hungary. But Austria holds no happy memories for Judie. She lost nine relatives in the Holocaust.

Mel and Judie have been on the road for seven weeks. Judie liked New Orleans the best. She wanted to tour rural Louisiana, but she and Mel were warned by other Jewish friends that they might run into trouble there.

"In 1994, can you imagine that?" Judie says.

"I can," I say, remembering the redneck last night in the bar. "I think you can go to any state and find pockets of people like that."

Judie and Mel are visiting Omaha tomorrow morning. In the afternoon, they are driving east to Dubuque, Iowa, to see Mel's sister. Judie says I'm welcome to ride along. I thank her and say I'll sure keep it in mind.

"If there's anything we can do for you, let us know," she says.

I crawl into my tent. I wish I'd asked Judie for a newspaper, but I don't want to disturb them now. I lie back and listen to the sounds of the city. A train bridge crosses the river just south of the campground. The creaks and groans of boxcars rolling over the tracks drift in and out of my slumber.

Condensation has turned my tent into a steam bath by the time I wake in the morning. My sleeping bag is soaked, as is my pillow, the old green coat that the painter in Oregon gave me. I set my things out in the sun to dry and head for the shower. Judie pops her head out of the trailer door.

"Would you like a cup of coffee?"

"That'd be great, thanks."

I don't like to drink coffee on an empty stomach because it gives me the shakes. But it's hard to refuse an act of kindness.

"Forgive me, but there are a few grounds," Judie says. "It's the last cup."

Judie runs a brush through her hair, brown and flecked with gray. The coffee is black and thick, and with each sip I tingle and fill with good cheer. I remember when I was a little boy, water always tasted better when the neighbor lady filled a glass from her tap and handed it to me. It's how I feel now with Judie.

"This is good coffee," I say.

"Well, it's old. It's yesterday's reheated. I drink my coffee until it's gone."

The campground shower is hot, the pressure strong. I hang a clean shirt in the stall and let the steam iron out the wrinkles. It feels good to put on a fresh shirt and roll up the sleeves for the first time. It's such a simple pleasure. I catch a whiff of the fabric softener Edie poured into her washer, way back in Idaho. I pull the collar to my nose and breathe in. It's like an old friend is here by my side.

I walk out into the brilliant day, down along the bank of the muddy Missouri. Factories across the river belch smoke into a sky the color of faded jeans. The limbs of fallen trees poke up through the murky water. A power boat cruises upriver, sending beer cans and motor oil containers ashore with its wake.

An unshaven man in a baseball hat tends three fishing poles.

"What are you fishing for?" I say.

"Catfish," he growls. "But I'm not catching any catfish."

He peels the cellophane wrapper off a cigar and throws it against the bank.

I feel like taking a walk.

"What's the quickest way across the river into Omaha by foot?"

The man jabs his cigar up at the train bridge. Water courses around its three stone pillars.

"There room up there?" I say.

"Oh yeah. There's two tracks, and there's usually only one train." He grins. "They don't like you crossing there," he says, "but I've seen guys do it."

He grabs one of the three rods and starts reeling. Something invisible tugs at the line, maybe only a snag.

"Or you can go across there." He points his cigar at the bridge for cars, about a half mile north. "That's where those two guys jumped from last week."

"What two guys?"

"They were running from the cops. They caught one right over there on that bank." He aims his cigar at a pipe that spews sewage into the river. "The other one drowned."

"He couldn't swim, huh?"

"Hell, it don't matter if you know how to swim or not in this fucking river. Look at those undercurrents. It's thirty-five foot deep out there.''

Indeed, the merciless brown water swirls and churns like a whirlpool, reversing course in some spots and flowing back upstream.

I walk away from the bank, then stop and turn around.

''What was their crime?'' I say to the fisherman.

''They stole a car,'' he says, then chomps down on his cigar.

I decide on the bridge for cars, even though the highway patrol might stop me, or worse. I climb a gate and walk down a dirt utility road that skirts the golf course. The road passes under the bridge, which is tattooed with graffiti. I scramble up the littered embankment. I slip through a hole in the chain link fence and pop out onto Interstate 80 like some sort of fugitive.

There is no sidewalk, only a slender cement berm, not even a body wide. The guardrail reaches my thigh. I take quick, but careful steps, the morning traffic whizzing by. I must duck under the sign at the state line to stay off the freeway.

Halfway across, I stop and stare down at the river. I think of the sorry bastard who jumped from here and drowned. He died stealing a car. Maybe he was a murderer who got what was coming. Or maybe he was just a petty thief who panicked and lost his life for a hunk of metal. I forgot to ask the fisherman if they ever found the guy's body. I wonder if he had a wife and kids? Was there anyone who loved him? Was he ever befriended by a kind stranger?

I'm glad to see Mel and Judie's trailer still parked at the campground. Council Bluffs sits amid a snarl of freeways. I'll ride with the Skokie couple and get out at a country road. I write in my journal at a picnic table until they return from Omaha in their van.

''Do you want that ride?'' Judie says.

''Sounds good.''

"What'll we charge him, Judie?" Mel says. "By the mile or the minute?"

I laugh and think, *If they only knew.*

Mel starts to hitch the trailer to the bumper. I ask if he needs help.

"No, thank you!" he says, leaving no doubt.

"When I ask if I can help," Judie says, "he says, 'Yes, stay out of my way.' "

We're soon rolling down the interstate, Mel at the wheel. I sit behind them. Mel calls back. He wants to know why I'm traveling across the country. I tell him about my penniless mission.

"No plastic?" Judie says incredulously.

"No cash, no checks, no credit cards, no nothing," I say.

"Oh, I feel so bad now," Judie says. "If I would have known, I would have had you over for dinner last night."

"Don't feel bad," I say. "I never tell people unless they ask. I don't want to come off like a con man."

"You're courageous," Judie says. "I could never do that."

"Judie complains if she can't watch TV," Mel says.

"Open that," Judie tells me, pointing to an ice chest behind Mel's seat. "You eat today. There's cookies and sodas and graham crackers, and I think there's a plum in there, too. We'll stop and get some real food out of the trailer if you want."

"No, this is good, thanks."

"Unfortunately, it's diet pop and nonfat cookies," Judie says, chuckling.

Every time I finish a cookie or a stack of graham crackers, Judie orders me to open the cooler for more.

"You've heard about Jewish mothers?" she says.

I nod.

"Well, it's true. We're always telling you to eat."

Outside the window, combines roll over golden fields of corn and soybeans. It has been a bountiful year. Even the ditches are green from the abundant rain. I think of what Ron told me yesterday—America at its finest.

Mel worked in his mother's clothing store in Chicago for eighteen years. Then he owned an auto parts franchise for another twenty-one years. Judie stayed home with the kids. In her spare time, she collected antiques. One day Mel came home and said, "Let's open an antiques store." He sold the auto parts franchise, and he and Judie started an entire antiques mall.

"It was very profitable, but a lot of headaches," Mel says. "After three years, we sold it."

"We didn't want to be the richest people in the cemetery," Judie says.

She looks back at me.

"Mike, open that chest, eat!"

Mel and Judie bought their first trailer in 1983. They roamed around the country for two years.

"Then we got back to Skokie," Mel says, "and it was, 'What are you going to do today, Mel?' 'Golf.' 'What are you going to do today, Mel?' 'Fish.' My wife told me to go get a job."

"No, Mel, I said, 'Go get some insurance,' " Judie says.

She turns to me. "Our insurance payments were killing us."

"So I started working in lumber yards," Mel says. "But only nine months of the year, because we go to Florida every winter. So I did that five years. And on July first, I turned sixty-five. So June thirtieth was my last day of work, and I said, 'See you later.' "

"Mike, have some more food!" Judie says.

Mel starts to change lanes. He doesn't see the little red sports car and we almost collide. Mel swerves. The trailer fishtails, rocking us in our seats.

"My fault!" Mel says, almost loud enough for the other driver to hear.

The near miss reminds me that I've been over this stretch of freeway before. It was fourteen years ago. I was just out of college. I had no plans. My brother was hired to deliver a car to Washington, D.C. I went along for the ride. We drove coast to coast in three days. I was scared back then. I mean, really petrified. My brother slept while I drove. When it was his turn to drive, I stayed awake, for fear that he would fall asleep at the wheel. When neither of us could drive anymore, we pulled to the side of the road. I was afraid to close my eyes then, too, knowing if I slept, a madman would walk up and fire a bullet into my head. On the plane home, I clutched the armrests, swearing to my brother that we were going down.

I entered a long, dark period in which I was paralyzed by the image of bodily harm. I feared the loss of an arm or a leg, a fate I surely knew was mine. Youthful ideals and dreams evaporated. At one point my greatest ambition in life was to die with all four limbs intact.

My fear of physical pain was eventually replaced by a fear of life in general. I was afraid of making the choices it takes to be content. There were things I thought I might enjoy doing, but I'll be damned if I could summon the courage to try them. Before I knew it, my life had stalled before it ever started. All the while I told myself, *This part doesn't count. You'll start your life one day. And when you do, life will be grand.*

A girlfriend who knew me all too well often said, "There are no dress rehearsals for life." I knew that in my head, but I could not convince my heart. I carried on as if there were no consequences to inaction. I behaved as if I had all the time in the world.

Years later I happened upon a quote by Franz Kafka: "From a certain point on there is no longer any turning back. That is the point that must be reached."

The words seemed to be spoken directly to me. I wrote them down on an index card. I memorized them. I repeated them to myself. No truth was ever so black and white. Yet still I could not stir my soul to act.

Years passed, and I acquired the trappings of a life. But it has been a sham. It is so easy to get by, and get by very well. But it is so hard to simply live. And though I had a life, I never really lived. And when the yo-yo flew off the string, I realized that all my worst fears had already come to pass. I was empty of passion. I was numb. I was halfway to nowhere. I was dead.

And so I walked out into the world with empty pockets. And I see now that that was the first true step. I know now that I will die. Die for real and die for good. But right now, I'm alive. I'm alive and I'm in Iowa, and that's not a bad place to be.

"You can't take it with you," Mel is saying. "They throw dirt in your face and say a few prayers.

"Do it!" Mel booms. "Do it now!"

TWENTY-ONE

I pull out my map and have a gander at southeastern Iowa. The town of Montezuma leaps off the page. I smile at the name, as I know instantly that it's my next stop on the Road to Cape Fear. I ask Mel to drop me at Route 63.

"Are you sure you don't want to be closer to Iowa City?" Judie says.

"Judie, the man knows where he's going," Mel says.

Mel pumps gas and Judie watches my pack while I use the restroom. When I return, I snap a photo of the couple standing by their trailer. Judie hands me a plastic bag filled with food.

"Mel and I want you to have this."

Inside are two sleeves of graham crackers, two cans of soda pop, two tins of tuna, two apples, and two pieces of chicken—a veritable Noah's Ark of sack lunches.

Hooray for Jewish mothers!

I draw a sign for Montezuma, eight miles south. A middle-aged couple pulls out of the gas station, the wife at the wheel. I can read her lips through the windshield: "Should we give him a ride?"

The man nods in the affirmative.

"We never pick up hitchhikers, but you look so nice and clean," the woman says.

"You going to Monty, are you?" the man says.

I tell them I'm traveling across the country, but I don't mention how. I just ask if they know of a safe spot I can pitch my tent for the night.

They put their heads together and come up with three possibilities. Any one will do, but they insist I take a look at all three. The only real campground is at Lake Diamond, but it's several miles north of town. The couple then drives me through Montezuma to a rest stop on the highway. The drawback is that there is no water, the woman says. They swing me by the city park. That would be the most convenient. Then I wonder aloud if the police would mind. We'll just go by the sheriff's office and ask, the woman says.

Montezuma is a town of about fifteen hundred people, with white clapboard houses and expansive lawns. In this harvest season, a jack-o'-lantern decorates every porch. It is a town that appears untouched by the dark forces that haunt so much of the rest of the country. The bell tower chimes "The Sound of Silence."

As I suspected, camping is forbidden at the city park. The couple assures me it's no trouble at all to drive me back out to Lake Diamond. I've heard it said that helpfulness in the Midwest is a trait born of necessity. The original homesteaders were so far removed from comfort and convenience, they had to rely on one another to get by. It is a trait that has been handed down over generations. By the time we reach the campground, the couple has spent an hour shepherding me around, making sure that a total stranger is not left wanting. It is a sharp contrast to life in San Francisco, where I don't even know my next-door neighbors.

*   *   *

I pitch my tent near the lake. The thick woods are painted by autumn's brush. I have the entire campground to myself. There is not even a ranger to offer my services to. There is not even any litter to pick up. All is clean and still and quiet.

I write in my journal in the fading light. A truck pulls up, and an old man steps out with great effort. He wears a camouflage jacket and carries binoculars.

"The geese come yet?" he says, ambling toward me.

"What geese?"

He cups a hand to his ear and cocks his head.

"What geese?" I say louder.

"Canadian geese. There were a hundred and fifty of 'em last night." The man smiles.

I've never seen Canadian geese. What would they be doing in Iowa? I wonder if the old geezer is having me on.

"That your house?" he says, pointing to my tent.

"For tonight it is."

"Where's home?"

"California."

"You're a long way from home."

"Yeah, I've come twenty-six hundred miles. This is my twenty-fourth day. I'm headed across the United States."

"You got a bike or something?"

"Nope."

He leans back and makes a sweeping motion with his thumb, like he's hitching a ride. The image is comical.

"I don't use a thumb," I say. "I've got a sign."

"You won't have any trouble. I can take one look at someone and tell right away what kind of person they are."

"What kind of person am I?"

"You're a good person," the man says, smiling.

The skin on his face is smooth and tight, radiating an inner glow. The man says he dropped his wife at the entrance, so she can walk down to the lake.

"I can't walk much anymore, too old. I've had two bypasses,

though I mowed the lawn today. I do some things I shouldn't do. I've got too much pride for my body and my pocketbook.'' He grins.

"You live in Montezuma?'' I say.

"Yep. It's an old house, but it's right on the town square. My wife looks at the Presbyterian church, and I look at the jail.''

An old woman hooded with a scarf walks up and gets in the truck without a word.

"What is your age?'' I say to the man.

"Guess,'' he says, standing up straight.

"Oh, I'm not good at this. Seventies?''

"Hah! I'll be eighty-seven.''

"Wow.''

He wonders if I'll be cold, then says I'm young and look like I'm in a good shape.

"What are you, about twenty?''

"Twenty!''

"Boy, I'm really off. What, sixteen?''

"You're joking,'' I say.

"Well, you must go to school somewhere.''

"I'm thirty-seven.''

"Boy, I was further off than you were with me.''

He looks at the sky.

"Well, it's dark,'' he says. "I better get going.''

He turns and shuffles back to the truck.

"What about the geese?'' I call to him.

"Oh, they'll be here.''

He grins wide and his eyes gleam. I know for sure that he's pulling my leg.

But when I see the taillights disappear around the bend, I hear a honk, and it's not the horn from the old man's truck.

I stare up at the blackening sky and see them. Seven geese flying overhead in a chevron, magnificent and graceful.

They are followed by another flock of forty, moving as one in a perfect wedge. Unbelievably, a hundred others appear, and then a hundred more. They keep coming, wave after wave, and I lose count. The birds glide through the air and touch down on the lake, the water now made white by their wakes. I step slowly to the water's edge and squint for a better look in the last of the light. The shadowy night fills with beautiful noise—the whoosh of wings, the splash of water, the honks of contentment. The music is deafening and lovely.

I am not cold, yet I shiver. I recall what the Indian told Linda about nature being kin. The Indian's language has no word for loneliness.

I am the only man on the dark shore, but I am not alone.

TWENTY-TWO

They are talking bumper crops this year in the Midwest. Iowa corn is yielding two hundred bushels an acre. Everybody has a vested interest in the land, but they don't call it that. They call it "ground." As in, "He owns that ground" or, "We're growing soybeans on that ground."

I pick my next destination the same way I did Montezuma. Purely by the sound of the name—Oskaloosa.

Drivers in rural Iowa acknowledge you like they do in Nebraska. But instead of a wave, it's an index finger raised from the steering wheel. Still, it's getting harder to flag rides.

Lots of cars pass me, lots of folks give me the friendly finger.

A white Cadillac stops across the road. It's aimed in the other direction. I recognize the car as one that passed me a couple of minutes ago.

"I ain't got all day," the guy hollers out the window.

He wears a red baseball hat and wraparound shades. A cigarette hangs from his lip, right above his poor excuse of a goatee. A punk.

I'm about to holler back (''Well, then why did you bother turning around and stopping for me?'') but this might be my only chance at a ride, so I hustle across the road.

Eric is a twenty-nine-year-old farmer from Oskaloosa, which he calls ''Osky.'' He asks where I'm from and I tell him. He says he was recently visiting his sister in San Francisco. That gives us a connection. Eric warms to me. He asks me questions until he has my whole story.

''So you're just seeing where the kindest people are in America?'' he says.

''Something like that.''

''Where has it been the best so far? The Midwest, I bet.''

I decide to have a little fun with Eric.

''South Dakota was great,'' I say.

He seems to take this as a personal challenge.

''It's quarter draft night out at the Country Corner. Stop by and I'll buy you a few beers.''

''Sounds good.''

''You can stay at my place.''

In the span of a few miles, Eric has transformed from a jerk into a nice guy.

Eric farms ten thousand acres with his father and two cousins. Corn and soybeans. On this day, another farmer has borrowed their dump truck, and Eric must retrieve it. We drive down dirt roads to a soybean field that rolls out to the horizon. A pair of giant green combines gobble up the crops like grazing dinosaurs.

We wait for the combines to fill the dump truck with soybeans. Eric yanks a plant from the ground and shows me how to shell the pods.

''I eat these by the thousands,'' he says, popping several round white beans into his mouth.

I try a handful. The beans taste bland, but I know they are rich in protein.

A garter snake slithers by my feet. The combines kick up dust over the land, creating an unreal sunset of pink and orange and purple.

Eric sits on the harvested ground near the dump truck. He worked eight years as a chemical salesman throughout the Midwest and the South. He returned to Iowa last year.

"Why did you come back?" I say.

"Settle down, I guess. Maybe find a wife with some Midwestern values. Not a woman who wants to burn her bra and get breast implants. I don't want a wife that'll just stay home and cook and clean. I'm a man of the nineties. But I don't need someone who's not fulfilled unless she's got a better job than me."

When the dump truck is full, Eric drives it to a grain bin. I follow in his car. After we unload the beans, we drive to Eric's farm. He nearly loses me, zipping sixty miles an hour down a dirt road.

He parks the truck and we drive his car into Oskaloosa. Eric lives with his mother and her second husband, a retired teacher. They own a modern ranch house, with a detached garage and a big backyard. Eric tells me to drop my pack in the guest room.

His mother, Irene, knits an afghan on the sofa, a fat cat sleeping next to her. Neither she nor her husband Joe thinks it odd that Eric has brought a hitchhiker home to spend the night. They greet me like a long lost son. Irene pours me a glass of iced tea and sets out a plate of freshly baked raisin bars topped with white frosting. She apologizes, but she and Joe have plans to visit some friends tonight. She writes a check for Eric and tells him to buy me dinner.

When they leave, Eric explains that his mother acts as his bank. He gives her all his money because he can't hold on to it.

Eric goes downstairs to his room to wash up. When he returns, he looks like a new man. He has changed into a neatly pressed button-down shirt. His hair is gelled. He now wears prescription glasses. The pathetic goatee has been shaved off. There is no sign of the smart-aleck punk I met out on the highway. He now looks scholarly, which, as it turns out, he is.

"Yeah, I'm a brain," he says, "or so they say."

Eric aced his college entrance exams and Iowa State gave him a full scholarship to study agricultural science. He played trombone in the marching band and graduated with a 4.0 grade average.

We drive to a restaurant called Dr. Salami's. Everybody greets Eric by his name. We have a beer at the bar. Eric sees two women he knows, nurses, and we join them at a table. We order more beer and pizza.

"This is Mike McIntyre," Eric says to Kim and Cheryl. "He's hitchhiking his way across America without a penny."

The nurses don't buy it. They insist I'm probably a cousin of Eric's from the next county over.

"Show us your ID," Cheryl says.

I reach in my shirt pocket for my driver's license. It's gone. I remember that I changed shirts at Eric's. Now I really look like I'm fibbing.

I give the women a day-by-day summary of my trip. Where I've stayed. Who I've met.

"How could I make all this up?" I say.

They still believe it's a tale as tall as me. They are the first people on this journey who don't believe me, or at least say so to my face. What is truly remarkable is not that they question my story, but that there haven't been more skeptics along the way. Let's see, a guy quits his job, gives all the money in his pocket to a bum and travels penniless across the country. I certainly wouldn't believe that fellow.

I don't know why it's so important, but I want the women to know I'm telling the truth. I answer all their questions, fill in all the blanks. But it's no use.

"I would never pick you up," Cheryl says.

"If you saw me on the road tomorrow, you'd give me a ride."

"No, I wouldn't," Cheryl says adamantly.

But now Kim has come over to my side. She smiles, her eyes sparkle with dreams. She drapes an arm around my shoulder. She rests her other hand on my knee.

"That's so romantic," she says.

"Cheryl looks at her like she's a traitor.

"That's so romantic," Kim says again.

Tonight is the first night of Oskyfest, Oskaloosa's answer to Oktoberfest. Eric and I drive to the fairgrounds, where the beer bash is underway in a giant exhibit hall.

"Both my mom and dad are superreligious," he says. "They don't approve of my extracurricular activities, but they don't say much, mainly because of my age."

A country-western band plays on the stage at the end of the building. Dancers do the Texas Two-step across the cement floor. Hundreds of other natives hover in groups at the edge, sipping beer from plastic cups.

Eric is the perfect host. He seems to know everybody, and he introduces me around by my first and last names. A simple introduction is powerful. It instantly transforms you from an outsider to one of the gang. I appreciate Eric's manners more than the pizza and beer. It feels good to be included.

Cheryl and Kim show up. Kim grabs my arm and stands on tiptoe to talk to me over the music. She is pretty, in a wholesome way, and if I didn't have a girlfriend waiting for me at home, I'd listen with a little more enthusiasm. I fantasize about life with Kim in rural America. But I know I am now romanticizing the Midwest, just as she is romanticizing my trip. As if to prove my point, Kim commences to rip on Oskaloosa.

"This town is like high school," she says. "Everyone always knows what you're doing."

Those who don't conform to the conservative small town ways are ostracized, Kim says. People talk. If they have to, they make things up. Right now, there are two conflicting rumors going around about Kim: She is a lesbian, and she is having an affair with a prominent male physician.

"This town is a high school," she says, growing more sullen.

"There's a reason she feels this way," Cheryl says.

"Tell me," I say.

"No," Kim says.

"Tell me, I'm a stranger, I'm just passing through."

"No, you'll think it's such a cliché," Kim says.

"Tell me, tell me." I keep goading Kim. "Is it a scandal?" I say.

Cheryl smiles and nods. Kim pouts.

"You're sleeping with another nurse?" I say.

"Close," Cheryl says.

"You really are having an affair with that doctor?"

Cheryl nods. Kim hangs her head.

"Is he married?" I say.

Kim bites her lip and nods.

"See, I told you you'd think it's such a cliché," she says. "Now you think less of me."

Ten years ago, I started talking to a woman at work. She was married. Talk led to lunch, and lunch led to flirting, and flirting led to a kiss at a New Year's Eve party as her husband dozed on the couch. We fell in love. The woman left her husband. This was it, this was the real thing, this was fate. Or maybe I told myself that to justify what I was doing with another man's wife. It is scary what we can rationalize. In the end, no new great love was created, only a marriage destroyed. A decade later, it is hard to picture the woman. I've tried, but I can't even conjure the feelings that led to my profound lapse of judgment. All of it has faded from my memory. All of it except for the pain I caused and the respect I lost for myself. That's something I can't forget.

"I was in one of these situations once," I tell Kim. "It happens. I don't think less of you. But I'll tell you, those things rarely work out. And if they do, they're not worth the price you pay."

*   *   *

The last stop of the night is the Country Corner. Eric circles the parking lot, looking for a car that belongs to a woman he's seeing. She's married. She's not here.

Inside, a cowboy sings karaoke on stage as thirty people do the line dance. The twenty-five-cent drafts flow, and pyramids of plastic cups rise from the tables. The music is loud, the air thick with smoke. It's a crude crowd of drunks, hayseeds, yahoos, and floozies. Eric joins a group of foul-mouthed men and sleazy women. They spend hours playing a drinking game, taking turns trying to flip a quarter into a cup. There isn't an ounce of intelligence on display at the table, and though Eric is a Phi Beta Kappa, he does his level best to fit in.

On the way home, Eric slows down and looks through the window of a coffee shop. He explains that he drops in to visit one of the waitresses whenever he gets the itch. She's married, he says, but her husband ignores her.

"She'll take you in back and fuck you. She's lonely."

I'll pass, I tell him.

I haven't had anything to drink since that long day back in Montana with J. D. and Kristin. When I wake the next morning at Eric's, my body feels like it's been poisoned. Irene and Joe are already gone, and Eric is running late. When I come out of the shower, I see that Eric has made a sack lunch for me and set it on the bed. There is a hoagie sandwich, three raisin bars, two bananas, an apple and a bag of potato chips. There is also a note, but I don't read it.

Eric drives me out to the south edge of town. After he takes off, I pull the note out.

"Mike, I will continue to pray for your safety as your journey eastward continues," it reads. "It was a pleasure for us to have you visit our fair city. Best wishes, and keep yourself safe and dry. Eric."

I think of the many looks Eric has shown me in the last eighteen hours. The punk, the brain, the gentleman, the scoundrel, the devout. The pressure to suppress your instincts and play the good ol' boy must be tremendous in these parts. I hope Eric will keep his own inner counsel and walk his own true path.

I've never understood what people mean when they say they have to find themselves. We know who we are. The hard part is being that person. It's always so much easier to be somebody else.

TWENTY-THREE

A farmer on his way to the bank to apply for a loan drops me in Ottumwa, Iowa, hometown of Tom Arnold, Roseanne's ex-husband. After Arnold, it must be a long drop down Ottumwa's celebrity ladder, because the local paper is eager to interview me. I pose for the photographer on the bank of the Des Moines River. A sign notes that last year's Great Flood crested at twenty-two feet, almost over the bridge. I hold the sign I started with in San Francisco, the one that says "America."

I walk a few miles south, past the John Deere plant and then some, to get to where the highway narrows to two lanes. The bridges have no shoulders, and I must quickly run across them, my pack pounding me into the asphalt, to avoid onrushing semis. When I return to the golden heartland, I write a sign for the next town, Centerville.

A blue Toyota pickup slams on its breaks and skids to a stop. I toss my pack in back.

"Push it all the way up," the driver says through a sliding window in the cab. He gives me a friendly smile.

I climb in front. The floorboard is heaped with dirty clothes and soda cans, leaving little room for my feet. When I manage to get the door closed, we're already up to speed.

"I hope you don't mind riding with a crazy man," the guy says.

He lets loose with a booming laugh. I figure it's a little joke, a conversation starter, but he keeps laughing, loud and unnatural. He won't stop. He laughs and laughs as he looks at me. The smile I first thought friendly now appears demonic. His teeth are yellow and caked with plaque. I must look spooked, as the man flips off the laugh like a light and says, "Nah, just kidding." He grins. I take my first breath of the ride.

He is a bear of a man, a University of Iowa T-shirt stretched tight over his enormous belly. Dark sunglasses hide his eyes. The tip of the first finger on his right hand is missing. That explains why he stopped. He wasn't able to give me the full Iowa index finger wave.

I ask where he's going.

"Home."

"What do you do out here?"

"I might go to Fairfield next week," he says.

He follows that nonsensical answer with the fact that he was an alcoholic and drug addict.

"Former?" I say.

"Oh yeah, I wouldn't touch a drop now for all the tea in China."

"How long you been clean?"

"Twelve years."

"That's great," I say, trying to sound cheerful.

"What I did then is the reason I'm not working today."

"How does something you did twelve years ago have an effect on your ability to work today."

"I'm a manic-depressive," the man says, flashing me a disturbing grin.

Oh no, here I go again, I think, remembering Barbara.

"Oh yeah?" I say, acting casual. "I stayed with a woman in Montana who is a manic-depressive. Bipolar, it's called, right?"

"Bipolar, yeah."

"Ted Turner is bipolar."

"I get terrible mood swings. I'm gonna pull in here and get a soda. That all right with you?"

"Sure."

"Well, it better be. I'm the driver. Hah, hah, hah!"

He parks in front of a convenience store on the edge of a cornfield.

"I won't be too long. Unless I get to talking. I talk a lot."

I step out of the truck to stretch my cramped legs. My gut tells me to grab my pack and hitch another ride. Instead, I follow the man into the store to see if anybody recognizes him. I don't learn anything new from the way the cashier rings up the driver's soda. What the heck, it's not that far to Centerville.

Back on the road, the man opens a twenty-ounce bottle of Coke. He swigs big gulps and spills some on his chest. He sets the bottle between his legs.

"I had a job that paid four sixty-five an hour," he says. A farmer hired me. He just wanted someone that wouldn't make him mad. I made him mad the first day and he fired me. So I'll go to Fairfield next week and make six dollars. Or I'll go to Mt. Pleasant and make six forty-five. Or I'll go to Drakesville! Or Albia! Or Chariton!"

A vein bulges from the temple of his red face and he grips the wheel like he is trying to strangle it.

" 'Cuz what the farmers don't understand is—"

He lets go of the wheel and balls his hands into fists. He raises his beefy forearms and pounds them down across the steering wheel, a blow punctuating every word.

"—they're . . . gonna . . . be . . . out . . . of . . . work . . . and . . . I'll . . . have . . . a . . . job!!!"

The rage subsides like a spent wave and the man grows eerily calm. Stunned, I stare out the windshield, hoping to see a road sign. How far to Centerville? If it's a mile, it's too far.

"I pick up hitchhikers," the man says. "I don't care. I picked one guy up one time, said he was from Fairfield. It was Fairfield,

New Jersey. Ha, ha, ha! He said, 'I'm from Juh-zee,' just like an aristocrat. Ha, ha, ha! There's a lot of Fairfields in the country.''

"Yeah, we've got one in California."

"I know!" he shouts. "There's a Fairfield, Connecticut; Fairfield, Florida; Fairfield, Idaho; Fairfield, Illinois. There's thirty-seven of 'em. I counted 'em up one day, 'cause I had nothing else to do. Hey, sorry for talking so loud back there. I talk too loud, that's my problem."

"Well, people can hear you better," I say, hoping I sound understanding.

"Tell them that! Ha, ha, ha!"

He raises the Coke bottle from between his legs and takes another sloppy swig.

"The stuff they have me on now puts me to sleep, right to sleep. That's why I gotta pull over all the time and get one of these."

He sucks from the bottle again.

"Know what the doctor told me?" he says.

"No, what?"

"He said he can't believe I'm even able to function."

I try to think of something to ask, but I'm afraid that anything I say might set him off. I nod and say, "Hmm," to whatever comes out of his mouth. I keep looking straight ahead. On the outside, I try to look calm. But on the inside, I cower like a whipped dog awaiting the next tirade by his master.

"I picked one guy up and he shot me. I said, 'What did you do that for?' "

He reaches across me into the glove box. *Oh, shit, this is it,* I think. I have a finger in the door handle. I look down out the window and see the blacktop whizzing underneath. I've often wondered what it's like to jump from a speeding car. Now I'll find out. I remember the article about me that will appear in tomorrow's paper. They can follow that with my obituary.

He pulls something from the glove box, but it's not a gun.

He pops the cassette into the tape deck. Jesus music blasts from the speakers.

"The thing with me is, *I don't care!* Ha, ha, ha!"

I see a sign. Centerville, three miles. *Just hold on.*

A car pulls out onto the highway ahead of us. We come up on it fast. I flinch and point. The guy waits until the last second before he hits the breaks. Tires squeal.

"I won't stop. You don't like the way I drive, too bad! I don't believe in laws. My daughter ran away two weeks ago. I asked a highway patrolman to help me find her. He wouldn't. You know what I told him?"

He raises his damaged finger and jabs it at me. I'm now the cop on the receiving end of his wrath.

"If I speed on the road, you don't know me. If you stop me, I'll take that gun away from you and kill you."

The man looks like he could reach over and squeeze the life out of me.

"Are you a pastor?" he says.

"A pastor?"

"Yeah, you're a pastor."

"No."

"But you could be one, right?"

I choose my words carefully.

"Well, in the broadest sense of the word," I say, "yes, I suppose I could be a pastor."

"Are you a Christian?"

I'll admit to being Judas Iscariot at this point.

"Yep," I say.

"I'm a Christian who cusses. A lot of people say that means I'm not a Christian."

"It's what's in your heart that counts," I say, hoping this doesn't piss the guy off.

"I just do my thing. I go where God tells me."

We race down the highway, Jesus music and fear banging on my eardrums.

"You're not in the good part of Iowa here," the man says. "You want to be over in Van Buren County. Lebanon, Keosauqua, Douds, Pittsburg. . . ."

I sense a detour coming up. I slip my finger through the door handle again.

Then all of a sudden we cross over a rise and enter the town of Centerville. I breathe easy.

"Where you want off?"

"Middle of town would be great."

He swings around the town square. The sidewalks are lined with people sitting in lawn chairs. Lady Justice is perched atop the old stone courthouse.

"This is good," I say.

"Nah, there's a homecoming parade today. I can't park here. I don't want to get in trouble. I've already been in trouble this week."

The parade hasn't started. There is plenty of room to pull over and let me out.

"Anywhere here is fine," I say.

"Nah, I'm gonna take you down a side street."

We stop at a red light. I wonder if I can hop out and reach my pack before it changes. But it turns green, and we're now driving down a road away from all the people.

There is no place to park. All the spaces are taken. No one is in sight. Everybody is in the town square, waiting for the parade. We're now heading out of town. *How long before I act?*

Suddenly the man pulls up to the curb and cuts the engine. I jump out like the truck is on fire and grab my pack.

"Hey, thanks a lot," I say.

The man slumps in the seat, grinning his demented grin.

"Well," I start in, but leave it at that.

"Yeah," the man says. "It'll be all right."

I don't know if he's talking about him or me.

TWENTY-FOUR

I had planned to reach Missouri today, but I'm too shaken to press any further. An Amish man rides by in a horse and buggy. I take it as a sign: Slow down.

I park myself on a bench on the courthouse lawn. Small town America, a parade, and Old Glory fluttering in the breeze. All that's missing is some apple pie, but the raisin bars Eric packed me do nicely.

A couple in their forties sit down one bench over. The man glances at my pack.

"How far you going?" he says.

"The East Coast."

"Just thumbing?"

"Yeah."

"Boy, I'd be afraid," the woman says. "I don't hitchhike, and I don't stop for hitchhikers."

"Yeah, well, I'm a little shaky now," I say. "I've had thirty-nine rides so far. Two of them were bad, one being the guy who just let me off."

"What was wrong with him?" the woman says.

"He was nuts. He just went berserk."

The man says he had some bum rides in his day. When he was in the Army, one driver took off with his duffel bag while he was in the restroom. Another time, a driver robbed him at gunpoint. That was in the sixties, when hitchhiking was considered relatively safe. Despite my fears nothing terrible has happened to me on this trip, nothing even remotely bad. I have no right to complain. The country has been more than kind.

The woman stays behind to chat when her partner leaves for

a closer look at the parade. Sally is quite attractive, with a trim figure, red hair and a bright smile that shows her gums.

"Are you from around here originally?" I say.

"No, we're from Wisconsin."

"Was that your husband?"

"No," she blushes, "he's my brother."

"So how did you end up in Centerville?"

"Norman blew out a brain aneurysm twelve years ago. I brought him over here and took care of him. Then when he got better, he moved into a place of his own. Then I got some brain damage myself, and he takes care of me. We both kind of lean on each other."

She smiles.

I ask what's wrong with her.

"Six years ago, I was robbed and beaten and strangled out at the market where I worked."

"Oh, no."

"I've lost a lot of my memory. I can't remember my kids' childhood."

"Well, you sure seem normal," I say. "You look great."

"Thank you." She smiles bashfully. "But if you'd seen me two years ago, you wouldn't have said that."

After she recovered from her physical injuries, Sally became a prisoner of her house. When she finally ventured out, she would get lost in public buildings. Even in tiny Centerville, she still looks for landmarks whenever she parks her car. She doesn't remember good friends from before her attack.

"A woman came up to me in the store the other day and gave me a hug," she says. I went, 'Ooh, get away.' She knew me from before. She said she knew what was going on, she understood. I've only recently started coming out. I usually don't talk to people. The only reason I'm talking to you is that Norman started visiting with you first."

If Sally hadn't told me, I would have taken her for the most outgoing citizen of Centerville. It's startling how outer appearances can so thoroughly mask the depths of inner trauma.

"So did they catch the person who hurt you?" I ask.

"Yeah, it was a husband and wife."

"Were they from here?"

"Missouri. They cased the market three times during the night before they held it up. I was working graveyard alone. I knew what they were up to. I told the police, but the cop that was on that night wasn't the regular one, and he wouldn't listen to me. The man strangled me, and the woman was clapping and yelling, 'Kill her! Kill her!' Then I woke up moaning and he bashed my head into the concrete floor. That's what damaged my brain. There was blood everywhere, all up the walls, 'cause he cut an artery. I think they thought I was dead. I crawled into the back room and locked the door."

Sally lay there bleeding for five hours before she was found.

The Missouri couple was released from prison after serving six years of a twenty-five-year sentence. A condition of their parole is that they stay out of Iowa. Sally was recently driving to Ottumwa when she spotted a car with Missouri plates in the rearview mirror. She pulled into the slow lane, but the car wouldn't pass her. On her way back to Centerville, she saw the same car. She doesn't know if it was them, but she is always looking over her shoulder.

Sally stands up from the bench. She says she's got to get going. She's enjoyed the visit, she says.

I ask if she knows anyplace I can camp.

"You can camp in my backyard," she says without a moment's hesitation.

Her offer takes me by surprise. I don't know how anyone who has endured what she has could even contemplate letting a stranger set foot on her property.

Sally gives me her address. She says she will be there all afternoon.

I spend the rest of the day in the town square, writing in my journal and jotting a postcard to Anne. At five, I walk down a wide, tree-lined street toward Sally's house. The air is humid; my jeans stick to my legs. I recall Sally's memory problem and wonder if she will have already forgotten me. I imagine her flipping out, hysterically yelling at me to go away.

I spot Sally washing down the side of her house with a garden hose. I take a few tentative steps up the walkway. She turns and flashes her big smile.

''Hey,'' she says.

She is a picture of calm and serenity.

Her house stands across the railroad tracks from a cement factory. It is made of cedar overlap siding, painted white. A porch swing hangs in front. The crawling roots of a massive maple tree buckles the sidewalk near the street.

The house was built in 1846 by the original homesteader. It caught fire twice and fell into disrepair. Sally picked it up a couple years ago for twelve thousand dollars. A contractor told her it would cost another twenty-four thousand to fix it. Sally, who once worked as an electrician, opted to do the job herself. It became her therapy. The makeover cost only fourteen hundred. A realtor offered Sally forty thousand for the place, but she refused. She had restored the house, and the house had restored her. They belonged together.

''Want to bring your stuff in?'' Sally says.

The question shocks me more than her original offer to let me camp in her yard. I wonder if she has a death wish.

The phone rings as soon as we're through the screen door. Sally answers it, motioning me to put my pack in a bedroom just off the living room. The house is tidy and small, the two bedrooms connected by the single bathroom. Tin foil covers the bedroom windows. In Sally's room, framed posters of Elvis Presley hang on the walls. The pictures are black and white, showing the young, thin Elvis, not the old, fat Elvis. I remember reading somewhere that Elvis put tin foil in his windows, too.

As Sally talks on the phone, she hands me a ginger ale from

the refrigerator and gestures for me to sit on the couch. She sits in the reclining chair, her feet tucked under her.

"He's from California . . . ," she says into the phone. "No, you don't know him . . . I don't know . . . *Becky*, I don't know . . ."

She smiles into the phone and says she has to go.

"That was Becky. She lives across the street. She knows how cautious I am. She says she's going to come over later and check you out."

Pictures of Sally's daughter and two sons hang on the living room wall. They are grown adults now, but all the photos show them as kids. I wonder if it's Sally's attempt to jog her memory of their childhood.

Sally was fifteen when she had Lisa, who is now thirty-two. Sally's boyfriend Steve was a soldier stationed in Korea when he learned that Sally was pregnant. He returned to Beloit, Wisconsin and married her. Their first son, Ted, now twenty-eight, lives near Centerville. The youngest, Scott, aged twenty-five, was diagnosed with cancer six years ago, around the time of Sally's attack. He lost his jawbone and lower lip to the disease. He later had brain surgery for the scar tissue sustained during radiation treatments. Scott lives in Wisconsin, but he is returning soon to move into the room where I set down my pack.

Sally's cat Aretha hobbles into the living room on three legs. Her mother chewed off her back left leg at birth. The owners were set to put the kitten to sleep when Sally stepped in and rescued it. Sally's disability check, her sole income, is less than five hundred dollars a month. Even so, she recently managed to pay a veterinarian to surgically remove a hair ball from the cat's intestine.

Sally sits down next to me on the couch and flips through a family album. The photos are yellow and faded. In one, she poses with Steve in front of a black convertible. It is their wedding day, and the future looks as bright as Sally's smile.

The marriage lasted twenty years. They were actually married twice. Sally divorced Steve both times for cheating on her.

She later married Doug, a county road crew supervisor. He was a tyrant. He beat Sally, told her when to eat and sleep, kept her from her kids. After her attack, he refused to let her seek long-term medical treatment. She wasted to seventy pounds.

Doug once pushed her from a moving car. Another time, he threatened her with a gun. Sally was afraid to leave him because if she did, he told her, he'd kill her children. But Sally's two eldest kids came to her aid. Ted kicked in the door of Doug's truck to try to get him to come out and fight. Doug wouldn't. Lisa later snatched a gun from Doug's hand and he backed down. Like all wife beaters, Doug was a coward.

"When I saw that he wasn't going to hurt my kids, that's when I ran," Sally says.

She moved to Wisconsin to live with Scott and stayed away six months. When she came back, she took up with a man from Kansas City. He was nice enough, but he moved to California. They kept a long distance relationship going for a while. Then the man lost all ambition and became a beach bum. Sally broke it off. She would like to marry again. She's not picky, she says. She just wants a man who won't drink and hit her. She hasn't been on a date in a year.

Sally asks if I'm hungry. You bet, I say. She sits me at the kitchen table while she whips up minute steaks, baked potatoes, and corn. She says she's not hungry and gives me both steaks.

Becky arrives from across the street. She is forty-five. Her jeans are so tight, it looks like she jumped into them from a second-story window. She appears to have had a face lift. She just broke up with her eighty-three-year-old boyfriend. She now dates another senior citizen. She's mad at him because he hasn't called in a few days.

"Becky, he went to a family funeral," Sally says.

"That's no excuse." Becky turns to me. "Are you a serial killer?"

"Nope."

"*Becky*!" Vicki says.

Becky asks if we want to go to a bar on the outside of town.

Sally is a teetotaler. She comes from a family of alcoholics. She helped her brother Norman get sober and still attends AA meetings with him. She doesn't like bars.

Becky begs Sally to go. She reminds her she needs to get out more. Sally asks if I want to go. If she does, I say. Becky says she will meet us there.

I wash the dishes while Sally gets ready. She emerges from her room dressed in jeans and a denim shirt. She wears white frosted lipstick of the kind favored by women in the sixties. At forty-seven, she still looks young and innocent and happy, baring no trace of the dark shadows cast over her life.

When we get to the bar, Becky is throwing darts at an electronic dart board. A country-western band plays, but nobody listens. Sally orders a Diet Pepsi and tells me to have anything I want. I ask the bartender for a Bubble Up.

The three of us play several games of darts. Sally has an unorthodox delivery. She squints her left eye, lunges forward, and thrusts her right leg back. When she lets the dart fly, her eyes open wide. It's an adorable sight, and I would be content to sit on a bar stool and watch Sally throw darts all night.

A thin man with black hair and a scowl stares from the end of the bar. Sally sees him and leans closer to me.

"He's been trying to get me to go out with him for a year," she says. "He's a beater, though. That's how he lost his last wife. I want him to think I'm with you."

It's after midnight when we drive home. I watch TV while Sally talks on the phone with Becky. When she hangs up, there is an awkward moment, as if Becky had been here in the room then left us alone. The house is still. Sally and I talk late into the night. I nod off momentarily several times, yet I'm curious what will happen next.

Finally, Sally says, "How hard is it to put your tent up?"

I sit up, a little relieved.

"Not hard at all. There are just two poles."

"I feel bad, not letting you sleep in the house, but I just wouldn't feel comfortable. I told Becky, 'He's such a nice guy, I don't know why I don't let him sleep in Scott's room.' But I just wouldn't feel comfortable."

"Hey, you don't have to explain anything," I say, getting to my feet. "After all you've been through, I'm amazed you'd even let me in the house."

"In the morning, I'll cook you breakfast and you can have a shower," she says, as if it's an apology.

"That'd be great."

I pitch my tent under the maple tree, holding my flashlight between my teeth. It is warm and windy, and my sleep is heavy with dreams.

Noise from the cement factory wakes me early in the morning. I pack everything up and sit on the porch steps. I hear music inside, but I don't want to take a chance on startling Sally.

She sees me through the screen door and says, "Well, come on in."

I shave and shower. Sally fixes me eggs, potatoes, bacon, and toast. I again eat alone.

"Becky gave me shit last night," she says. "She wanted me to try to get you in bed. I keep telling her no, I don't do that. See, that's Becky. I try to change her and she tries to change me and we both stay the same."

No one has ever bashed my head in, but there's a part of me that's damaged. That's the part that wants to go to Becky right now and hold her, then carry her into her room and lay her down on her bed, and afterward gaze up at the foil-covered windows and the pictures of Elvis.

I don't tell her any of this. Instead, I ask her how far it is to the Missouri state line, and she tells me thirteen miles.

"Are there good people down there?"

"A few," she says skeptically.

"Did you feel that way before your attack?"

"Yeah. Whenever there's trouble, it always seems to come up from Missouri."

There is an air conditioner in the living room window that Sally wants to store for the winter. I help her carry it out to a tiny shed off the garage. We set it on a pile of scrap wood and cover it with a piece of black plastic. The shed is dark, except for a few shafts of sunlight poking through cracks in the roof. I feel like we're kids, standing in our secret hiding place. My stomach stirs, but I again resist the urge to reach for Sally.

When we go back inside, I linger a while in the living room. It's been hard to say good-bye to people on this trip, but not like today. If I don't leave now, though, I'm liable to stay here forever.

"So, how many strangers have you had in your house?" I say on my way out the door.

"You're the first one since I got hurt," Sally says.

A tingle shoots down my spine.

"Why me?"

"I don't know. I just trusted you."

I can still hear Sally's stereo halfway down the block. When the radio changes songs, I stop in my tracks to listen to Billy Joel sing "The Stranger." Then I walk on toward Cape Fear.

TWENTY-FIVE

Kahoka sits in the extreme northeast corner of Missouri, twenty miles west of the Mississippi River. The town is so poor the local gas station doesn't even have a bathroom. I overhear the attendant giving passersby directions to the public restroom in the courthouse, and I tag along. When you're traveling without a penny, you never pass up free facilities.

The men's room in the basement of the County Courthouse is next door to the sheriff's office. I poke my head in and find the dispatcher, Mitch, slouched in an old overstuffed couch. He is forty-four, with gray hair and no uniform. His three-year-old daughter April, who is chatty and blond, rolls around on the floor.

"Someplace I can camp around here?"

"Which way you headed?"

"East."

"Well, the closer to the river you get, the more likely you are to find trouble."

"What kind of trouble?"

"Trouble is all. People are packed in like rats over there and they just go off. Pack rats, we call 'em."

Mitch mentions a campground several miles west, back where I've already been. I don't know if it charges. Besides, I've always had a hard time turning around.

"I tell you what," Mitch says. "My girlfriend gets off work in about twenty minutes. She lives nine miles east in Wayland. If she says it's okay, you can pitch your tent in her backyard. Just be sure to take my oldest step-daughter with you."

I wait on another sofa that looks like it was refused by the Salvation Army. It is pushed up against a wall papered with FBI "Wanted" posters. One guy is being sought for a string of murders. He doesn't look the type. He looks a little like me.

April scampers up onto my lap when I pull out my road atlas.

"Where's Mexico?" she says. She flips through the pages. "Here's Mexico."

"Hey, she's right," I say to Mitch.

"We're not raising no dummy."

Mitch was married three times but never had any kids with his wives. He and his girlfriend Teri live together but have no plans to marry. April was an accident. Mitch is fiercely protective of his only child. He won't let her stay with a baby-sitter. She spends four days a week with Mitch in the sheriff's office. The rest of the time, Mitch has her with him at his second hand store.

"I'm blunt," Mitch says. "Let me ask you two questions. One, do you have finances?"

"What's your second question?"

We both laugh.

"Are you having fun?"

"Yeah, I sure am."

Teri arrives to retrieve April. She is a heavyset woman in shorts, with permed dishwater hair and thick glasses. Her voice doesn't fit her body; it's soft and high. She looks at once sad and serene.

We pile into Teri's car, a rusted gas guzzler, and Mitch kisses her good-bye through the window. April sifts through sacks of groceries in the backseat. She asks me to open a bottle of juice.

Teri is employed as a factory seamstress. She works ten hours a day, six days a week.

"Lately, I've been doing everything but cut the fabric," she says.

We drive toward Wayland. Splattered raccoons mark our progress like mileposts.

"I really envy you, being able to just up and take off," Teri says.

She was born and raised in Missouri. She has never left the state. I was in Iowa this morning. I'll be in Illinois tomorrow. It's strange how people can spend their whole lives in one spot. Then again, they must think I'm odd, bouncing around the world like a bad check.

"I'm not just saying this, but you won't find a friendlier state than Missouri," Teri says.

She is so sweet and sincere, I almost forget there are forty-nine other states she has yet to visit.

Teri has two daughters. Missy is nineteen and Julie is seventeen. Teri is thirty-nine. She has already been a grandmother for two years.

"Missy was my wild one," Teri says. "I was always watching her. Then Julie goes and gets pregnant. I always said to her, 'Just be honest with me. Do you want to go on the pill now?' And she said, 'Oh, Mom, we're not ready for that yet.' Then she goes and gets pregnant. Not much you can do at that point.''

Julie and her boyfriend Kenny and their two-year-old son Dwight live with Teri and Mitch. Missy, who works at a convenience store, lives there, too. Missy is married to a man who is serving time for dealing drugs. She married him after he was sent to prison. The ceremony was at the courthouse. They were granted one night together, then Missy's husband was thrown back in the slammer. Teri thinks Missy married the guy to piss her off. It worked.

Teri divorced the girls' father a long time ago. There were some happy years in the beginning, then he took to drinking. Long weekends carried over into the work week. He was always disappearing, returning home only long enough to change his clothes. He prowled around. Teri counted fifteen different women. He brought one of them into the restaurant where she used to work. Teri hung in as long as she could. Then the battering started, and she got out.

She lives in a neighborhood of trailers, all with big backyards that converge into one. I pitch my tent under an oak tree that supports a swing. April runs out the back door of the trailer with a foam ball. She demands that I throw it as high as I can. I do. She orders me to heave it again. The drill continues until my arm feels like it's going to fall off. At last, Teri rescues me.

''Do you like wildlife?''

''Yeah.''

''There's a lake nearby. Want to go see it?''

''Sure.''

As we're backing out, Julie and Kenny pull up in an old Bronco with headlamps on the roof. Teri asks if little Dwight wants to come with us, and he climbs in.

Deer Ridge Lake is a long finger of water shrouded by oak, maple, and hickory trees. A pair of men float in an aluminum boat, their fishing lines disappearing into the dark pool. The scene looks like a calendar hanging on the wall of a hardware store.

"When I was a kid, we used to come over here and play for hours," Teri says. "In the fall, we'd get sacks and slide down the hills over the leaves, just like a sled."

She smiles at the memory.

"My kids today have TVs, stereos, and video games, but they always say they're bored," she says.

On the way back to Wayland, we see Julie and Kenny coming from the other direction. Teri stops to hand back Dwight.

"Just drop him at Marty's," Kenny says.

Marty is Teri's brother. He lives on a farm back toward the lake. Teri turns around and follows Julie and Kenny up a dirt driveway. A young boy throws a lasso around a sawhorse with a pair of plastic steer horns attached to the front.

"Don't be surprised if my brother doesn't talk to me," Teri says as we get out of the car.

We walk to the side of the house. Teri's sister-in-law Alice meets us at the sliding glass door and invites us in. A TV flickers in another room. I can't see the person watching, only a pair of cowboy boots propped on an ottoman.

"No, we better get going," Teri says.

April runs up a hill to the chicken house. Teri, Alice and I follow, passing a corral where two horses and a mule munch grain from a trough. We pass through a gate and duck into the dark chicken house. When we come back out, a man is approaching from the house. He wears jeans and a white T-shirt, and the cowboy boots I saw resting on the ottoman. He isn't smiling.

Alice walks down and intercepts him. He flails his arms, but I can't hear what he says. He stalks up the hill. He grips the top of the fence post and glares at Teri.

"What are you *doin'* out here?"

"Marty, we just came to drop off Dwight," Teri says softly.

"Well, you just give him to Kenny and Julie and *git!*"

He takes one step back from the gate, making room for us to pass. He shudders with rage.

"Bye, Alice," Teri says, hanging her head. "Come on, April, let's go."

When I walk by Marty, I give him a nod. It goes unreturned. He stares a hole straight through me to his sister.

"Sorry, Mike," Teri says when we reach the car.

I don't know what to say.

Teri heads back toward the lake and drives aimlessly along the dirt roads. It's the opening day of bow hunting season, and men step from the dark woods dressed in camouflage and stride empty-handed to their pickups. Teri points out the places where houses she knew in her youth once stood, their foundations now overgrown with brush. The forest gives itself up to the night. Teri keeps driving in a daze, long after there is anything left to see.

I want to know the reason for Marty's wrath, but I don't ask. We drive back to town in silence.

No one is home when we return. Mitch works until midnight. Missy is working overtime to pay for the six hundred dollars in collect calls her husband rang up in prison. Julie is who knows where.

"My kids are never here," Teri says. "Are you hungry?"

"Yes, I am," I smile.

"I'll fix supper then."

"Do you need any help?"

"No, thank you. You just sit down and watch TV."

Teri bakes potatoes and stirs up some Hamburger Helper. The kitchen table has only three chairs, one of which bumps against the refrigerator door. Teri eats quietly, her mind elsewhere. The only noise in the trailer comes from the TV, Robin Williams riffing maniacally in *Good Morning, Vietnam.*

I ask Teri how she met Mitch.

She says her old boyfriend, Dan, collected books and knew Mitch from the second hand shop. Teri lived with Dan for four years. He had been married. Before his divorce, he climbed a ladder to get his kids' kite down from a telephone pole. Dan brushed a live wire and was electrocuted. He fell twenty feet, landing in a sitting position.

"The doctors said the only thing that saved him was the fall," Teri says. "It jolted him back to life."

As a soldier, Dan had survived three tours in Vietnam. Now he was paralyzed, confined to a wheelchair. When he moved in with Teri, he outfitted the trailer with ramps.

"He hated sympathy," she says. "He was so good in that wheelchair."

He died of smoke inhalation in a fire in their old trailer. They figure he was trapped in the trailer and he couldn't get out.

"The only thing that kept me going was my kids," Teri says. People told me I'd get over it. You learn to deal with it, but you never get over it. I think about it every day."

"I'm so sorry," I say. "That's terrible. I've never had to face anything like that before."

Teri looks up at me. Her brown eyes go wet.

"I hope you never do," she says quietly. "I *hope* you never do."

She nudges the food on her plate and sets down her fork.

"I loved Howard, the kids' father," she says. "And I love Mitch. But I believe you have one real love in life, and Dan was it."

Teri stays with Mitch out of fear as much as love.

"He told me that if anything ever happened between us, he would do everything in his power to take April from me," she says. "I'm one of those people who if you take my kids from me, you might as well put a gun to my head, 'cause I'd be through."

Teri is being so candid, I decide to ask her about Marty.

"So that was your brother, huh?"

She sighs. A couple of years ago, her father and Mitch got into an argument—over what, nobody remembers. Just two stubborn and opinionated men, neither willing to back down. "If you weren't holding that baby," Teri's dad told Mitch, "I'd deck you." Mitch handed April to Teri, and Teri's dad came at Mitch and they got into it. Mitch used his connections in the sheriff's department to get Teri's father arrested. Mitch later asked that the charges be dropped, but it was too late. Teri's dad was convicted, fined, and placed on probation. He told Teri to never set foot in his house again. He eventually made up with Teri, but Marty still carries a grudge. He thinks Teri should leave Mitch, out of family loyalty. But with Mitch holding April over Teri's head, that is an impossibility.

Julie, Kenny, and Dwight roll in around ten. Julie and Kenny scoop Hamburger Helper into their bowls and sit down at the table. Dwight plays in the living room, snot running from his nose.

"Dwight eat yet?" Teri says.

"No," Julie says.

"You're sitting there feeding your face and he hasn't eaten yet? You get up and feed him something!"

It's the only time I hear Teri raise her soft voice.

I take the local newspaper out to my tent and read it using my flashlight. By the time I wake in the morning, Mitch has already returned home and left again for work. Teri sees me packing from the back window.

"Do you like sausage gravy?" she says through a hole in the screen.

"I love sausage gravy."

"Well, I'll get breakfast started then."

On my way in, I stop to visit with Kenny, who is washing his Bronco. The best way to get a man talking is to compliment his wheels, so I do.

"I know it'll rain, now that I've washed the car," he says.

He has a shag haircut and rotting front teeth. He works as a laborer, digging holes for telephone poles. He still keeps a room at his parents' house, down the road in Luray, but he spends most of his time here in Wayland.

"There are fewer blacks over here," he says.

I don't know if Kenny assumes I'm a bigot like him, or if he just doesn't care. Either way, I've heard enough, and I go inside.

I sit at the kitchen table, sipping a cup of coffee while Teri cooks breakfast. She tells me Missy got home after midnight and got a call from a guy she met on a 900-number party line. She fell asleep during the call. Kenny discovered the receiver off the hook this morning.

"This one boy from Texas calls Missy a lot," Teri says. "I heard him talking to her one time. I couldn't believe the things he was saying. He kept calling her. She wasn't home one time and I answered the phone. 'I been trying to call Missy,' he said. I said, 'I know you have, and I don't like what you say to her.' He said, 'Do you know what Missy does for me?' I said, 'No, what?' He said, 'She masturbates over the phone.'

"I just hung up," Teri says, flushing red with embarrassment.

At last, I meet Missy. She walks out of her room, which is separated from the kitchen by a torn accordion-shaped partition. She wears a St. Louis Cardinals baseball jersey.

Teri tells her how Kenny found the phone off the hook. Missy mumbles something about the Texas trash talker having enough money to pay his long distance bills.

Teri's biscuits and gravy are the best things I've tasted since San Francisco, but they sit in my stomach like hockey pucks. I feel like I may stay full clear to Cape Fear. She offers to make me some sandwiches, but I tell her I'm good.

The sky is dark gray. All through my time in the Midwest, they've been calling for rain, but I've managed to stay a day ahead of the storms. I haven't got wet since Oregon, and I see no point in getting soaked in Missouri. I say my thank-yous and grab my pack.

Thirty yards up the road, I turn around to take one last look at Teri's trailer. I'm surprised to see her standing at a window, staring at me. Our eyes lock. Even at this distance, I can see tears welling, the way they did last night when she told me about Dan.

It dawns on me that so many of the kind strangers I've met are women who have suffered great heartache and tragedy. They are fierce survivors. They have taught me lessons in perseverance and compassion that will stick with me long after this journey is over. But what have I given them in return?

Jerry, the man back in Idaho who bought me a motel room, said that people who help me have their own motivations. As I turn away from Teri's wet gaze, I can only hope he is right.

TWENTY-SIX

My Magic Marker is fading. I've put a lot of miles on it. I use the last of its ink to write "Quincy" on a sheet of paper and tape it to my dog-eared piece of cardboard.

A man stops for me. He has gray hair and gray pants and two toothpicks in his mouth. He's going to Quincy, across the river in Illinois, to church. He used to own a drugstore there. But the Wal-Marts and Kmarts moved in, and he was forced out. He now runs a drugstore in Memphis, Missouri. Half of his customers are on welfare. No one has a job, he says, but they've got slews of kids.

"It's their meal ticket," the man grumbles. "I've got a solution to it. It may sound extreme to you, but the answer is orphanages. They'd reduce the welfare rolls and give these kids a better chance than with their deadbeat parents."

I see the top of a steel bridge in the distance and my stomach flutters with excitement. I told myself before I left that if I made it to the Mississippi, I'd know I'd make it the whole way.

"All this was under water," the man says, recalling the terrible flood last year.

"How about that Phillips 66 station?"

"That's new. The old one washed away."

This part of Missouri was looking good until some nut broke the levee. Officials said it would have held. Instead, thousands of acres of crops, along with buildings and homes, were destroyed.

"If the farmers could get hold of him, they'd hang him from the highest tree."

We cross the Big Muddy, the grated bridge humming beneath the tires. I feel like a racehorse turning for home.

Quincy, site of one of the famous debates between Abraham Lincoln and Stephen Douglas, occupies a hill above the river. It is an old town of brick storefronts and stately houses. The druggist parks at the Episcopal church at the eastern edge of the city. He recommends Highway 104, the scenic route.

The scenic route is lined with the chain stores that chased the druggist across the river. If somebody knocked me out and dropped me here, there would be nothing to let me know I was in Quincy, Illinois, when I came to. I could be in California or New York or Texas. Every city in the country is starting to look the same. America has been malled.

This section of Route 104 has four lanes—two too many. I'll walk until it slims down to a friendlier width.

The strip malls give way to fields of corn. Some ears stand taller than my own. But the scenic route still resembles an interstate, so I keep walking.

At noon, I rest at the entrance of a motor speedway. I shed my long-sleeved shirt and drink half the water from my bottle. I eat the banana Eric gave me and the last of the raisin bars.

Food has almost become a nonissue on this trip. If I don't meet another kind stranger, I could ration my provisions and still limp into Cape Fear with something in my belly. As of today, my food bank includes two cans of tuna from Mel and Judie, four nutrition cookies from Pete and Doris, a brick of sweaty cheddar cheese from the Montana Rescue Mission, a can of beans and two tins of lunch loaf from Pastor Larry, the nine energy bars from my friend Bruce, and somewhere at the bottom of my pack, down near my winter gloves, the big bag of trail mix Linda bought me way back in Redway, California. The stash is reassuring, a hedge against a downturn in the kindness market. The drawback is that my pack now weighs seventy pounds. I feel like I've got a pantry strapped to my back.

I walk against the traffic. A few motorists wave, but most folks glare at me, as if menaced by the sight of a man walking down the highway. My left arm goes numb. I poke my thumbs under my backpack's shoulder straps to relieve the pressure. I buckle the hip belt to shift the weight. I undo it a hundred yards later. I alternately tighten and loosen the shoulder straps. I fasten and unfasten the chest strap. I reach behind and support the bottom of the pack. Nothing works for long.

A plane swoops down over the cornfields. A crop duster, I figure. But when I reach the crest, I see runway lights and an airstrip. A sign says "Quincy Municipal Airport." After two hours of walking, it's mighty discouraging to see a mention of Quincy. I drink the last of my water.

I keep passing campaign signs for some fellow named Allan Witte. He is running for treasurer. I know there's a thing or two I could teach him about saving money.

After ten miles, the highway thins to two lanes. But now there's no shoulder to stand on, no place for a car to stop. With highway dollars, it's always feast or famine. I decide to walk straight on through to Liberty, another ten miles.

The road cuts through a forest, tree limbs meeting above the blacktop and forming a tunnel. Traffic is light, so I follow the center line. When the occasional car happens by, I hop up onto the bank, watchful for snakes in the grass.

I round a bend and a bull-necked dog rushes me from a gravel driveway across the road. I freeze in my tracks.

"Buddy! Buddy!" shouts a man working under the hood of a

car. Then to me: "He won't hurt you." But Buddy looks like he's still making his mind up. He veers off at the last instant, right before my body language was about to admit that I was dog meat.

I stumble down the road, barely able to lift my feet. At last I see a water tower perched on stilts, the ubiquitous symbol of the rural Midwest. A sign at the edge of the village reads: "Welcome to Liberty, America's Freedom Town." I take a look around. Liberty is free, all right. Free of a drinking fountain, free of a bathroom, and free of a campground. At least it is also blessedly free of a Wal-Mart.

I cross the town park, aimed for a bench under a shelter. Kids rake leaves into piles and wade through them like snowdrifts.

"Hey, what are you doing?" a boy calls to me.

"I'm on a trip."

"How far you goin'?"

"All the way."

"Clear across Adams County?" he says.

"Yeah," I chuckle, "and then some."

Jay, who is ten, and his brother Ricky, nine, drop their rakes and follow me to the bench. We are soon joined by Trudy, a seven-year-old with freckles and a gap-toothed smile.

"So what do you guys do for fun around here?" I ask.

"We love watching cartoons," Jay says.

"Yeah, we can name every cartoon on TV," Ricky says. "One time I woke up at three in the morning, I wanted to watch cartoons so bad."

"But they're not on then," I say.

"Yeah, I know," Ricky groans, disappointed all over again.

"Even when I get old," Jay tells me, "I'm gonna watch cartoons."

"Nah, when you're twenty, you won't want to watch cartoons," Ricky says.

"Uh-huh, when I'm a hundred, I'll watch cartoons," Jay replies.

Trudy has nothing to add to the debate. She is content to sit close to me, like I'm her new biggest, bestest buddy.

I ask Jay and Ricky what their dad does. I cringe when they tell me he's dead. And their mother?

"She lives in Clayton," says Ricky, like that explains it all.

The boys live with their aunt. The three of them recently moved to Liberty from Quincy.

"We couldn't keep the house," Jay says. "Our uncle died last month."

"Our aunt adopted us," Ricky adds.

"No, she *is* adopting us," Jay corrects him.

The boys seem so carefree, as if they are untouched by the losses in their lives, though I know that can't be true. If I were to return to Liberty in ten years, I wonder, what kind of young men would I find?

Jay and Ricky take turns trying to lift my pack off the ground. Trudy stays by my side. I look up and see a man down the street barbecuing in his yard. He keeps staring over at us. I can guess what he's thinking: *Some pervert is in town to molest our children.* I don't mind. If I ever have kids, I'd like to live in a place where my neighbors kept an eye out for them. I'm sure the man is relieved when my three little friends spring up and run to the swings.

I rest my aching feet and write in my journal. Around sundown, a father and his four boys drive up. They carry ice chests to a picnic table and spread out their dinner.

The man asks where I'm going. I tell him.

"Where you staying tonight?"

"Don't know yet."

He laughs.

After he's through eating, he comes over to my bench.

"So, what's your purpose?" he says. "What's your goal?"

"If you really want to know, I'll tell you."

I figure that will scare him off, but he sits down and leans forward, ready to listen. He's about my age, with black horn-rimmed glasses. He is the custodian at the local school. His name is Brian.

"I know where you can stay tonight," he says after I've finished my story.

"Where?"

"At our church," he says, smiling. He and the boys are heading there now. His wife is already there, attending a meeting. "They have snacks afterwards. You want to come?"

"Sure," I say. "I could use a little spiritual nourishment."

Bible study is in session when we enter the Liberty Christian Church. About thirty people sit in the middle pews, huddled around the preacher. He hands out photocopies of a timeline that shows how Christianity has been corrupted by various denominations since the time of Jesus. He says the word of the Lord was rescued only in the last century, when fundamentalist churches such as this one returned to a literal interpretation of the New Testament.

"I don't mean to put down other religions," the preacher says. I have to bite my cheeks to keep from laughing. It's always the same: *Ours is the only carnival selling tickets to the ride to heaven.*

The preacher excuses himself to prepare for a baptism. He appoints a member to lead the congregation in a few hymns. The man wears blue jeans, a T-shirt, and red suspenders. He loses his place in the hymn book and we sing "Rock of Ages" twice.

A red velvet curtain opens behind the altar, revealing the preacher and a woman named Sue. They stand in a hidden pool of water, a painting of a forest over their shoulders. Sue is dressed in a white smock. The preacher says a few words and dunks Sue in the water as she holds her nose. The curtain draws to a close, and, like that, another soul is saved. It seems so easy.

I'm not sure what to say to Sue in the receiving line. My stock lines to brides at weddings—"You looked so beautiful up there"—doesn't seem appropriate. I shake her hand and say, "Congratulations."

There are cookies, cake, popcorn, and Kool-Aid waiting downstairs. Brian has already spread the word about my trip. The congregation swarms me. It seems that everybody saw me walking down the road today. They press close, asking questions, offering me more snacks. I feel bad about stealing Sue's thunder, and me a heathen at that.

The preacher sits down next to me. He is young and energetic, fresh out of Bible school. He offers to let me sleep in his office.

"I'd let you stay at my house, but my wife runs a child care service out of our home, and the authorities might—"

"Not approve of a stranger in the house," I finish for him.

"Right."

When the reception breaks up, the preacher shows me to his office, pointing out the men's room on the way. He pulls a box of religious cassette tapes from the shelf and sets them on his desk next to the tape player.

"In case you get bored," he says.

His wife goes next door to their house to fix me a steak sandwich. The parishioners file out. I ask the preacher if he wants me to lock up. He says no, the church door is always open. Now, that is faith.

After the preacher and his wife go home, a tall man with salt-and-pepper hair and friendly eyes comes through the church door. He is one of the people I met at snack time, but we didn't visit much.

"Would you like to sleep in a bed tonight?" he says.

I follow Jim outside, where his wife Linda waits in their new Cadillac. I get the idea that they left and returned to extend the invitation after grappling with their collective conscience.

Jim is a contractor, and Linda is a school librarian. They live in one of the nicest homes in the area. The sprawling, two-story brick house is set back among the woods outside of town.

Their eldest son, Jim Junior, is away at college. Jim says I can have his room.

"I get to go upstairs first," Linda says, worried I might find a mess.

I start a load of wash. Jim and Linda's other son, Andy, returns from his job at the YMCA in a nearby town. We all sit around the table talking about my journey.

"Boy, I could never do that," Andy says.

"Your mother would never let you do it," Linda says.

"Yeah, I was afraid to tell my mom," I say. "I told her I was traveling across America, but I skipped the penniless part."

Mercifully, the conversation steers clear of religion. If my hosts think I'm going to hell, they keep it to themselves.

Jim grew up in Texas, the youngest of twelve children. He might be the most mellow, even-tempered man I've ever met. Linda was raised here in Liberty. She and Jim met in Washington, D.C. Jim was in the Navy, and Linda was a secretary for the FBI, recruited right out of high school.

I've been in their house only an hour, but I am totally at ease. A month ago, this would have been an impossibility. Now I feel at home anywhere in the country.

I doubt that my sense of comfort is ever completely matched by my hosts'. No matter their ability to judge character, their gut instincts, their faith in humanity, surely there must always come a moment—perhaps in bed, after they've turned out the lights— when an inner voice asks them, *Can we really trust this stranger with our lives?*

I say good-night. On my way upstairs, I stop and turn back to the family.

"You were leery about letting me stay here, weren't you?" I say.

"Yeah, we thought about it a while out in the car," Jim admits.

"Well, I sure appreciate your hospitality—and your trust."

"Yeah, I'm glad we invited you home," Jim says.

*   *   *

In the morning, Linda and Andy are rushing to get to school. Jim sits at the kitchen table, his usual calm self.

I'm midway through my bowl of cereal when he says, "You want to go golfing, Mike?"

I love to golf, but the image of teeing it up during a penniless journey hits me as comical.

"I didn't bring my clubs," I say.

"No problem, I've got an extra set in the garage."

Jim first must run some tools to one of his construction crews at a job site. He leaves me at home, alone. The beautiful house contains the family's worldly goods—all of them now entrusted to me. Despite mounting evidence to the contrary, the benefit of the doubt is still alive and well in America.

When Jim returns, we drive his Cadillac out to Arrowhead Heights, the local country club. The morning is slightly overcast and crisp—my kind of golf weather. Jim buys us coffee to go. The coffee warms my hands as we zip over the rolling fairways in the cart. We are the only people on the course. We say little to each other, but few words are necessary on a golf course. It is all understood.

I've never been a very good golfer, but golf is the one activity in which I can completely lose myself. On a golf course, the only thing on my mind is the next shot. I forget everything else. I forget life's uncertainties. I forget any troubles or worries. And for a few glorious hours here in western Illinois, I even forget that I just may be a crazy man on a crazy quest.

Before I left California, I was having difficulty controlling my driver, so I started using my three iron off the tee. Today, I also leave my driver in the bag—until the back nine, when my caution strikes me as ludicrous.

"I mean, after all the risks I'm taking on the road, I guess I can afford to take one on the golf course," I tell Jim.

"Yeah, it's safer if you miss out here," he says.

I reach for the biggest club in the bag and let her rip. As I see the ball sail out over the fairway, straight and true, I know that, if nothing else, the Road to Cape Fear has cured me of my phobia of the one wood.

Back at Jim's, we fix ourselves sandwiches from cold cuts and eat them with pickles and potato chips. Afterward, we cut ourselves pieces of chocolate cake and wash it down with iced tea. It's the perfect end to a perfect morning.

"Let me ask you something," I say to Jim. "Do you ever get mad?"

"No, I try not to."

"I guess you could say you're a contented man."

"You could say that," says Jim, his brown eyes beaming wisdom and peace. "I've been lucky. If you find the right woman, it's real good."

I think about Anne. I've thought about her a lot on this trip. Usually, it's after I've met a happy couple who have been married a long time. If Anne and I had followed through with our wedding plans, we would have been married a year by now. That's a year I'll never have back. If I really want what Jim and Linda have, what am I waiting for? So many times out on the highway, I've imagined asking Anne again to marry me. Perhaps this is how the journey is destined to end. On the Road to Cape Fear, maybe I'll lose my fear of commitment.

I help Jim clear the table. Then I fold my clean clothes and put them in my pack.

Jim asks if there's anything I need, anything at all.

"Could you spare a Magic Marker?"

TWENTY-SEVEN

I take nothing for granted. No matter how good it gets—my own room, a hot shower, plenty to eat, a round of golf with a fine fellow—I've got to start from scratch each day. There are no guarantees of kindness on this journey.

I've now traveled penniless for three thousand miles. The trip is working. Still, I can't allow myself to think I'm just going to waltz the rest of the way in. Perhaps it has all been sheer luck, like making your number twenty consecutive times in a game of dice. If I am on a roll, I only hope I reach the end before crapping out.

I use the felt pen Jim gave me to snag a ride to Meredosia, a blue-collar town on the eastern bank of the Illinois River. I drop by the town hall, a storefront on the main drag, and ask about camping options. There are none, comes the reply from Bonnie, the receptionist. When I tell her I'm not picky, she wonders aloud whether I can pitch my tent in the front yard of the boat club. She calls all over town, trying to secure permission.

"He's a real clean-cut guy," she says when she tracks down a club member.

Bonnie's word must be golden because the man on the other end authorizes my night's lodging. Bonnie gives me directions. She says she'll have the police check on me during the night.

The boat club is only three blocks away, but I somehow get lost. I stop to get my bearings from two men talking in a yard. One of them starts to give me directions before the other one cuts him off.

"I'll take you over there," he says.

"That's okay, it's only a couple blocks," I say.

"Throw your stuff in back and hop in," he says, walking toward his pickup. "I'll show you what it's like."

After I climb into the bed of the truck, I look back at the other man. He wiggles his hand, as if to say that the situation I'm now in is a little shaky.

The man drives toward the river at the speed of a snail. The boat club turns out to be a lopsided cabin, shaded by an oak tree. The man eases past the building and continues through the parking lot all the way to the concrete boat ramp. A tug boat maneuvers a string of five barges under the bridge and down the lazy river.

I walk around to the cab to thank the man for the lift. I now see that he's drunk. His eyes are bloodshot and his speech slurred.

"What are ya da'wn? Campin'?"

"Yeah."

"How far ya ga'wn?"

"The East Coast."

"Ya got more money'n brains."

I look at the man. He stares back at me through angry eyes.

"Ya got more money'n brains," he says again.

Though I don't have a penny in my pocket, the man just may be right.

A retired bulldozer operator stops for me in the morning. He lives in Jacksonville, seventeen miles east. He drove over to Meredosia to buy some comb honey. He's a native of Tennessee. I tell him I'll probably be in Tennessee next week.

"Cops may warn you 'bout hitchhiking in Kentucky and Tennessee," he says.

"Is it illegal?"

"No, it's legal. They just may warn you. And if they do, take their advice. You just be careful down there. I don't mean to scare you, but some people take rides and disappear. You just be careful who you get in a car with."

"What's the problem?"

"Oh, some of them boys can't hold their liquor and put a show on. You just be careful."

Ever since I left California, folks have been warning me about someplace else. In Montana, they said watch out for the cowboys in Wyoming. In Nebraska, they told me people aren't as nice in Iowa. In Iowa, they said I'd find trouble in Missouri. No one ever says anything bad about their own part of the country. Evil in America is always down the road.

I walk through Jacksonville, out past the Kraft food factory, and draw a sign for Waverly, the next town east on Illinois 104. A new green Saturn passes me, then the driver turns around and comes back.

"Do you really need a ride to Waverly?" the woman says through the window.

I search my mind for one other reason a guy would stand on the side of a road with a sign that says "Waverly." I come up empty.

"I sure do," I say.

"Well, if you're not a rapist, a robber, or a murderer, climb in."

The woman appears to be in her forties. She works for an answering service. It's her day off.

"You're only the second hitchhiker I've ever picked up."

"I'm honored. Why did you stop?"

"Because you're so clean-cut. I thought you were about my son's age. He's twenty-three. I was going to give you a lecture. But now I see that you're too old to lecture."

When she drops me off, I give her my own brief lecture.

"Don't pick up hitchhikers."

As I move east, it takes more rides to travel fewer miles. Every driver is going only to the next town, and the next town keeps getting closer.

A woman with a thick German accent drives me from Waverly

to Auburn, a trip of eleven miles. The front seat of her Volvo is piled with papers, so she tells me to ride in back. She doesn't say another word. Instead of a pauper, I feel like a millionaire being chauffeured through the countryside.

A beefy man hauling a flatbed of pesticides picks me up in Auburn.

"Nobody will stop for you out here," he says.

So how is it I've come three thousand miles? I wonder.

The man is due to get laid off from the chemical plant next week. Then he'll have a couple months' work in the fields during harvest. After that, who knows? He carries me five miles to Pawnee.

A cute young blond in a Mustang whizzes by, eyeing my sign for Assumption. Not a chance, I figure. But she pulls a U-turn.

"Where in Assumption?" she says.

She's even prettier standing still. She gives me a big smile. My gaze falls to her smooth legs extending from a skimpy pair of cutoffs. I lapse into the male hitchhiker's fantasy.

"Anywhere," I say.

Natalie is nineteen. She studies psychology at a junior college in Decatur, about fifteen miles north. Today she cut school and called in sick to her day-care job. She's hiding from her mother until dinner. She says her stepfather "owns part of Assumption." She smokes like a fiend and drives like a demon, almost ramming into the back of a lugging combine.

"What's that playing?" I say over the stereo.

"Smashing Pumpkins. Ever hear of them?"

"Oh yeah."

"Do you know Green Day?"

"I've heard of them, but I don't know their music."

"I love Green Day," Natalie says, pulling the CD from under her bare leg. "I *love* Green Day."

The J.C. is her third college in two years.

"I missed two months of school last year. I was hospitalized."

"Oh no, what was the matter?"

"I was on the psychiatric ward. They were giving me electro-shock therapy. Ever hear of that?"

She turns to me and smiles.

"Yeah, but I didn't know they still used it."

"Oh, they still use it, all right. It makes you have a seizure."

I think of all the people I've met on this trip who have seizures. Edie's granddaughter Laura, Barbara, her brother-in-law Mark, Sally in Iowa, now Natalie. It's either a strange coincidence or there are a lot more people than I thought with seizure problems.

"Did they have a name for your condition?" I say.

"Depression is what it was. I tried to kill myself three times."

I almost start to cry. A few miles ago, I was lusting after this girl. Now I'm wrought with sadness for her.

I've never wanted to commit suicide. But there was a time when I wouldn't have minded never waking up again. I was in college. Suddenly and inexplicably, life was terrifying and over-whelming. I locked myself in my dorm room and didn't go to class for a month. I felt completely alone. I lost all sense of control. A giant wave of despair had me pinned to the bottom and wouldn't let me up. I got better only with counseling. When the episode passed, I swore I would never feel that way again, and I never have.

I tell Natalie all of this in the hope that something in my story might help her.

We reach Assumption, Natalie bouncing her knee to Green Day.

"You can almost see my house. There's my mom, as a matter of fact, painting."

I look beyond somebody's backyard to see a woman painting a house in the next block. It's a nice-looking house, a nice-looking mom. I wonder what went so horribly wrong.

Natalie drops me at a gas station at the edge of town.

"Don't kill yourself, all right?" I say.

"Okay." She smiles.

*   *   *

The couple that stops for me next has come to Assumption to buy their daughter a dress for the high school homecoming dance. They are on their way home to Pana, nine miles south. I put my pack in the trunk, careful not to wrinkle the formal gown enclosed in the clear plastic garment bag.

I ask the people what they do.

"I'm on disability," the woman says. "An injury I got back in 1969 has returned. I was a driver for the state, and I've been driving and having seizures and not even knowing it."

When I ask the next driver who picks me up where he's going, he says Shelbyville—but I swear it sounds like Seizureville.

TWENTY-EIGHT

There are some towns where I instantly know I'm not destined to get invited home with anybody. Shelbyville, Illinois, is one of them. It's a pretty place, set near a lake in the center of the state. But it exudes an air of self-sufficiency, a quality I suspect it also admires in its drifters.

I sit on a bench in a little brick square and open a can of beans with my Swiss Army knife. As I eat the cold beans, I recall where I got them—Pastor Larry—and that gives me an idea.

It's dark when I start knocking on church doors. The Catholic priest is the first to answer. I ask Father Joe if I can borrow a pew.

"I can't let you for several reasons," he says. "But we'll work something out."

Father Joe invites me into the rectory. He was recently sent here, and his office floor is covered with boxes yet to be unpacked. He's about eighty, with a halo of white hair. He was ordained in San Diego, where I once lived for five years.

"I'm on a sort of spiritual journey," I say, and tell him about my trip.

"That's quite an adventure, Mike, but it's getting too cold for you to be sleeping outside."

He calls a local hotel and says he's sending me over. As he fills out a voucher, he tells me about a priest who often picked up hitchhikers.

"We always told him he was going to pay for it, and he did. They found him dead."

My situation also reminds Father Joe of another priest. This one took his vow of poverty to the extreme, refusing to even touch money.

"When he rode the city bus, he'd get other people to pay his fare," he says, chuckling at the image.

He jots something on a church envelope and hands it to me. It's good for six dollars in groceries at the local supermarket.

"You still won't have to handle money, but you'll be able to replenish your pack."

I appreciate Father Joe's help, but I wish he'd called one of his parishioners rather than the hotel. I guess my hunch about Shelbyville was right.

The Lidster Hotel is the town's closest thing to a flophouse. I'm led to a dank basement room, with a chipped tile floor, an industrial gray metal desk, and a stained bedspread.

A portable humidifier drones violently in the hallway. When I go out to investigate, I find an old man standing in front of an opened refrigerator that's streaked with spilled liquids and food. The Lidster has been his home for sixteen years. He lives on his Social Security payment of $299 a month. Mention of my road trip prompts him to name every relative who ever died, and how each met his demise. Several were "knocked over the head." The list goes on for five minutes.

He bids me good-night with, "Watch you don't get knocked over the head."

* * *

In the morning I exchange the church envelope at the market for a box of crackers, a package of sliced turkey, an apple, and some grapes. I return to the bench where I ate the beans and start a letter. A heavyset man in overalls and a baseball hat walks up and demands to know my "purpose." I tell him straight.

"Have you accepted Jesus Christ as your personal savior?"

Father Joe didn't say a word about religion when he set me up with a place to stay and something to eat. I guess this fellow is here to settle the account. As the saying goes, there's no such thing as a free lunch.

Lee is sixty-three and a former Marine. He farmed most of his life and later ran a hardware store in town. He says he's read the Old Testament twice and the New Testament thirty-one times. I listen politely as he recites several spiritual poems he wrote. Every one ends with the word *repent.* After he finishes a poem, he says, "What do you think of that one?" or, "How's that for a hillbilly?"

He runs out of poems and wanders off.

He returns a minute later. "I'm back."

I look up from my letter.

"You told me you don't have a penny. How 'bout I buy you dinner?"

It's 11:30 in the morning. Besides, I've got a pack full of food. I tell Lee thanks all the same.

He says God told him to buy me dinner. "God said, 'You fed his spirit, now feed his stomach.' "

"Well, I don't want to get you in trouble with God," I say.

I follow Lee around the corner to a storefront cafe. He says, "Hey buddy," to everyone who greets him. The special is fried chicken, mashed potatoes and gravy, cole slaw, cottage cheese, and brown bread and butter.

Lee won't let up on the God talk. If God is so powerful and loving, I ask him, then why do bad things happen to good Christians?

Jesus suffered, is his answer.

He tells me his wife lost her left breast to cancer last year. He tears up during the story and his lip trembles.

"I held her in my arms and told her it don't matter what she look like. I'll always love her."

Tears stream down Lee's rosy cheeks. He removes his glasses and wipes his eyes with his hands.

Out on the sidewalk after lunch, Lee cocks his head and says, "Your face looks familiar. I've seen you before. Are you a preacher?"

"No, not yet."

He gives me a closer look. "You're not run of the mill," he says. Then he says it again.

He pulls his wallet from his overalls and offers me money. I tell him I can't accept it. He gives me his number and tells me to call collect if I get in a jam.

"I want to take someone to heaven with me. What good is a carpenter if he never builds a house? What good is a fisherman if he never catches a fish? What good is a Christian if he never converts one soul? You're too good for hell. You know what the Bible says about strangers?"

"No, what?"

"They're angels in disguise."

Eastern Illinois is littered with towns that look tiny on the map, but that jump up and swallow you when you reach them. The city of Mattoon spits me out onto Route 16, a four-laner thick with rush hour traffic. I walk twelve miles to Charleston, home of Eastern Illinois University. I keep walking until I've passed the last gas station and fast food joint.

An auto mechanic named Jim stops for me. His hands are as greasy as his face is kind. He's going home to Kansas—Kansas, Illinois.

"This is my wife's car. I was supposed to fix it, but I got tired."

"It sounds like it's running good to me," I say.

"There's a few things wrong."

Mechanics can always find something wrong, even with their own cars.

I ask Jim if there's any camping in Kansas. He suggests the city park. I tell him the cops might have a problem with that. "You have police, right?"

"Yep, one day and two night."

"Is there a secluded place I can pitch my tent where they won't bother me?"

"Well, if you really want to camp, you can camp in my backyard."

Kansas is one of those blink-and-you'll-miss-it towns; you can throw a rock from one city limit sign to the other.

Jim pulls into a driveway alongside a big white house. We walk around back to a yard that borders a pasture. A picnic table sits below a maple tree.

"I'd let you stay in the house, but it's a mess," Jim says.

I know it's a weak excuse. Still, I can't fault Jim. He's known me for fifteen minutes, which means he doesn't know me at all.

"You sure your wife won't mind?"

"I don't know," he says with a chuckle.

Jim asks if I want to take a shower, but I already had one today. He and his wife leave for work early, so I know there won't be time for one in the morning. He says to knock on the back door if I need to use the bathroom. On his way inside, he points to a garden hose coiled on the side of the house. "If you need water." He gestures to a table covered with garden tomatoes. "There's even some free tomatoes here."

He pauses in the doorway. "It's gonna get down to forty-seven tonight."

"I'll be fine. I've got a down bag."

I set up camp before Jim's wife has a chance to change his mind.

I walk into town for a look. A grain auger lugs corn to the top of a bin. The marquee at the Kansas State Bank reads: BEST

WISHES FOR A SAFE HARVEST. The counter at the Crazy Corner Cafe is full of coffee sippers in baseball hats.

A left turn takes me down the main drag. Downtown Kansas stretches out for an entire block. There's a second-hand store, the post office, an upholstery shop, a boarded-up saloon, and an American Legion Hall. No town in the Midwest is too small for a veterans post.

I continue along past the Methodist Church, down a residential street. Kids in Kansas don't leave their bikes in the front yard; they leave them on the sidewalk. I stop outside a house and watch TV shadows flicker on the living room wall.

I return to my tent and crawl in. As I lie in the dark, I wonder what Jim and his wife think about the stranger camped out beneath their bedroom window. I imagine Jim's wife at work tomorrow saying, "You're not gonna believe what Jim did last night. . . ."

I fall asleep listening to the comforting purr of the grain auger.

Jim and his wife have left when I wake in the morning. I stick my head under the garden hose and eat a tomato from the table.

Jim probably thought what he did for me was nothing. I bet he doesn't know what a patch of grass, a hose, and a tomato mean to me. I write him a thank-you note and pin it under a cement statue of a dog sitting on the front porch.

At the post office, an old lady is waiting in the lobby when I step in to mail a letter. She stands expectantly in front of the wall of mailboxes.

A female voice calls to her from behind the boxes.

"Mail's all out, Mary."

The old woman inserts her key into her box yet another time, as if she can't believe the clerk. An empty mailbox stares back at her. She snaps it shut and limps away. I hold the door open for her.

"Thanks," she huffs. Then she mumbles, "Kids don't know how to write anymore."

"What's that?"

"That daughter of mine doesn't take the time to write."

She limps down the sidewalk, leaves swirling about her feet. It will be winter soon.

I blow east out of town with the wind. Like Dorothy, I have a feeling I'm not in Kansas anymore.

TWENTY-NINE

The man who drives me into Indiana is a construction worker in a shiny new Dodge pickup. A sling holds his right arm, so he steers and lights cigarettes with his left one. He's heading for a car wash in Terre Haute. He lives outside of town.

"There's my house, right up there," he says, pointing with his good arm to a cabin on a wooded hill. "Yeah, it's nice out here. No niggers out here. Them niggers ruin everything. Run the value of your house down, everything."

When he drops me at the car wash, I see an African-American pulling out in a Porsche. I take a few steps before realizing he's the first black person I've seen since leaving California.

I have a good friend who is black. He's often told me that there are entire regions of the country he'd rather see from an airplane. I always thought it was hyperbole. Until now. How sad it is that you can travel through ten states and encounter only white Americans along the way.

Three-quarters of the people who give me rides say they never pick up hitchhikers. An equal number tell me I'm "clean-cut." I knew appearances would count for a lot on this trip. But every time I shave and shower and put on a fresh shirt, I never think about the one aspect of my appearance I can't change: the color of my skin.

If a clean-cut black man set out from San Francisco on a penniless journey and followed my exact route, how far would he get? I'd like to think he'd be standing here with me, in Terre Haute, Indiana, but I fear that may not be the right answer.

I walk south out of town, past another Kmart and Wal-Mart, and set my pack down near a stoplight. Traffic is bumper to bumper, so I know I'll be standing here a while. For some reason, the time it takes to get a ride is inversely proportional to the number of passing cars.

A van pulling an aluminum fishing boat drives by. I don't bother making eye contact with the driver. Tourists never stop. When the van pulls to the shoulder, I figure it's for a reason other than to invite a stranger on board. But a man steps out of the passenger door and waves me down.

He makes room for my pack behind the front seats.

"Don't squash my tortilla chips," the driver says as I load my pack into the van.

The driver's name is Frank. He's a large man with a jowly face and a stomach like a medicine ball. He is semiretired from his hose and brass fittings business. The passenger, Phil, is a retired farmer. He's short and trim and wears a Purdue Boilermakers baseball hat. Both men live in Kokomo, north of Indianapolis. Phil has fourteen years on Frank, but it looks the other way around.

"You go to school here?" Frank says.

"No, I'm from California."

"Shoot, I saw your sign say 'Sullivan.' I thought you might be able to tell us something about the fishing down there."

Frank and Phil chuckle about how the one hitchhiker they decide to pick up turns out to be a know-nothing out-of-towner.

Frank says he needs a smoke. He asks Phil to find a coffee and cigarette stop on the map. It is Phil's van and he doesn't allow smoking.

Frank pulls into a Hardee's on the outskirts of Sullivan.

"Come on, we'll buy you a cup of coffee," Phil says.

"Yeah, come on in with us," Frank says.

Coffee with cream and sugar sounds good, even though I have an empty stomach and I know I'll get the shakes.

It's noon, and every line inside the Hardee's is a dozen people long. My eyes lock in on a copy of the *Indianapolis Star* newspaper on an empty table. I snatch it up quickly. Every section is here, even the sports page. It's the find of the trip.

Frank buys three large coffees and we take a table by the window.

"I once hitchhiked to Newark, New Jersey," Phil says. He pronounces it *"New Work."* "That was in 'forty-two, way before you were born."

"It was so long ago, Phil had to stop along the way and make peace with the Indians," Frank says, his belly jiggling at the joke.

Frank snuffs the butt of his cigarette in the ashtray. Phil stands up to leave.

"One more cigarette," Frank says.

"Frank is trying to quit smoking," Phil tells me, rolling his eyes.

Phil quit cold turkey ages ago.

"I had a nightmare. A good buddy of mine was laying on a slab of cement in the morgue. He had a cigarette in his mouth and the smoke was drifting up over his head. He was dead as that tobacco. He died a few months later of a heart attack."

"I used to smoke two packs a day of Camel unfiltereds," Frank says. "Now I'm down to six a day of these filtereds. I have two in the morning, two around now, and two before I go to bed."

"He quit for three weeks," Phil says. "I told him there's no need to start up again."

"I had a heart attack September eleventh," Frank says. "That one scared me. I'm trying to take better care of myself."

He takes a long drag on the cigarette. The heart attack three weeks ago was his fourth.

"Have you had surgery?" I say.

"Yeah, I've had 'bout everything done to me."

He smokes the cigarette until there's nothing left, then he sucks on the filter like it's a marijuana roach.

"Frank, good thing them cigarettes have filters, or you'd be burning your fingers right now," Phil says.

Frank smiles with embarrassment. He knows he's hooked. He changes the subject.

"What do you do?"

"Before this trip, I was working as a journalist," I say.

"You gonna write a book about this trip?"

"I hope to."

"Well, write your name down and the name of the book so I can get it when it comes out."

I write "The Kindness of Strangers" on the back of the Hardee's receipt, but I don't put down the penniless part.

I ride with Frank and Phil a few more miles until we come to the turnoff for Route 54.

"Good luck with the fishing."

"Have you got money for food?" Frank says.

"The point of my book is to go across the country with no money."

Frank reaches for his wallet and draws out a ten.

"No, thank you. I can't accept any money."

He holds the bill out to me. "Take it."

"I appreciate it, but I can't. I've got to get across America without a single penny."

"No wonder you're skinny," Frank says. "If I'da known that, I woulda bought you something to eat back there at Hardee's."

"I've got food in my pack. Thanks for the ride and the coffee, though."

After they drove off, I wonder if I should have taken the ten from Frank and given it away. It would have meant ten fewer dollars for cigarettes. It could have been my act of kindness to a stranger. Then again, I think Frank has enough money to smoke himself into an early grave. I doubt he'll even be around long enough to buy this book.

I have plenty of vices, but smoking has never been one of them. When I was seven, I asked my great-grandmother for a puff from her cigarette. I was fascinated by the way she held the burning stick. To my astonishment, she started a new one and handed it to me. I asked her how many puffs I could have. As many as I wanted, she said, it was my cigarette. I took one drag and just about coughed up a lung. It was by far the nicest thing my great-grandmother ever did for me.

I walk east along Indiana 54, a narrow two-laner that threads a thick forest of hickory, spruce, and oak. The air smells clean, and it feels good to be back in a part of America that has yet to be malled.

My foot almost comes down on a package of cigarettes lying on the side of the road. It's a full pack, newly opened. A driver must have gone to light up then decided, *That's it, no more,* and tossed the bad habit out the window. I pause in the woods and wish the brave soul good luck.

I stop at a jog in the road guarded by a gas station. Before I've finished writing down the name of the next town, a man pumping gas offers me a ride. A woman sits in the front seat. I climb in back. The door is smashed in and I must slam it several times to get it to close.

"My husband used to hitchhike," the woman says. "He was a professional hitchhiker. We both worked for carnivals. He's been all over the world. Well, he's been to the Virgin Islands."

The man stops the pump at three dollars and slides behind the wheel. He has a pocked, unshaven face framed by a greasy shag hairdo. His scary looks are tempered by his friendly manner.

"I told him you were a professional hitchhiker," the woman says.

"Well, I guess I was," he says, turning back to me as he drives. "I had this army ammo box, see? And I put a motorcycle battery in it. Then I connected a CB radio to it. I'd talk to truckers and get rides. I'd make money at it, too—polishing the tanks, unloading the trucks. I'd do that four months a year and work for the carnival eight months.''

We drive thirty miles to Bloomfield. The man drops his wife at a nursing home, where she works as a nurse's assistant. They met four years ago at a carnival in the South.

The man ran away from home at fourteen to join the circus.

"I worked with elephants for a year," he says. "Well, I shoveled elephant shit.''

He switched to carnivals—where he operated rides and ran games—because they paid better. When he tired of the road, he and his wife returned to her hometown, Sullivan.

"I figure after sixteen years, it's time to settle down," he says.

Settling down at the moment means unemployment. Jobs in this part of Indiana are as scarce as bearded ladies.

The man drives me to a private campground outside of Bloomfield.

"If this don't look good, you can ride back with me to the house. We don't got much there, but you can have a ham sandwich.''

I thank the man for the offer but tell him I'll be fine. Once again I'm amazed at how often it's the ones with little to eat who are quick to share their food.

THIRTY

H oosier Park hugs the shore of a clear lake formed from an abandoned coal pit. The campground is empty but for a couple of RVs, their owners nowhere in sight. A giant maple tree creeks in the wind like an old man's bones. Leaves fall from the sky like brown snowflakes.

I knock on the door of a simple cabin. The fellow who answers is a bowling ball of a man, round and heavy. A pair of glasses rests on his pug nose. A strand of hair sweeps across an otherwise bald head covered by a baseball hat that bears an Indiana road map. A fat cigar pokes out from his mouth over a double chin.

"All right if I camp here?"

"Yeah, but it'll cost you."

"How much?"

"Two dollars for campers is all."

"How about I do some clean-up work for you?"

"That low, huh?"

"Yeah, I'm traveling across the country without a penny."

"How you do that?"

"Pretty well, actually."

"Yeah, why not? We don't have any campers now anyway."

The campground lacks a shower and a sink. I ask the man if he has a container I can use to shave. He comes out a few minutes later with a pan.

Arnie, who is sixty-five, is a retired basketball coach. It is fitting that my host has a basketball connection, as the sport is the leading religion of Indiana. Arnie has two passions in life—his son Todd, and basketball—which converged into one obsession when Todd led the high school basketball team Arnie coached to a state championship. But Todd is grown and off on his own now, and this is Arnie's first year away from the game. He bought the campground to see him through his twilight years, but it's killing him. When the school buses started up this fall, he nearly cried.

He grew up poor in southern Indiana, the son of a man who died in a coal mining accident. Arnie ran off and joined the Marines when he was sixteen. He was sent to mainland China after World War II to help train Chiang Kai-shek's troops, who were fighting Mao's communists forces. Mao's army was assisted by the Soviet Union, and Arnie says he fought against Russians—a claim not yet acknowledged by history books. One night when the trains he was guarding came under communist attack, Arnie was separated from his company. He roamed through China with the nationalists for eight months, engaging the enemy numerous times. He was captured when he wandered into a communist-held village, later liberated by U.S. artillery. He then walked for several weeks around the Great Wall to evade the communists.

"They talk of Mao's great thousand-mile march," Arnie scoffs. "Hell, I walked eleven hundred miles."

When the communists finally closed in, Arnie had only four hours to reach the sea. He jumped in a Jeep and maneuvered his way through the hordes of fleeing nationalists. He reached the docks just in time to board the last U.S. ship to pull out.

"You say you're out looking for interesting people," he says to me. "Well, you came to the right place. There ain't a hundred people in the world been through what I have."

He chomps down on his cigar.

"Hell, it's storybook," he says.

I pitch my tent and sit at a picnic table. An hour later, Arnie walks out the door toward his Jeep pickup.

"I'm going into town for a sandwich," he calls over. "I know I'll have to buy, but you're welcome to come along."

We drive into Bloomfield to a diner called the Huddle. Arnie heads straight for an eight-seat table in the middle of the restaurant and plops down.

"Might as well have room," he says.

He orders chopped steak, string beans and the salad bar. He swears he's got to lose the forty pounds he's put on since he quit coaching. I order the all-you-can-eat buffet.

After China, Arnie returned to Indiana and went to college. He got his teaching credential. He later served with the Marines in Korea and Vietnam, where he was an underwater demolition specialist. He instilled in his son a love for scuba diving, and last summer the two of them ran a diving school at the campground's lake.

When Arnie graduated college, he became an industrial arts teacher and the basketball coach for an Indianapolis high school.

His teams were consistent winners, always ranked near the top in the basketball-crazy state.

It was at his first job that he met his wife, a teacher named Katherine. She was a stunning woman, bright and beautiful. It was forever a mystery to those who knew them how the homely jarhead managed to snare the most fetching female from Greene County, Indiana.

Arnie got malaria during the war and suffered from a low sperm count. It took Katherine ten years to get pregnant. When Todd finally did come along, Arnie set a basketball on the baby's chest the day he was born. His future was never in doubt. He became the coach's lifelong student.

"I worried that Todd was an unpopular kid," Arnie says. "What I found out was, none of his friends wanted to come over to the house 'cause I was always drilling him."

As Arnie pursued his single-minded goal of a state championship, Katherine got behind several liberal causes. She worked for Indians, blacks, Latinos, and any other groups she saw as disenfranchised.

"She wanted to turn our house into an international village," Arnie says. "She never had anything bad to say about anyone. She was caring. She cared so much about everyone else, she left her own family."

The night Katherine told Arnie she wanted a divorce, he demanded custody of Todd. He'd do anything to keep him. "I won't lose you both," he said. Katherine resisted. Arnie didn't wait for a court to decide. He skipped Indiana with an Oldsmobile, $120 and Todd. He left the house and everything else to Katherine.

He wouldn't tell her where he was taking their son. He said relatives in Indiana would alert him if she made a move against him. If she did, she'd never see Todd again. At one point, Arnie pulled off the freeway and called about teaching jobs in Australia. Months later, when he heard that Katherine had agreed in court to let him have custody, he called to tell her that he and Todd were living in Kansas.

Arnie never remarried, raising Todd on his own.

"Just me, him, and the world," he says.

He got a high school coaching job in Kansas. He did nothing but win. He moved up to bigger schools and always had his teams in the top ten. When Todd entered high school, Arnie was at last his son's official coach. And in Todd's senior year, father and son combined to win it all. In the state final, Todd scored thirty-four points, grabbed twelve rebounds, had five assists and four steals.

"We were up by one with about a minute and a half to play," Arnie says, recalling the game as if it were last night. "That's a long time to hold the ball. Todd came over to me on the sideline and shook my shoulders and said, 'It's over!' And he went out and scored the last four points of the game. He could never dunk a ball. But in the last seconds of that championship game, he went baseline and just jammed that sucker through."

Arnie pauses.

"Hell, it's storybook," he says.

Father and son weren't finished. They went to Southeast Kansas State University in a package deal. Todd was the rookie sensation and Arnie was the new coach. They had four good years. Todd set a national free throw record for small college players and was named an All-American. Arnie left his own mark. In a game against a Canadian college, he pulled his team off the court when the hosts refused to play the American national anthem. The controversy caught the attention of Bob Knight, Indiana University's legendary, chair-throwing basketball coach. "That guy's crazier than I am," Knight reportedly said. From then on, Arnie's team had a standing invitation to scrimmage with Knight's squad whenever they were in Indiana. And Arnie could often be seen sitting behind Knight in the best comp seats at IU games.

When Todd graduated, he moved to Indiana to start his career as a high school basketball coach. Arnie stayed with the college in Kansas a few more seasons, then lost heart. His number-one recruit was gone, his favorite team had disbanded.

Arnie needed three more years in the Indiana school system to qualify for a pension, so he returned to his Hoosier home and signed a contract with a high school in South Bend. He did the best with what he had, taking a team ranked 428th to the top fifty. But high school had changed in the years he was away. Arnie was now a dinosaur. His disciplinarian methods didn't fly with the young, liberal principal, and he was reprimanded more than once.

Kids had no respect for Arnie. They called him "Crip" because his arthritic knee caused him to limp. The proud Marine had to take their abuse. His retirement was bittersweet.

It's dark when we get back to the campground. Arnie builds a fire in a ring next to his cabin and we pull up a couple of chairs. A hoot owl joins the conversation from a nearby tree.

After he quit coaching, Arnie moved to Bloomfield, where he knew the mayor. The land near the lake was owned by the city. Arnie figured it would make a good campground and he struck a deal.

The only problem was that the wooded area had been the hang-out for a gang of drug dealers. When Arnie cleared the ground for campsites, he found fifty syringes in the grass. Gang members tore through the park at night in pickups to try to scare Arnie off. When he built a gate at the entrance, they drove around from the other side of the lake. Arnie felled a tree across the dirt road, but they took a chain saw to it and came marauding through. The next night, Arnie was ready for them.

He blocked the road with another tree. The gang again sawed through it and drove in. But this time, Arnie had dug a pit on his side of the tree with a backhoe and covered the hole with branches. It later would take three tow trucks to pull the pickup out. As the gang members stomped around the lip of the pit cursing Arnie, he watched from the woods. He then lit up the night with a floodlight aimed on himself. What the hooligans saw was one frightening Marine. He wore a helmet and camouflage face paint, and stood at attention with a smuggled AK-47 on his shoulder. Arnie clicked off the light and eerily faded into the black night. The gang never came back.

"Hell, it's storybook," Arnie says.

When Arnie moved to Bloomfield, he befriended a fifteen-year-old girl, the daughter of a welfare mother who kept company with various unsavory men. Arnie thought he could save the girl, Keri, from a life like her mother's. He told her that if she avoided the wrong crowd at school, he'd provide for her. He bought her clothes and shoes and other gifts. Then one day he saw her standing on a corner snuggling up with a boy Arnie knew to be a drug dealer. Arnie cut Keri off. His last advice to her was to get on the Pill. Keri went to Arnie for help a few months later. She was pregnant. Arnie now gives her money for diapers and baby formula. He always demands a receipt. Tomorrow he's taking her shopping in Indianapolis.

Arnie gets up and throws another log on the fire.

I ask him why he never remarried.

"I know the girl I shoulda married. She was from Hollywood." Arnie met her on a weekend pass when he was in boot camp on the West Coast. "I took her to the prom. We stayed in touch when I was in the Marines and after I got back from China. She wanted to get married, but I wasn't ready. She wrote to my mom for years." Four decades later, Arnie decided he had to find her. "She once told me she had an uncle who worked at Soldier Field. I wrote the Chicago Parks Department twice. They wrote back and said they had no such name on their retirement roles. I placed ads in the *Los Angeles Times*. When my mom died, I searched for the letters, but she had thrown them out. I've been looking for her for the last ten years."

Like his father, Todd is a bachelor. He had the same girlfriend for eight years, all through high school and college.

"Then she broke it off a month before the wedding," Arnie

says, shaking his head. "She was a cousin of that mystery writer up there in Maine . . . Stephen . . ."

"King?" I say.

"Yeah. It was gonna be the biggest wedding ever."

The fire rages. All this talk of lost loves gets Arnie started again on Katherine.

"People always told me I didn't deserve her. Well, they were probably right. But no one did." Arnie stares into the flame. "I've never gotten over it, not really. I don't sit around and mope. But when I'm feeling ill, or I go to bed with a pain in my side, I get this nightmare. . . . I'm young again, and everything's good. Then it turns bad. I relive that awful feeling. And I wake up, usually at two or three in the morning. And, boy, when that happens, that's all the sleep for that night."

In the end, Katherine was the coach's greatest trophy. But it was a trophy he never really won. He only got to hold it for a while.

Arnie rubs his eyes, and the tears on his cheeks glisten in the glow of the flame.

As frustrating as his final years of coaching were, he's got to get back in the game. "I can't let go," he says. He plans to send resumes to five hundred high schools. He knows most of them will reject him on age alone. Maybe he'll change his birthdate from 1929 to 1939, he says. Anybody can get one digit wrong, right? He wants a school near the ocean. Maybe that would entice Todd, a scuba diving fanatic. The team would be reunited.

"I'm gonna take a class in political correctness and learn sensitivity," Arnie says. "I think I can update myself, be able to take the kids' shit. Maybe I'll even see a psychiatrist. Maybe he can tell me some shit. I'm gonna lose forty pounds. Hell, it'll work. Someone wants a winner."

The flames die out. Arnie struggles to his feet. He invites me inside.

When I step through the cabin door, my eyes go wide. The room is furnished almost entirely with memories.

"This is the sanctuary," Arnie says.

It is a shrine to Todd and glory past. The walls are laden with basketball memorabilia—plaques and photos and framed newspaper clippings. Shelves are lined with trophies, draped with nets cut down from rims in victory. The basketball Todd scored his one thousandth point with sits on the television, next to the one he used to sink his fifty-fifth consecutive free throw. The VCR is loaded with a tape of the Kansas state high school basketball championship.

My gaze falls to a framed black-and-white photo on the end table. In it, Todd is surrounded by college teammates accepting a trophy. A pretty cheerleader kneeling at his feet looks up at him adoringly.

Arnie sees me staring at the picture. He picks it up.

"That's the gal Todd went with for eight years. She's the one who broke his heart, and mine. Tore the shit out of me. The only reason I keep it is Todd's in it."

He returns the frame to the table.

"Yep, he made all his daddy's dreams come true. I always wanted to be a Marine, and I wanted to have my son win me a state championship. Thirty-four points, twelve rebounds, five assists, and four steals. Mr. Basketball.

"Hell, it's storybook."

THIRTY-ONE

Many folks I meet in Indiana have no concept of distance. When I tell them I'm crossing America, they often say, "You're gonna see a lot of country." Or, "You've got an awful long way to go." It's as if they believe Indiana still sits on the western edge of the United States. I guess they haven't heard of the Louisiana Purchase.

The preacher and his wife stop for me in Stanford, Indiana. I know he's a preacher before I meet him because the tailgate of his truck is branded with pinstripe that reads, "The Preacher."

"What kind of preacher are you?" I say.

"Nondenominational."

"By the Book?"

"It's the only way."

The preacher wears a black cowboy hat and a string tie. He's got a voice made for radio. Before he became a preacher, he was a used car salesman. When I think about it, it's not that huge a career change.

He and his wife have moved back to Indiana after twenty years in California. They hated living in Fresno.

"Only twenty-eight percent of Fresno is white now," the preacher's wife says.

Tens of thousands of Southeast Asian refugees have immigrated to Fresno since the end of the Vietnam War. The preacher's wife has a friend who works in Fresno's subsidized housing office.

"She told me they don't even know how to use the refrigerator," she says. "They put boxes of dirt in them. It's terrible how they treat those apartments."

I tell her that refugees are among the most hard-working, productive citizens of our society. As for their confusion over the use of Western appliances, I point out to her that the world is full of cultures whose home furnishings she would find equally baffling. I smile to myself when I imagine the preacher's wife encountering a *hammam,* the seatless, bowl-less, and tissueless Arab toilet.

The preacher loves his new church. There isn't a single black among the congregation. Next week he will share his vision of God with third-graders at the local public school—something he admits he could never do in California. He's excited that the separation between church and state is a concept foreign to his part of the country.

I ask the preacher why he picked me up.

"Based on your appearance," he says. "You hate to say that, but that's the way it is. I'll tell you the truth, now, if you had long hair and a beard, no way I would have stopped for you."

"You mean long hair and a beard like Jesus?" I say.

The preacher can only smile.

We reach Nashville, Indiana, a country-western tourist trap patterned after the real Nashville in Tennessee. The preacher pulls into a Hardee's and says come on in.

"I don't want you to put in your book that the preacher wouldn't buy you lunch."

I can't get away from the antiques shops of Nashville fast enough. An angelic young man with long blond hair stops for me. His mountain bike rides in the back of a Jeep Wrangler decorated with a Grateful Dead bumper sticker. I feel like I've been transported back to California.

Darryl is taking a semester off from college to work construction and save some money. He lives in a cabin without running water. He's driving only a couple of miles, to a state park. I think it must be a good spot to ride his bike, but he says he going to the campground to take a shower.

The mention of hot running water pricks up my ears. I haven't had a shower in three days—the longest stretch of the trip.

"Do the showers cost anything?" I ask.

"They're supposed to," Darryl says, "but I never have to pay."

He agrees to let me come along. We stop at the entrance to the Brown County State Park. The ranger in the booth recognizes Darryl and waves us through. The forest is a sunburst of reds, oranges, yellows, and purples. It looks like a rainbow exploded and dripped on the trees.

The shower is piping hot, and I linger under it long after the dirt has melted away. After I change into clean clothes, Darryl drives five miles out of his way to drop me at a market in Gnaw Bone.

Columbus is the next town east, and that's how I feel. Like Columbus, out discovering a new world—a world without money.

A rusted beater pulls up in front of the store and a young man with shaggy hair and a greasy tank top steps out of the passenger side. His buddy remains in the car. When the fellow comes out of the store, he gives me a long look. I watch out of the corner of my eye as the men talk. They drive away, only to stop fifty feet later behind an ice locker. I can't see what they're doing. A couple minutes later, they turn around and stop alongside me.

"You goin' to Columbus?" the driver says.

"What?" I say, stalling for time to think of an excuse.

"You goin' to Columbus?"

"Yeah," I say. "Hey, no offense, but I only ride with single drivers. I appreciate it though." I give his door a friendly rap.

"Oh, 'cause we're goin' to Columbus. I was just gonna give you a ride, is all." He shoots me a smile absent of sincerity.

"Thanks anyway."

"Well, I hope you get a ride."

It's the first ride of the trip I've refused. When the men drive off, I congratulate myself for saving my life.

By late afternoon I'm in Vernon, in the southeast corner of Indiana. The sign on Route 7 for the Muskatatuck State Park bears a symbol for a campground; it says nothing about a fee. I walk down a road covered by a canopy of branches. It climbs the other side of a ravine and skirts an open grassy plateau the size of a polo field. From the look of the facilities, I know it's too nice to be free. A worker with a rake in his hand confirms this. I tell him I don't have any money and ask about other campgrounds in my budget.

"Oh, you can stay here free," he says, "only because you're a backpacker."

I sleep great. When I poke my head out of the tent in the morning and look at my neighbor's campsite, I see a deer hanging from its neck by a rope. The rope is thrown over a tree limb and secured to the ball hitch of an old blue Chevy pickup. A man about my age is skinning the deer with a knife. Blood covers his hands and forearms. He puffs on a cigar as he cuts.

"You get that this morning already?" I say on my way over.

"No, last night. But it's gonna be warm today. I gotta get her in ice."

Tom is married and the father of three. He's a foreman at a steel fabrication plant up in Gary. I ask him if he's originally from Indiana.

"Yep. If you ain't a Hoosier, you're a loosier." He smiles wide around his cigar.

Tom shot the deer with a bow and arrow. He works quickly, slicing long strips off the animal's back and storing the meat in a plastic garbage bag.

"It's wanting to stick to the bone, but it's still cool," he says. "Here, touch."

I put a tip of my finger to the purple meat. It's cool and grippy.

"How far away were you when you let the arrow fly?" I say.

"About fifteen yards. It went through both lungs and the heart. She didn't suffer a bit. This is one of Jesus' prettiest creatures, and I'm just glad He allowed me to have one."

The deer has all the dignity of a captured cattle rustler in the Wild West. Its brown eyes are now cloudy, its tongue stiff and jutting to the side. Tom reaches up into the cavity and cuts out the tenderloin.

"Yeah, people spend lots of money for drugs to get the same feeling I get from bow hunting," he says. "It's exhilarating."

Tom carefully packs the animal's hide. He saws off the hooves and wraps them in newspaper; a Mexican man he knows will use them for bullwhip handles. He slices out the windpipe, which he'll later turn into a deer caller. Not much will go to waste.

I've never hunted, let alone fired a gun or shot an arrow, but

I admire Tom's sense of conservation. He's a breed apart from the hunters I once interviewed for a story on the notorious exotic game ranches in Texas. Down there, people shot tame animals from the back of a pickup hauling a trailer that dribbled corn feed. When one hunter missed badly and only blew a hole in a Sika deer's belly, he didn't bother tracking the wounded animal and putting it out of its misery. It was getting dark and he had paid to kill two more.

When Tom learns I'm penniless, he offers me some deer meat.

"You might get hungry," he says.

I politely decline. There's no room in my pack, I say.

He stubs the dead ash of his cigar on the picnic table and relights it.

"What do you miss most?" he says. "Besides your girlfriend, I mean."

I don't answer.

"Cable TV?" Tom says.

Still nothing comes to mind. "You know, I'm so busy meeting people and trying to get down the road without money that I haven't had time to miss anything," I say.

I don't miss TV. I don't miss movies. I don't miss beer. I don't miss any of the things I usually use to numb my mind and pass the time. This has been the only extended period of my adult life that I have not been bored. If I could only make it last.

I shake Tom's blood-stained hand. He makes a final offer to share his deer meat. I thank him and return to my campsite to break down my tent.

"Hey, what's the name of your book?" Tom yells over.

I tell him.

"It's hard to believe we're all strangers," he says, "when we're really all brothers."

THIRTY-TWO

The citizens of Vernon, Indiana, are making ready for their annual festival when I walk through town. Vendors erect booths along the street for an arts and crafts show. Boys rake leaves on the courthouse lawn under a gray sky. One kid reclines on a park bench, his rake idle in his hands. The supervisor tells him to hop to.

"You see, I told you, boy!" a lecherous voice cackles from a cell window in the nearby jail. "Git back to work! Hah!"

At the edge of town, a Toyota brakes to stop for me. I grab my pack and start to run, but the car speeds on.

A few minutes later it returns. A young, chubby couple sits in front; a boy rides in back. There's also a dog, a caged parakeet, and a pile of blankets and clothes. I don't know where I'll fit myself or my pack. The man apologizes for passing me; there was no room to pull over. He rearranges his cargo. The boy, Kyle, aged six, sits on his mother's lap.

The man served five years in the Navy before he was kicked out for a bad back. He now attends pharmacy school up in Indianapolis. He and his wife are originally from Madison, Indiana, on the Ohio River. They are going there now to visit their parents.

"I've got a big brother," the boy says.

"Kyle, you big fibber," his mom says.

"Do you have a kid?" Kyle asks me.

"No, not yet. Someday."

"In two weeks?"

"No, I don't think that soon."

"In about four weeks?"

"No, a little longer than that."

"Five weeks?"

The mom rescues me.

"*Maybe,* Kyle," she says.

The dad turns down a country road outside Madison. They need to drop the dog and bird at his mother-in-law's before continuing on to his parents' house in town.

As soon as we're out of the car, Kyle grabs my arm.

"I show you gwama's garden," he says. "We gotta go akwahs da bwidge."

He clutches a stuffed bear in one hand and my hand in the other as he leads me over a footbridge. We wade through a bank of tall grass that opens onto a gourd garden. The gourds are immense, some the size of laundry baskets. Kyle tramples through the garden, kicking up vines. The patch is out of sight of the house. I tell Kyle maybe he ought to leave his grandma's gourds alone. It's a timid request, as I don't want to make their boy cry. At the same time, I don't want to get blamed for killing a blue-ribbon gourd.

Kyle's dad calls us. It's time to go to town. I only hope we get away before the damage is discovered.

"So, you're going to see your folks for the weekend?" I say to the man as his wife says good-bye to her mother.

"Yeah, well, I got word my grandmother died at six this morning."

"Oh, I'm so sorry."

"That's okay. You had no way of knowing."

When I think of all the woes on this man's mind, I'm surprised he made the time to take on one more problem. Not to mention, he had to turn back and pick it up.

"Was it unexpected?" I say.

"She had lung cancer, but she went fast. I saw her two weeks ago, and she was good old Grandma. My dad called me this week and said she wasn't feeling well. We were gonna drive down last night, but classes ran late. I figured I'd see her this morning, but I didn't make it."

He raises his eyes heavenward.

I'm lucky. Both my grandmothers are still alive. They're in their eighties, but remain sharp. Even so, you never know. I decide I'd better write them both from the next post office I see.

The family drops me in the new part of Madison, on a busy boulevard up the hill from the historic center of town. The road is without a shoulder. What's worse, they're repaving, so there's even less room to walk. I pass a golf course and fondly remember my round in Liberty with Jim. Three men stand on the tee, taking practice swings. I lapse into a daydream: The golfers call to me. They need a fourth. I climb the fence, drop my pack, and pick up a one-wood. There's a big bet. My partner says don't worry, he'll cover me. I play magnificently. We win, and the losers buy me a hotel room and dinner.

I'm knocked from my fantasy by a rock that hits me in the face. It must have shot up from under the tire of a passing car. It hits me above my right eye. A half inch lower, I would have stumbled into Cape Fear a cyclops. I touch my forehead. No blood, but there's a knot the size of a golf ball.

Madison's Main Street is one of only three Main Streets in the United States on the National Preservation Registry. The wide avenue is lined with Greek Revival, Italianate, and Federal-style buildings. The red brick and clean sidewalks gleam in the sun.

The bridge across the Ohio River ends at the base of a wooded bluff. There is no sign of life on the other side. Kentucky looks foreboding—the edge of the mysterious South. Stereotypes race through my head. I have visions of hillbillies chasing me through the forest. I recall a disturbing scene from the movie *Deliverance*. I think of backtracking and detouring through Ohio.

I scold myself for being so ignorant. I know better. I've traveled all over the world and have found good people wherever I've been. On this trip, I've been treated with kindness in every state for the last thirty-five hundred miles. I'm ashamed that even for an instant I believe Kentucky will offer up anything less.

A "Pedestrians Prohibited" sign guards the north side of the bridge. I write "KY" on a sheet of paper. I don't bother affixing it to my cardboard because my roll of tape is running thin.

"We'll take you to Kentucky," a smiling woman says through a car window.

She's driving and her daughter rides in the front seat. I sit in back. The daughter is twenty-one. Her mother is three months pregnant.

"I can size someone up pretty quick," the mother says.

"All her boyfriends are in prison," the daughter hoots.

"Melissa!"

The daughter watches me through the vanity mirror in the visor. "Yew hitchhiking all the way across the country?"

"Yep."

"Yew got balls." She snickers.

"Melissa, watch your mouth!"

The bridge arches over the wide green river, and my head spins from the height. When we reach the other side, Melissa asks her mother to stop at a gas station.

"Yew like Coke?" Melissa says.

"Sure."

While Melissa drops coins in the soda machine, her mother leans over the seat.

"My daughter's got a mouth on her, but she's kind."

Melissa hands me a twenty-ounce bottle of Coke; the soda machine charges thirty-five cents. I've either traveled back in time or Kentucky is the state inflation forgot.

Mother and daughter have no plans; they're just out driving. They drop me at a gas station in Bedford, thirteen miles south of the river on Route 421.

"There's some real good people here," the mother says. "They'll give you a ride."

There is a new feel to the land. I'm still in the United States, but it's a different country. The abrupt change reminds me of crossing from California into Mexico. The blacktop is potholed. There isn't a new car on the road. People wear tired looks and tired clothes. What little they have is paid for with sweat, and it's obvious there aren't enough jobs to sweat over. Northern Kentucky is as depressed as a recent widow.

I sit on the tall curb of the Country Store Super Market—an oxymoron if I ever heard one. An old, stooped man shuffles out the door to his pickup. He casts a cloudy eye in my direction.

"You want me to take you down the road a couple miles?" he hollers.

I stand and meet him at his truck. John is frail, with a cough like a baby rattle. He holds himself up against his truck with a bony hand. In his other hand, he pinches a burning cigarette. His fingernails are stained orange from nicotine.

"You a tobacco farmer?" I guess.

"Three hundred years my family's been doin' it." He gasps for air. "You cain't lose money if you do it right."

I ask John if there's a spot in Bedford a traveler can pitch a tent. He rubs his whiskered chin and comes up with a park on the other side of the gas station.

"They may investigate, but no one'll bother you."

He gives the pack on my back a sideways glance.

"There aren't many *real* hobos left," he says. He recalls a man who passed through here in the seventies. "I called him the plastic hobo. He carried everything in a plastic bag, and he used the bag for a shelter."

After John leaves, I cross the road to look for the park behind the gas station. There may have once been a park there, but not in my lifetime. I'm sure that to a man of John's years, it was here only yesterday.

I walk back across the road to reclaim my seat at the Country Store Super Market.

John returns in his pickup. He flicks an ash from his cigarette out the window.

"I thought of a place where you can camp. The back side of

my farm is on 421. There's a wooded area there with a creek. Put your pack in back and I'll show you.''

He drives down the road at a comfortable fifteen miles an hour. We pass a string of places I'm hard put to call homes. They are twisted trailers and sagging shacks. Laundry waves in the breeze like flags of surrender. The shabby yards are littered with pieces of dead automobiles and machinery. A giant old-fashioned cash register sits in a rutted dirt driveway, its drawer open and empty.

We clear the squalor and drive several more miles.

"Is there a creek there?" John asks, squinting into the woods. "My eyes aren't too good anymore."

"Yeah, I think so."

He parks and tells me to check it out. I slide down a ravine to a stream that trickles over slabs of shale. There isn't a flat spot in sight. I climb back out. I'll ride back to Bedford with John.

"How's it look?" he says.

"Well, it's pretty, but it's all rocky."

He says the ground is flatter across the creek. It's his neighbor's land, but he won't mind, John assures me.

Storm clouds are gathering. I've already conquered my fear of sleeping in the forest in the rain. There's nothing new to prove here. Besides, this is my first time in Kentucky; I don't want to hide like a hermit. But John is so eager to accommodate me, I worry I will appear ungrateful, maybe hurt his feelings. So I tell him I'll be fine here and thank him for the ride.

He reaches into a paper bag on the truck seat and hands me four tomatoes from his farm. After he disappears around the bend, I start the long walk back into town.

THIRTY-THREE

I return to the curb at the Country Store Super Market and eat one of the tomatoes. It's vine-scarred, but juicy and sweet. Rusted clunkers roll by, knocking and belching. It sounds like all of Trimble County needs a tune-up.

A barrel-chested man with a salt-and-pepper beard sits down beside me.

"Lemme show you somethin'."

He pulls a knife from a leather sheath, but it doesn't look like any knife I've ever seen.

"I carved that out of black granite," he says.

I run my fingers along the cold smooth blade and whistle in admiration.

"How long did it take you to make it?"

"Aw, I worked on it an hour or two a night for a couple months."

Rex was born and raised in Bedford. He is a welder. He's divorced, the father of eight grown kids. He lives above the store. The sidewalk is his front porch, and he gives a friendly wave to all who pass.

A black Trans Am pulls up and the driver leans across his girlfriend to talk to Rex. I can't hear what they say over the roar of the engine.

"Be good!" Rex shouts at the end of the conversation.

"I work for his dad," he tells me. "He's crazy."

"The dad or the boy?"

"The boy. He's had three totals already and he's not yet eighteen."

Rex nods at an orange 1965 Ford pickup parked at the curb. With its makeshift top, the truck looks more like a van.

"There's my vehicle down there," he says. "A friend of mine used to own that. He died ice skating on a pond. They never found him."

At the funeral, the man's wife recalled that Rex was fond of the truck. She asked him if he wanted to buy it. He did. She asked for $3,500, a price too steep for Rex. She let the truck sit in the barn. A year after her husband's accident, the woman died of a brain aneurysm. At her funeral, the woman's mother asked Rex if he was still interested in the truck. He was. She let it go for $150. Rex dropped a new battery in it and it came back to life.

The firehouse siren pierces the air. The tanker truck screams past, red lights flashing. It's followed by a state trooper. "She gives tickets for even two miles over the speed limit," Rex says. The auxiliary fire truck and an ambulance bring up the rear. Rex can't tell if there's a fire or a wreck.

A man drives up from the direction of the cause of the commotion.

"There's a guy standing in his yard waving a gun," he says.

He notices a light on at the mortuary down the street. "Who's in the bone house?" he says.

Rex answers with a shrug.

A young man missing a front tooth walks up and sits down on the other side of Rex.

"I've learned the secret to meeting women," he says. "Elbow 'em in the jaw and take 'em home." He laughs. "It works. That's how I got laid last night." He was shooting pool at a bar. A waitress came by with a tray of drinks. When he moved out of her way, he swung around and caught another woman in the mouth. It was lust at first smack.

"Well, I gotta go," the man says, and he does.

Another man in a pickup pulls up. He says he's driving across the river into Madison and asks Rex if he wants to come. Rex climbs in and they leave me alone on the curb.

I write in my journal by the light from the store. I nod hello to everyone who comes and goes. A woman steps out from her car.

"Hey, mister, I saw you over in Madison," she says in mock accusation.

"Me?"

"Yeah. You came in and asked to use the bathroom at the gas station."

"Oh yeah. You told me there was a bathroom at the visitors' center. It was a real nice one."

For some reason, my scintillating conversation fails to engage the woman, and it looks like I'm destined for a night in the rain.

Rex's friend drops him off an hour later.

"Ya still holding that curb down?" Rex says.

He sits down next to me. Bedford is silent. There are no more cars, no more curbside gossip. Just two strangers sitting in the dark.

I glance at Rex's orange truck. That would sure keep me dry.

"So that's really a truck, huh?"

"Yeah, it's just got a top on it. It's got paneled walls, insulation, everything."

"Hey, you think I can sleep in your truck tonight?"

"If you can find some room. I got pretty much everything in there—boots, tools, fishing rods."

Neither of us speaks. Rex gets to his feet to use the pay phone outside the market. After he hangs up, he walks by me without a word and climbs the stairs to his apartment.

Rex's excuse about the clutter in his truck reminds me of Randy in Garberville, California. When I asked if I could crash in his greenhouse, he said it was way out in the woods. I guess people are loath to just come out and say no.

The night air is damp and chilly. My breath fogs in front of my face. I wish I hadn't forgotten my sweater in the back of J. D. and Kristin's pickup in Montana. I wonder how Kristin's abortion went. I wonder who's wearing my sweater.

When the first raindrops hit my head, I hoist my pack and hunt for shelter from the storm. I come to Bedford's community center—a corrugated metal warehouse. A white stretch limo is parked in front. I hear people inside shriek and holler. It can only mean one thing: A celebrity preacher has come to town to whip the faithful into a frenzy. But when I step inside, I find in progress a sham of another sort—a professional wrestling match. Two hulking men in tights bounce off the ropes, taking turns slamming each other into the canvas mat.

I ask the ticket seller if I can use the rest room and he says okay. When I come out, a pack of youths yells at me.

"Faggot!"

"Turd burglar!"

I have no idea what I've done to prompt their fury. But then I see that they are hurling the epithets at a target behind me. I've stepped in front of a wrestler retreating from the ring.

"Faggot!"

"Turd burglar!"

He wears a hooded black robe—the bad guy, I presume. He stalks me through the angry crowd like the Grim Reaper.

Outside I find a picnic table beneath a roof next to a church. At least I'll stay dry for the night.

I spot Rex walking down the street. My eyes follow him to the other end of town, where he goes into an all-night convenience store. He comes out and strides back through town. I'm pretty sure I'm hidden by the shadows. Just in case, I turn away to save us both the embarrassment of eye contact.

A moment later I hear footsteps. I look up.

"Hey," Rex says.

"Hey."

We make small talk in the dark. Neither of us says what's on our minds. There's an awkward silence.

Finally Rex says, "Where you sleepin' tonight?"

"I figured I might lie down right here," I say, patting the table.

"Well, you're welcome to come upstairs and sleep, if you don't mind sleepin' on the couch."

A man is talking on the pay phone when we reach the market. "Hey, Rex," he says.

It's got to be a tough situation for Rex. Plenty of folks saw us sitting together on the curb. It's a small town. There's bound to be talk. I admire Rex's kind gesture.

The front door of his apartment is without a knob. Rex fishes a key from his pocket and undoes a padlock. Inside he ties a string from the door handle to a nail on the jamb. A double-barreled shotgun rests against the wall.

"It ain't fancy," he says. Then: "Plop down where you like."

A threadbare rose-colored sofa and matching chair face each other in the cramped living room. I sink into the chair, which has popped a couple of buttons. Rex disappears behind a wall into the kitchen. I hear the microwave run. He walks back out and hands me a cup of tea. When I hear the microwave start up again, I figure it's for Rex's tea. But he returns and presents me with a mini sausage pizza. When he comes out of the kitchen for the last time, he carries tea and pizza for himself.

Rex flips on a portable TV sitting on a table in the corner of the room. A documentary on aviation plays on TNT. Neither of us pays any attention. We quietly munch on our pizzas, our feet nearly touching in the space between the furniture.

The walls are crowded with sketches and paintings of Native Americans. Among them hang framed collections of arrowheads. Rex's grandmother was a full-blooded Cherokee. Her hair grew to the floor, plus another two feet. She raised Rex from the age of three, when his mother passed away. Rex's father was always off chasing work. Rex's grandmother died when he was thirteen, and he was on his own.

"I notice you was writin' down there," he says.

"Yeah, I'm keeping track of where I've been."

"I had a heart attack here 'bout four years ago that set me down for a good while. I wrote a story then."

He rummages through a pile of papers on the floor beneath an end table.

"I ain't got a good education," he says, handing me the product of his search. "You probably can't even read it."

I unfold the two sheets of white ruled paper. "The Boy," as the story is titled, is written with smudged pencil in a child's scrawl. The grammar is awful and the spelling atrocious, yet it is a touching tale about a poor lad of ten in New York City. As snow falls on him, he stares enviously through a department store window at a display of shoes. A rich woman in a chauffeur-driven limousine pulls up to the curb and asks the boy what he is doing. He tells her he's asking God for a new pair of shoes. The woman takes the boy into the store and buys him a new pair of shoes. The story ends with the boy saying to the woman, "Are you God's wife?"

When Rex's grandmother died, he dropped out of the eighth grade to find work. "I know that's why I haven't been able to git better-payin' jobs." As a father, he made sure all eight of his kids graduated from high school.

Rex removes a gold chain from around his neck. A gold arrowhead dangles from the end. He twirls the necklace around his finger, then untwirls it back out—over and over. He says he has no regrets.

"If I die tonight, well, I've had a full life. I've had good things and I've had bad things."

"What bad things?" I say.

"Oh, just bad things."

Rex slumps on his side on the couch, as if it's uncomfortable for him to sit upright. He slips one of his rough hands under his suspenders and holds his belly.

"I lost a girl," he says. "She was fifteen months old. I git up one day to go to work. I picked her up from her crib to set her in bed with her mother like I always did. I noticed she wasn't crying like she usually was. It was four in the morning, dark still. I went out to the kitchen to make some coffee. Then I heard a sound like nuthin' I've heard in this life. Jo was screamin', 'Nancy's dead!' "

Rex pauses. "She had an enlarged heart. We never knew. It just burst in her sleep. Jo clutched that girl for four hours. Sat in a rocking chair, wouldn't let no one near her. Finally, the doctor came over. He talked to her 'til he was able to git up close to her. Then he give her an injection in the arm and she went to sleep. Then we took the baby over to the coroner's office. Jo never did git over that. I kinda think she blamed me for it."

Rex shifts his weight on the couch. He stares at the far wall, but I don't think he's looking at arrowheads.

I'm lost for words. Before I say anything, he starts in again.

"The worst thing that ever happened to me, I was over in Milton. I was in the coffee shop, drinking coffee. A man come in from up near Indianapolis. He had a little girl 'bout three. Cute thing with brown hair. She was bouncing around the restaurant like a rubber ball. He come over to talk to me. Says his wife is divorcing him. Says he won't ever git to see his little girl again. 'No, they can't do that,' I tell him. 'Yes they can,' he says. He says, 'Will you do me a favor?' I tell him, 'Well, if I can.' He says, 'Follow me 'cross the bridge into Indiana.' So I git in my truck and follow him over the bridge. Then 'bout half-way 'cross, he stops his car. Before I know it, he's got his little girl clutched in his arms, and he jumps off the bridge into the river."

I feel my cheeks and ears tingle.

"They dragged them up before dark," Rex continues. "His arms were still wrapped around the girl." Rex hugs the air to show me. "Boy, I've seen that picture a thousand times. It's been twenty years and I still have nightmares. If he'da told me he was gonna kill himself, I don't know if I woulda stopped him from jumping off that bridge or not. But I'da saved that girl. When you lose one'a your own, . . ." he begins, then trails off. "I saw him stop and I figured he was comin' back to tell me somethin'. I didn't even have time to git outta my truck. Why he had to kill that girl, I don't know. I've played it over in my mind a thousand times, tryin' to see what I coulda done dif'rent. I don't know why that had to happen.''

I had taken Rex for a simpleton. But I now see that his simple ways mask the depth of his emotion. And because his anguish has come from out of nowhere, his revelations are all the more haunting. I sit in the chair, numb.

''There are some things in this world that just can't be explained,'' I say, groping for something to soothe Rex's soul. ''Some things just happen for no good reason. There's not a thing different you could have done.''

After he goes into his room to bed, I curl up under a blanket on the couch. Rain pelts the window, but I am dry and safe and warm. I think of Rex and wonder what the night holds for him, if the demons will visit his dreams. I arrived a stranger in Rex's humble home and I will leave that way. He doesn't know I'm traveling without a penny. He didn't ask what brought me over that bridge today. I guess he doesn't worry about the ones who make it all the way across.

THIRTY-FOUR

Rex leaves for work at seven on this Sunday morning. It's too early and too cold for traveling, so I write in my journal in the outer lobby of the post office. A young, gregarious man wearing a tie comes in and offers me a ride to New Castle, twenty miles down the road. He's the pastor of a church there. When we reach New Castle he says I can finish writing in his office above the rectory.

The pastor, Matthew, and his wife, Shelley, check on me an hour later, and I tell them about my penniless journey. I mention that several kind strangers have been Christians. I see the light go on above Matthew's head, and I'm soon agreeing to speak before his congregation.

I tailor my speech to the audience. I confess that I had no religious upbringing, yet on this trip I've been to church more times than in the rest of my life. I tell the flock that many of the people who have fed, sheltered and transported me have been good God-fearing folks like themselves.

After the service, the faithful hover around me. I feel a hand dip into my pants pocket. I reach in and pull out a ten-dollar bill. I stare at the money in horror. I push it toward a man with slicked-back hair and long sideburns.

"I can't take your money," I say. "I'm doing this trip without a penny."

He tries to force my hand and the money back into my pocket. As a struggle ensues, another hand slips into my other front pocket. I wheel around. I pull out a five and practically fling it back at a man in a powder blue suit.

"I can't accept money," I say.

I back away from the two men, who keep lunging at me with the bills. My retreat is interrupted by a bony, veiny hand that stuffs a twenty in my shirt pocket.

"No, please, I can't take it," I tell the old woman.

"But you've got to stay *somewhere*," she says.

During my talk, I told the crowd several times that I'm traveling without money. Either they didn't understand or they didn't believe me. Or maybe they took my allusions to the kindness of Christian strangers as a personal challenge.

They keep coming at me. I back away between the pews, deflecting the laying of moneyed hands. I want to run, but I'm cornered. I'm the lion being fed to the Christians.

I manage to escape penniless only after agreeing to accompany the congregation next door to the local coffee shop.

I take a seat next to a perky choir member named Tammy. She and the others eat pumpkin pie. She asks if I want lunch. I'm hungry but I decline. I'm sure many of the churchgoers thought I took the money. I don't want to appear greedy, like some swindling televangelist. To placate Tammy, I accept a piece of pumpkin pie.

A man slaps me on the back.

"Be sure he eats some lunch," he says to the table.

"We offered him lunch," Tammy says, "but he wants *py-uh.*"

Someone introduces me to Dean, a teddy bear of a man. He's not from the same church; he's a Lutheran. He just happens to be in the restaurant.

"We've got a guest room that doesn't get used often enough," he says.

And just like that, the question of tonight's lodging is settled.

We drive out to Dean's place, where I meet his beautiful wife, Marla, a florist, and their adorable nine-year-old daughter, Emily. They live in a house straight out of *Southern Living* magazine, rich with antiques and a mahogany baby grand piano.

Dean is an executive with a large Kentucky corporation. His ancestors settled in the area two centuries ago. Many of New Castle's buildings bear his family name.

Dean is a man in love with his town. In his spare time he heads a one-man beautification project. He has planted hundreds of trees and thousands of annuals in the last five years. He strings lights every Christmas in the town square. He started a local harvest festival, which now draws ten thousand people a year. He and Marla also give money and cars to several of the area's disadvantaged college students.

"I grew up here, I was educated here, and I just want to give something back to the community," he says.

Dean plans to spend this Sunday afternoon planting flowers on the courthouse lawn. I offer to give him a hand.

We stop for sodas at the convenience store.

"Hey, Dean," says a fellow by the refrigerator.

"Hey, Buddy," Dean beams. "Stay out of trouble. And if you get in trouble, give me a call. I'll help you out."

"That go for me too, Dean?" says another man in the store.

"Yeah, Bobby, as long as you don't cost me too much."

I like how Dean knows everybody. Back in the truck, I tell him I'm doing my best to travel through small towns.

"Television tells us that New York and L.A. and Miami are America," Dean says. "That's not America. This is the real fabric of the country out here."

We kneel in the dirt, tearing up the dying petunias around the courthouse lawn. Then as Dean digs holes with a trowel, I drop in tulip bulbs, alternating rows of red and gold.

"I'm not building a monument to myself, but I'd like to think that I can leave something that will outlast me," Dean says. "If I died this winter and never got to see these tulips come up, I hope that folks would see these bulbs and say, 'Hey, I miss Dean.' "

When we get back to the house, Marla and Emily have gone to church for choir practice. Dean and I wash up then drive into town for dinner. We discuss religion over plates of shrimp and twice-baked potatoes.

I ask Dean the eternal riddle: Why does God bother putting us here if there is only one right answer?

"You know, you're so nice, Mike. I haven't heard you say a negative thing. You don't swear, you're sincere and personable. It's hard for me to believe that's possible without you being a Christian."

He looks genuinely puzzled. I feel the Bible Belt cinch a little tighter around my journey.

Marla and Emily have yet to return from church when we get home. I pull my clothes from the dryer and fold them in the guest room. Dean walks in.

"Can I give you a hug?" he says.

Earlier at the coffee shop, Tammy hugged me when she stood to leave. When Dean and I were driving around later, he asked if that surprised me. Yes, I said, a little. "I'm a hugger," Dean said. I let the remark pass. Now I wish I hadn't.

Some men are huggers. Me, I'm a firm handshake kind of guy. Dean may hug everyone he meets. It's probably no big deal. But because I've known him all of six hours, I'm not positive about his intentions, and I can only think the worst.

I tighten as Dean embraces me. It is a simple hug, over soon and free of anything untoward. Yet it changes everything. I no longer feel comfortable in Dean's house. I hope his family will come home soon.

Later, when Marla and Emily have gone to bed, Dean returns to my room. I'm sitting on the bed, setting the alarm clock. He sits down beside me. He wears long johns and a red V-neck sweater.

"Let's pray, Mike."

He takes my hand in his and prays aloud. I cannot hear the words because I am distracted by the sight of my hand held to Dean's leg, Dean now squeezing and rubbing my fingers intently. Again, I fail to see the innocence of the gesture.

When Dean leaves the room, I turn out the light. But it is a good while before I fall asleep.

It's still dark out the next morning when Dean drives me into town. We're meeting a friend of his who works in Frankfort, the state capital. He's my next ride.

Neither of us speak. I think Dean senses my discomfort. He finally breaks the pregnant silence.

"I've never had a brother, Mike. If I would have had one, I wish it could have been you."

We shake hands goodbye and I get into his friend's truck.

"Well, you just stayed with the Samaritan of New Castle," Dean's friend says, driving along Route 421. "There's not a finer person in Henry County. Yeah, old Dean doesn't know a stranger."

At the start of his journey I wondered if America was too suspicious to let a stranger into its heart. But on this day I wonder if it is the stranger who is too suspicious to allow America into *his* heart.

THIRTY-FIVE

A trucker who hasn't picked up a hitchhiker in ten years stops for me in Danville, Kentucky. I don't even have a sign out. Just another lucky day in America.

Burley is driving to Macon, Georgia, to deliver a load of shortening to a restaurant chain. Route 127 twists through the Cumberland Mountains. Men with bushy beards stare from shacks on the side of the road.

"Look at them 'billies," Burley says.

Across the Tennessee line, framed notices are nailed to every telephone pole. "Jesus Is Coming," they read. "R U Ready?"

I step down from Burley's truck on the loop outside of Jamestown, nineteen miles south of the border. Burley sends me packing with a bag of lemon drops, an apple, and a cluster of grapes.

Jamestown lies in Fentress County, one of the poorest in the nation. The screen at the drive-in movie is overgrown with vines. A mobile home dealer on the edge of town advertises trailers for as low as $129 a month. "Making Your Dreams Come True," the sign says.

The Chamber of Commerce occupies the former jail, a stone building from the last century. I try the door but it's locked. I see a man inside jump up from a cluttered desk.

"Come on into my house," he says with a smile.

The Chamber president, Baxter, is fifty-nine. He wears a tweed coat, khaki pants, and a plaid tie. His dark, curly hair touches the collar of his blue, button-down shirt. A plaque given to him by the Rotary Club reads: "To a chicken fightin', chicken pluckin', over the fire barbecue expert."

I ask him about camping in the area.

He unfolds a map of the Big South Fork National River and

Recreation Area, ten miles away. When I hesitate, he hands me a brochure for a campground closer in. I see it costs twelve dollars. He hands me another flier.

I thank him.

He follows me out the door. He sees my pack sitting on the porch.

"Would you like me to call one of those campgrounds for you?"

"Oh no, that's all right. I'm not sure what I'm going to do, just checking things out."

Baxter looks me in the eye.

" 'Most anybody around here will let you pitch a tent on their land, if that's what you want."

Now we're talking.

"Any particular direction?" I say.

"Tell you what, I've got a big farm about ten miles south of here. I've got to pick my son up at football practice, but if you're here at five-thirty, you can ride out with me. Then you can ride into town with me in the morning." He smiles. "We may even find a barn for you to sleep in."

I wait across the street at the Mark Twain Park. It sits in view of Mark Twain Street, near the Mark Twain Inn and Mark Twain Apparel. Twain's father was a Fentress County judge before moving west. And though the famous author was born in Missouri, locals take great pride in knowing that he was conceived in Jamestown.

Baxter returns for me at his office an hour later.

"Practice isn't over, but I knew you'd be sitting out here in the cold," he says.

I get in his truck, a collection of rusted dents rumbling through its second quarter of a million miles. We drive to the York Institute. The state-supported high school was the dream of Sgt. Alvin C. York, the World War I hero who killed 26 Germans and captured 132. He was born in nearby Pall Mall.

Baxter's son Bryan is twelve. His older brothers are twenty-five, thirty-two, and thirty-three. The doctor told Baxter's wife Carol she'd better sit down when he told her Bryan was on the way.

We drive along a pine-studded plateau out to Banner Springs. The entrance to Baxter's farm is marked by a harvest display of pumpkins, gourds, cornstalks, and an orange bow. A dirt road leads to a magnificent country house perched on the edge of a gorge. I can hear the Clear Fork River rushing eighty feet below.

Sam, a mix of rottweiler and boxer, bounds up and nearly knocks me over. He holds himself up against my chest and licks my face.

Baxter says come on in. I follow him along a porch that wraps clear around the two-story house. There isn't a barn in sight. I realize he has just invited me to spend the night.

The bed in the guest room belonged to Baxter's great-grandparents. Their house was commandeered by Confederate soldiers during the Civil War. A Union bullet is still lodged in the bed's headboard.

Carol is cooking pot roast when we walk into the kitchen. Baxter quickly dons an apron and makes a sheet of biscuits from scratch, using a chilled wine bottle for a rolling pin. They've been married thirty-five years but remain as fresh as newlyweds.

Carol is a seventh-grade science teacher. She is a picture of Southern grace and charm. She is nine years younger than her husband. Baxter was Carol's Sunday school teacher. He often showed up at her family's farm under the pretext of helping her dad and brothers.

"He scared all those other boys away," Carol says, beaming at Baxter.

"It worked, it worked," Baxter says.

The family is an anomaly in these parts. Both Baxter and Carol have college degrees. The only television allowed on in the house is the McNeil-Lehrer News Hour. And while they may not be the wealthiest people in Tennessee, it's obvious they skew the per capita income of impoverished Fentress County.

This fall, Baxter took twenty-nine local youths to a Tennessee Tech football game in Cookeville, about fifty miles away. Only four of the boys had ever been out of the county before—all of them with Baxter to a previous game.

Baxter calls folks around here "mountain stay-at-home people." He considers himself one of them.

"We rarely entertain in our house," he says. "When we do, it's usually kin."

The revelation makes my night here all the more special.

I ask Baxter what he likes best about his part of the country.

"The people," he says. "If you come here and say you're the King of Siam, that's who you are—'til you screw up."

Baxter leases out his land to Mennonite farmers. He has run the Chamber of Commerce for the last nine years.

"They fire me every so often, then they ask me back."

After dinner, we go for a walk in the woods with Carol's sister and her husband. The night is clear and crisp. The bright stars look so close, I think I can grab a handful and put them in my pocket.

The simple pleasures of country living.

When I come downstairs in the morning, Baxter is frying sausage and eggs, while Carol grades papers at the kitchen table. She asks if I'll come to school today and tell her class about my trip. I'm worried I'll give her students the wrong message. I don't want to be the cause of a bunch of seventh-graders hitchhiking across the United States.

But Carol says the kids should be exposed to what else is out there. "They need to know." She wants me to tell them the good and the bad.

She teaches at the elementary school in Allardt, an old German community outside of Jamestown. Baxter swings me by at nine.

I prove a hit with Carol's students, so she asks if I'll stay and talk to Bryan's class. Before long, I've agreed to talk to every class in the school.

The kids are very well mannered and attentive. I pull the U.S. map down over the blackboard and show them my route. I ask how many of them have been to California. Hardly a hand goes up all day.

The questions keep coming: Where are people the kindest? How many pairs of shoes do I have? Am I carrying a gun? Has anybody tried to run me over? Is there racism in other states? Are the pigs' feet as good in other parts of the country? Have I fallen in love with anyone? What am I most afraid of?

And my favorite, from a meek little girl with glasses and freckles, who raises her hand and says, "Yew wanna eat lunch with us?"

The women in the cafeteria load me up with a huge tray of chicken strips, macaroni and cheese, two rolls, Jell-O with whipped cream, green beans, milk, and an ice cream sandwich. Carol introduces me to the school principal, a thin man with white hair and long brown sideburns.

"Mike, when you're through with your trip, maybe you oughtta come back and settle right here," he says. "We'll treat you so many ways, you're bound to like one or two."

"I just might do that."

Carol tells me that one of the kids I spoke to is slightly retarded. He is ordinarily quite shy. But she says he came up to her in the cafeteria and said, "I want to grow up to be a journalist and go all the places he's been."

I'm touched by the story, but I'm also concerned that I've made such a strong impression on someone without knowing it. When I left San Francisco, I was thinking only of myself. I never gave a thought to this trip impacting a child in Allardt, Tennessee. I am reminded that no matter how hard we try, nothing we do is in a vacuum.

A patriotic tone runs through the talks I give in the afternoon. I tell the students how my faith in America has been renewed. I tell them how proud I am to live in a country where people are still willing to help out a stranger.

I keep looking at the map. I see "Cape Fear" written in the blue part, where the country bumps up against the Atlantic Ocean. My journey is almost over. Only one more state to go. I am excited, and sad.

Then all at once a realization hits me. It's so simple. . . .

It took giving up money to have the richest experience of my life.

At the end of the day, kids press around me. They wish me luck. Some of them ask for my autograph.

After I say good-bye and walk out the door, one of them pays me the highest compliment conferred in elementary school. I'm in the hallway when I hear a boy tell his classmates, "He's cool!"

THIRTY-SIX

My celebrity lasts only to the curb, where I again turn into a nobody. The few drivers who pass by eye me with suspicion. My lecture stop means a short travel day, and I lose another hour crossing into the Eastern Time Zone. By nightfall, I'm lucky to make it thirty miles closer to Cape Fear.

Huntsville, Tennessee, is the home of former U.S. senator Howard Baker. His house is easy to spot. It's the one with the front yard the size of a golf course. I consider pitching my tent on his lawn, then figure it might be best if I just tell local law officials they have a new vagrant in town.

The deputy chief looks straight out of central casting. His gut hangs over a belt that displays his badge. The gun in his holster almost reaches his armpit. When I ask him where I can camp, he keeps me waiting for an hour on a sofa outside the jail. I'd settle for a cell, until I learn that the cozy stone jail houses an overflow of murderers and rapists from the state prison system.

A road worker who shares the couch with me asks where I'm going.

"North Carolina."

"You better cross them Smokys durin' the day, boy!" he says. "Them Smokys get cold."

The deputy chief finally returns and says I can camp at the baseball field outside of town. The park is set back in the woods. I walk along a remote road through the dark. I fight gusts of wind to pitch my tent in the farthest corner of the field. The night is bitter cold, and I crawl into my sleeping bag fully dressed.

In the morning, I take a look at the map. I'm so close to the end, I figure it's a good time to call home to Anne.

I find a pay phone in the courthouse. Handcuffed prisoners in orange suits are led through the hallway. It feels funny to hold a receiver to my ear. I tell the operator I want to place a collect call to San Francisco.

I hear the phone ringing on the other side of the country. I'm excited—and nervous. I haven't talked to Anne—or anyone I know—for nearly six weeks. I've been completely cut off. There was no way to reach me. I fear that something terrible has happened, and I almost hang up before the call goes through.

I'm relieved when Anne answers and tells me that all is well. It's great to hear her voice, but our conversation is awkward. I don't know what it is. I decide that it can wait until I get back.

Before I hang up, I ask Anne to mail my ATM card to me in care of general delivery at the post office in Wilmington, North Carolina, the last city before Cape Fear.

The transcontinental connection leaves me unsettled. I'm in limbo, neither here nor there. I force my mind back to the journey. I have 450 penniless miles to go.

I get the feeling I could be stuck for days in the mountains of eastern Tennessee. Huntsville is not on the way to anywhere. It's all local traffic. Caryville is the next town of any size, and that's what goes on my sign.

A dented Ford panel van stops across the street from me. Like so many strangers who have offered me rides, this fellow passed me then turned back. The driver says something, but his voice is so soft, it's lost in the wind.

"What?" I say, cupping my ear.

"I'm goin' right past Caryville," the man says.

And then some. He's going clear across the Appalachians into North Carolina.

Eldon, twenty-six, is from nearby Oneida. He's a ceramic tile layer. He drives to jobs throughout the South. He has to be in Gastonia, just west of Charlotte, tonight. I'm in luck.

His van is packed with tools, a dolly and several Army surplus sleeping bags. I throw my pack on top of the heap and climb in.

Eldon's appearance screams backwoods. Most of his upper teeth are worn down to pointy nubs. His one full-length tooth fits perfectly into the gap formed by a missing tooth in the bottom row. His ears stick out at right angles from under a Tennessee Volunteers baseball hat. He pulls cigarettes from the pocket of a sleeveless khaki shirt. His arms bear patches of skin with no pigment. He would be downright scary if it wasn't for his doe brown eyes and painfully shy voice.

I ask Eldon why he turned back for me. He says that not so long ago, his van broke down thirty miles from home. He stuck out his thumb. No one stopped, not even people who knew him. He walked home in the dark.

"When I saw you, I thought about that time I walked."

Something about Eldon strikes me as so sweet, I almost cry. He reminds me of Forrest Gump, the slow-witted but big-hearted character from the blockbuster movie of the same name.

A cooler full of RC Cola rides on the floorboard between our seats. Eldon offers me one, but it's too early in the morning for me.

Outside Knoxville, we pick up Interstate 40. The freeway climbs a summit just outside of the Great Smoky Mountain National Park. Wisps of fog rise from the forest like spot fires. Rain hits the windshield. It feels good to be on this side of the wipers.

I tell Eldon that money hasn't touched my hands in nearly six weeks.

"That's the way it'll all get done here pretty quick," he says.

"How do you mean?"

"The Book of Revelation," Eldon starts in. He tries real hard but stumbles over the Scripture. "I forget the exact words," he says. He alludes to the mark of the beast. He says everyone will soon need money cards with numbers, like the kind you use at the Safeway. "It's gittin' to where we cain't use cash anymore." He stammers, fumbling for the right passage. "There's a Bible in that glove box," he finally says.

I fish through the compartment but come up empty. I remember the small Gideons Bible that Pete gave me back in South Dakota. I pull it from my pack and flip through Revelation.

"Here it is," I say. I begin reading: "And that no man might buy or sell, save he that had the mark, or the name of the beast, or the number of his name. . . ."

Many of the Christians I've met on this trip were force-fed their faith as children. They did not come to it as a choice. I am not impressed by their convictions. But, like me, Eldon had no religious upbringing, so I am curious as to how he came to believe.

"Three or four years ago, I was just layin' in bed one night and I just knew," he says. "Jesus Christ done died for my sins."

"How did you know?"

"It's the only thing I've ever known for sure. You can tell me my name is Eldon Wallace. I think my name is Eldon Wallace, but I don't know it for sure. But that feeling I got is the one thing I know for sure."

"What did it feel like?"

"It was a glowin' feelin'. I reckon it was the best feelin' I ever had."

I ask Eldon what his life was like before.

"I was headed down the wrong track." He made thirty thousand dollars in three months, then blew it all on women, drugs, and booze. "It don't matter what you do. All you gotta do is believe. Like that guy who died on the cross next to Jesus. All he said was two words, 'Remember me.' And Jesus said, 'You will live forever,' or somethin' like that. I'm as low-down as they come, but I believe."

We stop for gas in Asheville, North Carolina. The cashier in the minimart sits in a bullet-proof booth, something I haven't seen since leaving San Francisco.

"Get you somethin' to eat if you want," Eldon says quietly, almost like he's embarrassed. "I don't mind."

I tell him I'm okay, but he insists. I grab an egg salad sandwich from the refrigerator.

We leave the freeway for Route 74, a road that twists through lush mountains covered with kudzu plant. The rain continues to pour, and we pass three wrecks within twelve miles. I spot a yellow "Dead End" sign out of the corner of my eye. Is my worst fear still out there waiting for me?

When at last we reach the flatlands, I see the first new crop since Nebraska. Corn has been replaced by cotton. The bolls are so white it almost hurts my eyes.

Eldon is meeting his father-in-law and brother-in-law at the job site in Gastonia. They're driving up from Alabama. It will take two days to lay the tiles. The men will sleep at the job site to save on expenses. That's why Eldon carries the sleeping bags. He says I'm welcome to stay at the job site with them.

The job site turns out to be a Burger King. When we arrive, electricians, carpenters, and wallpaper hangers are working swiftly. The restaurant is due to open in a week. Eldon and I sit in a booth, trying to stay out of the way. Eldon's tiles won't arrive until tomorrow morning.

Nail guns, drills, and country-western music bombard my ears. The floor is cluttered with tools, boxes of furniture, and stainless steel cooking equipment. A layer of sawdust covers everything.

The guys doing the finish work are a group of hard partiers called the Zoo Crew. One of them wears a baseball hat emblazoned with the Confederate flag. ''American by Birth,'' it reads. ''Southern by the Grace of God.''

The superintendent, Gene, pulls up in a pickup. He's followed by a fat black lab with a white beard named Matlock. The dog is friendly; Gene does the barking. He keeps the crews hopping. I hope he doesn't notice me. The floor of a Burger King may not be the perfect bed, but at least it's dry.

Eldon's in-laws haven't arrived by six, so we walk next door to the McDonald's. We bring our Big Macs, fries, and Cokes back to the job site. I don't think that's what Burger King has in mind when they say, ''Have it your way.''

After the workers leave for the night, I have a closer look at my newest digs. There's no heat or hot water, but a sink works in the pantry. I sweep the kitchen floor and unroll my sleeping bag next to the Frymaster. Eldon sets out his three Army surplus bags in the men's room.

Eldon's brother-in-law, Keith, finally shows up around eleven. His dad and the other helpers are stuck in Georgia. The windshield wiper motor on their car broke. They'll drive up in the morning.

We all sit in a booth and talk. I thought it might be hard to get enthusiastic about sleeping in a Burger King, but I'm exhausted. I ask if I can flip out the lights in the kitchen and leave the ones in the restaurant on.

''Hell, turn 'em all off,'' Keith says.

I find the electric panel. There are two rows of light switches. I hit them all at once. The building goes dark—except for a glaring bulb over the Frymaster and my sleeping bag.

I carry my bedding into the pantry and spread it out by the meat locker. The floor slopes down into a drain, and a ventilator hums obnoxiously overhead. I have one of my best night's sleeps of the trip.

The tile truck comes at seven in the morning. I don my poncho and help Eldon and Keith unload the boxes. A carpenter arrives and says that one of the Zoo Crew was arrested last night for drunk driving. When Gene hears this, he takes it out on the workers. He glares at a couple of trucks parked in a section of the parking lot that has turned to quicksand.

"I don't know why in the hell you boys gotta drive in that mud," he growls.

But the sight of the neatly stacked boxes of ceramic tiles changes his mood. He pulls a ten-dollar bill from his wallet. He tells Eldon and Keith to buy themselves breakfast at McDonald's. Eldon tells me to come along.

"Get Matlock a sausage biscuit," Gene calls after us.

We slosh through the orange mud. Keith says Gene always buys his dog human food—that's why he's so fat. I order an Egg McMuffin and a large coffee. For once on this trip, I've actually earned my meal.

We get the food to go and run back to the Burger King in the rain. When we unload the paper bag, Keith realizes he forgot Matlock's sausage biscuit. Gene is none too happy. I wolf down my Egg McMuffin before he takes it away from me and gives it to his dog. Matlock paces around with a look that says, "Which one of you flunkies screwed up?"

The rain won't quit. I keep staring out the window, as if that will do any good. My choice is to either get wet or spend a very long day in a half-finished Burger King. I pull a plastic garbage bag over my pack and walk out into the storm.

THIRTY-SEVEN

North Carolina 74 is six lanes wide for the twenty-three miles between Gastonia and Charlotte. There is no shoulder, nowhere to stand and hold out my sign. I wade through the tall, wet grass. My boots are soaked. The rain is unrelenting, and the mud on my pants now looks like blood. Drivers in warm, dry cars whiz through puddles and spray me. I am cold and wet and miserable.

I come to a long stretch of strip malls. Cement islands rise between the two directions of traffic. They taper at the ends so people can make left turns into the Wal-Marts and Kmarts. I dart through rushing cars and step onto an island. I stride briskly down the center of the road, hopping from one island to the next. To all the Kmart shoppers, I must look like a moron.

A man with a big piece of cardboard under his arm watches me from the entrance to a strip mall.

"Where you headed?" he calls to me as he crosses three lanes to reach my island.

"Cape Fear," I say.

The man follows me. I have to slow down for him to keep pace. His clothes are grubby and he needs a shave, but he seems harmless.

"Where are you going?" I say.

"Oh, nowhere. I just had my sign out for a couple hours."

"What's your sign say?"

He unfolds the cardboard, and I read it as we walk:

"Homeless, Disabled, Hungry, Please Help, God Bless You."

"Are you really homeless?"

"No, I have my own home."

This disgusts me. I walk faster, but keep my comments to myself. The man hustles to keep up.

"The reason I put my sign out is I'm disabled and my government check is only three eighty-eight a month. I need the extra money to pay my bills."

He looks perfectly healthy. He has all four limbs. He's walking. He's talking.

"How are you disabled?"

"I had a broken arm."

But I see he doesn't have trouble hefting around his giant sign.

I once wrote a story about panhandlers. Most of the 20 or so I interviewed were able-bodied and said that bumming change was their chosen profession. A few were earning more than a hundred tax-free dollars a day. I know there is a legitimate homeless problem in this country. But ever since that story, I've been wary of all beggars.

My new friend scampers behind me like a puppy.

"I used to do what you're doing," he says, "hitchhike all over the country."

I stop in my tracks. The man bumps into me. I snap in his face.

"Buddy, I don't think you've ever done what I'm doing. I'm crossing America without a single penny. I haven't touched money in six weeks."

He looks at me in disbelief.

"I need my money to live," he says apologetically.

I walk faster down the island. The man falls behind.

I finally reach a spot in the road where there's room to stand. I hold my umbrella over my head and stick out a thumb.

The man with the sign catches up to me ten minutes later. He carries two McDonald's cheeseburgers.

"I brought you some food," he says.

He hands me the two burgers, their yellow wrappers wet with rain.

The man runs back across the road. He yells to me that I should come up to his trailer if I get tired.

"Number fourteen," he says. "Top of the hill."

For a moment, I feel guilty about judging the man. Then I remind myself that the money that bought the food was obtained fraudulently.

I wait until the man is out of sight before I throw the burgers in the trash.

A teenager in a station wagon stops for me. His name is Cam. He lives in Belmont, a suburb of Charlotte. He quickly volunteers that he is half white and half black. He wants to be a cop and work with dogs in the K-9 unit. He attends a junior college, but he cut class this morning to play video games.

"I love Mortal Kombat," he says.

Cam says he has a friend who works at a motel where I can stay for free. But he withdraws the offer before I can accept.

"You probably wouldn't like it. It's all black people living there."

I assure him I have no problem with that, but he insists it's a bad idea.

He says he has a black friend who lives with his grandmother. I can spend the night at her house.

"She's not racist or anything," he says.

As badly as I'd like to get out of the rain, I tell Cam that I can't just show up at another person's house.

He suggests I hop a freight train. He drives me to the switching yard to check a schedule he says is posted there. But when we reach the station, there is no timetable and no train.

He says he will drive me to Cape Fear. It's only four hours. He was there last weekend.

Cam is eager to help, but I finally realize he's unrealistic. He has to return his dad's car soon. He must also pick up his girlfriend from high school. His girlfriend is white, he says. Her uncle belongs to the Ku Klux Klan.

Cam drops me back out on Route 74. At least there is a sidewalk.

He warns me to watch out in Charlotte.

"If you get stuck there, stay downtown," he says. "It's lighted and the cops patrol there. There's white people and black people together down there."

My clothes are still wet when I step out of Cam's car. I lean my umbrella into the driving rain.

After a few miles, I can see the Charlotte skyline through the clouds. But cities look closer than they really are when you reach the edge of them, and I must walk several more miles. Unfortunately, the sidewalk runs out before I hit town.

Parts of America are inhospitable to pedestrians. I continue on along a one-foot wide swath of grass that runs between the guard rail and the highway. I walk slowly, careful not to trip over vines and stumble into oncoming traffic. In some places, I must walk around bushes that hang over the road.

Route 74 crosses above a freeway near downtown Charlotte. The rail on the bridge only reaches my knees. The cars rushing below combine with those passing inches from me on the bridge to give me vertigo. The wind blowing my pack adds to the whirling sensation.

I'm so angry, I almost smash my umbrella against the guard rail. It's the first time I've been mad on this journey. I'm no longer taking the trip. The trip is taking me.

I navigate a series of slippery on ramps, off ramps, bridges, and medians, until at last I reach the Queen City.

I was last in Charlotte in 1989, covering the trail of Jim Bakker, the televangelist who swindled millions from his followers. I stayed in a nice hotel then and ordered room service. Today I'd settle for Bakker's dry prison cell and some gruel.

Charlotte is the first real city I've been in since passing through Omaha last month. The tall buildings, the crowded sidewalks, and the endless stoplights confuse and annoy me. The whole world suddenly seems in my way. All I want is to get in the clear.

A damp doom descends on me. I feel like my luck just ran out and washed down the gutter. I already wrote Anne today. Now I scribble a hasty message to her on a postcard, noting where I am and the exact time, then drop it in a mailbox. Just in case.

I walk along East Seventh Street to the edge of the city. I walk with my eyes on the wet sidewalk. When I lift my head, I see I'm now in the midst of a housing project. The looks people give me say there aren't too many gangly white guys with backpacks who walk down this road.

A man pulls over, even though I don't have a sign out. He tells me to hop in. This is no place for me, he says.

"I knew you weren't from around here, walking where you were. You were in the crack part of town."

As if to underscore his point, the topic on the call-in show playing on his radio is crime. One caller says that the United States has more mass murderers and serial killers than any nation in the world.

The man delivers lights for a manufacturer. His last stop is in Matthews, the next town east of Charlotte. He drops me on the highway outside of town. I make a sign for Monroe, thirteen miles farther.

The road is clogged with rush hour traffic. No one stops. It's getting dark.

A Union County sheriff's deputy drives by. I watch him make a U-turn. A couple minutes later, he pulls up on my side of the road, blue lights flashing. He gets out of the car.

"Are you hitchhiking?" he says.

"Am I doing something wrong?"

"No, I was just wondering what you were doing out here. You got any ID?"

I reach in my shirt pocket for my sole piece of identification, my California driver's license.

"The extension is on the back," I say.

I hand him the license, pointing out the new date of expiration taped to the other side.

"So what are you doing out here?"

I tell him the truth, all except the penniless part.

He takes my license with him back to the patrol car and gets on the radio. He's in there a long time. It's not getting any lighter.

He finally returns.

"You got a valid license?"

"This is valid."

"No, it says it expired in 1991." He points to the expiration date on the front.

This could be bad. A dumb cop.

"Like I said, the extension is on the back."

He scrutinizes the license.

"Am I doing anything wrong out here?" I say again.

"No, but we get calls. People don't like to see hitchhikers on the road."

"So, someone called about me?"

"Yeah, everyone's got a mobile phone these days, so I had to check you out."

I almost ask what he'd do if I called up and said I didn't like the look of a particular car. But I hold my tongue. Besides, I know he wasn't responding to a call. He passed me, turned around and came back.

"So, why aren't you driving?" he says.

"Like I said, I'm a writer traveling across the country to research a book."

"I know, you told me that. But why aren't you in a car?"

I don't know if it's true, but I've heard that the police can pick you up on vagrancy charges if you don't have any money. That's why I don't tell him I'm penniless.

I decide to go on the offensive.

"I'm a little confused here, officer. If I'm not doing anything wrong, why are we having this conversation? It's getting dark, and I don't feel safe traveling after dark, and I've got a ways to go.''

The cop steps back.

"Okay, I'll get out of your way. Good luck, Mr. McIntyre.''

The guy leaves me on the side of the dark road, seething. I'm reminded of my dislike of cops. I was once busted for eating a sandwich I brought into a movie theater. Two sheriff's deputies came for me during *Terms of Endearment.* One held his baton to my throat. "You can make this hard, or you can make this easy,'' he said, just like in the movies.

I'm still seething three hours later when I walk into the Monroe police department. I ask the officer on duty if there is anywhere I can camp for free. I'm sure he will arrest me. But the officer couldn't be more helpful. He says to pitch my tent in the city park, and he gives me directions.

I'm forced to rethink my feelings toward policemen. I guess they're not all bad. After all, I did travel all the way to North Carolina before getting hassled by one.

The rain subsides to a drizzle while I pitch my tent beneath a scrawny tree in the park. I open a can of tuna and eat it with some crumbled crackers. When the storm resumes, I sit up in my sleeping bag and wait for the water to pour through. But the tent holds.

For a while.

All at once, it's as if a rain cloud has burst inside the tent. Water seeps from every fiber. I scramble out of bed and drag my wet things to a cement slab that is covered by a roof. I drain my tent and crawl back into my sopping sleeping bag. I am very close to Cape Fear, but the travel gods won't let me finish in comfort.

THIRTY-EIGHT

Cape Fear is less than two hundred miles away. I'm so close I can see the end. And with that knowledge comes a heightened sense of risk. I feel like a short-timer in the Army. My tour of duty is almost up, but I'm still walking point. My sole objective now is to avoid the land mines.

I don't know how it's possible, but my boots actually feel wetter than they did yesterday. My toes have more wrinkles than a relief map of Appalachia. I squish on back out to Route 74. It's still raining.

My first ride is a red-headed fellow originally from southern Indiana. He asks where I slept last night. I tell him the Monroe city park.

"You were in a dangerous place," he laughs. "Right by the train tracks there, bodies turn up dead there all the time."

Maybe the Monroe cops aren't so nice, after all.

A trucker from Alabama stops for me. Truckers drive forever. Maybe this one is going all the way to Wilmington. But it's the shortest ride of the trip. The trucker carries me six miles to Wadesboro.

A husband and wife who recently moved here from Oklahoma pick me up. The woman does all the talking. She just had surgery and her jaw is wired shut, but she can't keep quiet. She wipes drool from the corners of her mouth as she talks. They're Mormons, she says. She mentions this several times. I don't bite. I'm too wet and cold to talk religion. They drop me at a gas station in Rockingham, east of the Pee Dee River.

The gas station is in the middle of the town, not a good place to catch a ride. I would walk to the outskirts of Rockingham, but it's pouring. I stand beneath the eaves of the gas station's min-imart, holding a sign for Wilmington. I'm sure I look pathetic.

I want to finish at Cape Fear tomorrow, Saturday. The post office in Wilmington closes at noon tomorrow. If I don't get there in time, I'll have to wait until Monday to pick up the ATM card Anne sent me. The prospect of officially ending the journey, yet remaining penniless for two extra days is a nightmare. I must keep going.

The problem is not the rain so much as my pack. It now feels like a seventy-pound tumor on my back. If it didn't belong to my brother, I'd ditch it. I do the next best thing. I jettison most of its contents. I'm like a damaged airplane dumping fuel to fly just far enough to reach the runway. The only items I keep are my clothes, sleeping bag, and an energy bar.

I now feel light enough to run—and I do. I run through Rock-ingham in the rain.

A fellow from Arkansas pulls over. He's only going twenty-five miles to Laurinburg. He offers to drive me five miles farther to Maxton. There's a truck stop there, he says. But when he drops me off, there is only one trucker ready to roll out—and he's heading west.

The worst news is that Route 74 has turned into a freeway. It's illegal to hitchhike. Most people driving seventy miles an hour aren't inclined to stop anyway.

I stay dry beneath an overpass. But it's so dark, I don't think anyone can see my sign until they're right up on me. My only chance at a ride is to stand out in the rain. The passing eighteen-wheelers spray me with water and blow my umbrella inside out. My jeans cling to my shivering legs.

At last a trucker pulls over. He locks his brakes and skids along the grass shoulder.

The trucker is a jolly fat man who was once robbed at knife-point by a hitchhiker.

"But I hate to see a man stand out in the rain," he says. "People don't have no heart anymore."

He is from South Carolina. He says folks in North Carolina aren't friendly. I don't know if that's true, but the kind strangers I've met in this state have all been from someplace else.

A good friend of mine says America is hard on the edges and soft in the middle. He may be right. None of this journey has been a cakewalk. But the country was more accommodating in the states between California and North Carolina.

The trucker warns me about pneumonia. When he stops outside of Lumberton to turn south on Interstate 95, he recommends a cheap motel I should go to if no one stops right away.

"You have money for a motel if you get stuck out here?"

Even now, at the end, I am weak. The image of a hot shower and a dry bed flashes in my head. I can't be tempted by the trucker's response to the truth.

"Yes," I lie.

A black man picks me up at the freeway on ramp.

"I was in the Air Force twenty-two years," he says before I get in the car. "I ain't afraid of nothing."

He's only going thirty-three miles to Whiteville, but I know I'm safe for yet another ride.

The man emigrated from Jamaica when he was twelve. At sixteen, he hitchhiked from Los Angeles to New York. He kept a diary of the trip.

"Someone will read it," he says.

We splash through the driving rain, windshield wipers slapping and the defroster losing its battle with the fog on the window. As the man talks, I get this eerie feeling that I know him. I don't recall his face, nor do the details of his life sound familiar. It is more a sensation of his presence, the way a blind person can tell when someone else is in the room. I can't explain, but it seems as if this man has been shadowing me all along, like some guardian angel. And now our parallel paths have converged for one brief ride. I feel like we're floating, and I wipe the fog from my window to check and make sure the car is still on the ground.

"Have we met before?"

The man turns to me and smiles.

"Could be."

No one is going far. I'll have to nickel and dime my way to Wilmington.

A junior college administrator drives me eighteen miles to Bolton. Like the others today, he's originally from somewhere else: Germany. A box of bottles rattles in the back. The guy must be going to a party. But he says the bottles contain vinegar. He is coming from the college TV station, where he taped a special.

"I've watched all the cooking shows, and I've never seen one on vinegar," he says.

The last person to pick me up today is from North Carolina. A Tar Heel at last. She drives like Junior Johnson.

"Fasten your safety belt and don't be scared," she says. "I'm late for work."

She has her sports coupe up to ninety in nothing flat. She weaves in and out of traffic. We come up on cars like they were parked. I grip the armrest, my knuckles turning white.

"I'm Angela," she says, "And you are . . . ?"

"Petrified."

"Relax, I'm late for work every day."

"Where do you work?"

"I deliver pizza for Dominoes."

"Boy, no wonder you guys can get it there in thirty minutes or less."

The closer we get to Wilmington, the more cross-traffic we encounter. Vehicles pull slowly onto the highway. Angela almost drives up the backs of several cars. She doesn't seem to know how to use the brake pedal. If the fast lane is blocked, she swerves into the slow lane. It's all a blur of pavement and metal. Earlier I was worried I wouldn't make it to Wilmington today. Now I'm afraid I won't make it there alive.

But soon we are crossing the bridge over the Cape Fear River, and Angela actually stops the car in downtown Wilmington. I step out, grateful to be standing still. Patches of blue poke through the cloudy sky. Now that I don't need a ride, it has stopped raining.

Cape Fear is twelve miles farther. After I drop by the post office in the morning, I'll head out there and make it official.

Only one more night.

THIRTY-NINE

Wilmington is the biggest city I've had to spend the night in since Billings, Montana. I can't count on the kindness of strangers. No shelters are listed in the Yellow Pages, so I get the address of the YMCA. Maybe they'll let me sleep there.

The Y is twenty-seven blocks away. I start hoofing it. Naturally, it begins to rain. My umbrella snags on branches as I walk in the dark. I make it twenty-three blocks, then the sidewalk runs out. The shoulder of the busy boulevard is flooded. I walk back downtown.

I find the police station inside a brick building near the riverfront. The officer at the desk gives me directions to the Salvation Army. But when I get there, every bunk is taken. The receptionist calls Wilmington's other shelter. They are full, too. She tells me the police will let me sit in the station.

"I'm back," I tell the officer when I return. "The shelters are full. All right if I sit in here until daylight?"

The room glares with fluorescent lights and the chairs are wooden. But at least it's safe and dry.

"I can't let you stay here," the cop says. "It's against policy."

"Oh, shoot, the lady at the Salvation Army said you let people sit in here."

"It's up to the sergeant on duty. The sergeant's policy tonight is no."

I gaze over the cop's shoulder at the sergeant, a stern-looking black woman hunched over paperwork inside a glass office. From the way she grips her pencil, I know her policy is ironclad.

I ask the officer if there is an open public building in town where I can stay out of the rain.

The cop leans over the counter and whispers, so his sergeant can't hear. He says there is a closet in the lobby of this building. I can stay there.

It sounds like a crazy idea, and I wonder if the cop is kidding, but I thank him and go looking for tonight's lodgings.

I find the closet next to the automatic door that opens to the street. It stands across the lobby from the restrooms. It's about the width of a coffin, but not as long. The space is made smaller by the presence of a single sofa cushion, a two-by-four board, and a music stand.

After I remove my pack, there is barely enough room to curl up on the floor. I take off my shoes and socks and lay on top of my wet sleeping bag. My hip is bruised from sleeping on the cement slab last night in the park. I wish I hadn't thrown away my pad.

The closet door won't click shut. It's warped and keeps popping open. Light from the lobby filters through the crack. I toss and turn, trying to find a comfortable position. My feet press against the door, and my head rests on the base of the music stand.

I finally doze off.

I don't know how long I've been asleep when I hear the automatic door swing open. I listen for the footsteps to turn toward the police station, but they come my way. Still groggy, I bolt upright. The closet door is open an inch. A human shadow dances on the closet wall. It gets bigger. I place my feet against the door and try to lock my knees, but I'm too late. Whoever is on the other side barges in.

I spring up, reeling with panic. The intruder flicks a cigarette lighter. There is suddenly an angry black man in my face, attacking me with eighty-six-proof breath.

"What the fuck are you doing in here???!!!" he shouts.

I stumble back into the music stand.

"Who are you?" I say. "Who are you?"

He steps back out of the closet without a word. He's unshaven, and the cuffs of his baggy pants are frayed from dragging on the street. He stumbles across the lobby and drops in the doorway of the men's room. He lays his head on the greasy athletic bag he carries with him.

I shut the closet door and stand in the dark. I try to wedge the two-by-four against the door but it won't hold. I place the cushion between my feet and the door, as if that's going to keep anybody out. I sit up on my sleeping bag. I worry about what's happening on the other side of the door. I don't make a sound. I'm afraid to even shift. I don't want to remind the guy I'm in here. When I hear him snoring, I lay back down.

The automatic door rumbles open a while later. Someone leans on the closet door.

"Hey!" I shout, trying to sound scary.

"Oh, excuse me," says the man on the other side.

I hear him sit down next to the other man. He spreads out some newspaper and lies down. The man mutters something I can't hear, waking the guy with the lighter.

"There's a white guy in there," the man with the lighter says.

The new man is talkative, but he's hard to understand. I pick up snippets, wondering if any of it pertains to me.

"Night of the living dead . . . Lies in disguise . . . Revelation, chapter nine . . . Lies in disguise . . ."

The man rambles on, growing loud and belligerent. If he keeps it up, the cops will hear him and come kick us out in the rain.

Sure enough, the doors from the police station open at around one in the morning. I hear the authoritative click of heels start across the Linoleum floor.

"You can't sleep here!" a woman barks.

It must be the sergeant.

"Let me see the chief," the new guy grumbles.

"I'm in charge here tonight. You gotta sleep somewhere else. People come in here and see you, they get scared. Not everyone who comes here is a criminal. There are some people who come here for legitimate reasons."

"Can't I just sit here, to avoid the elements?"

"How did you avoid the elements last night?"

"I slept in a friend's car at his apartment building."

"Well, I suggest you do the same tonight."

"He ain't there."

"My heart goes out to you, but you can't stay here."

A new voice enters the conversation.

"We get treated better by white people!" shouts the man with the lighter.

"Who is that talking behind that corner?" the sergeant snaps.

I hear the man with the lighter roll into the sergeant's view. He starts in about injustice, but the woman cuts him off.

"Who keeps the bathroom open for you? You get on out of here. I don't want to see you here again. You come back here when there's white folks working."

The two men gather their things and leave.

"You think this is funny," the talkative one says to the sergeant on his way out the door.

"No, I don't. I think it's sad. All the black people who died fighting for civil rights, and you ending up like this. . . ."

"Civil rights! Whatta you done for civil rights? I marched in Mississippi for civil rights! You ain't done nothin' for civil rights! Don't go talkin' to me 'bout civil rights! . . ."

The argument carries on out into the street. I listen through the closet wall. My fellow vagrants don't rat me out. When the sergeant walks back into the police station, I try to get some sleep.

It's not long before the two homeless men return. They try to keep quiet, but their voices echo like they were camping in the

Taj Mahal. The automatic door keeps swinging open as more bums stagger in. A few try the closet door. "Hey!" I shout over and over.

Finally the commotion is too great. The sergeant marches back into the lobby. This time she has help. The officers escort everybody out of the building. The night is again quiet. I breathe easy. Then somebody pushes on my door.

"Who is that in there?" the sergeant growls.

"Me."

"Who's 'me'?"

"Mike McIntyre."

"Come on out of there!"

I walk out of the closet rubbing my eyes. The sergeant glares at me. The officer who told me to crash in the closet stands behind her.

"How long you been in there?" the sergeant says.

"Since about ten," I say.

"What are you doing coming in and sleeping in the building without telling anyone you're here? You could be cited."

I don't tell her how I found the closet.

"Damn, he knows the building better than I do," the cop says with convincing amazement.

I drag my sleeping bag and pack out of the closet. I put on some dry socks and step back into my wet boots.

"Where are you from?" the sergeant says.

"California."

"California! And you end up in *Wilmington?*"

"Yep, it's the end of the line."

"California," she says, shaking her head.

It seems like a good time to laugh. And we do.

It has stopped raining when I leave the police station. I've got a few hours to kill before the post office opens. I walk down along the river. Wind whips clouds across a slate gray sky over water the color of gun metal.

I peer through the window of a news rack at today's paper. The lead headline is no surprise: It rained seven inches in twelve hours yesterday. A new record.

The only other story above the fold recounts a tragic incident in Chicago. Two youths dropped a five-year-old boy from a fourteenth-story window because he wouldn't steal candy for them.

I'm sickened to the core. I'm also racked with guilt. All of the time I've wasted in my life. The boredom, the despair. The false starts, and the times I never started at all. I may never get it right. But I'm still here. There is hope for me yet—and that now seems so unfair.

I grieve for the boy who will never see Cape Fear.

FORTY

The biggest scare on the Road to Cape Fear comes at the hands of the United States Postal Service.

"I'm sorry, sir, but nothing has arrived for you," the clerk at the Wilmington post office says when I reach the counter.

That's impossible, I tell him. Anne sent my ATM card by two-day priority mail. It should have arrived yesterday at the latest. The man shakes his head. He looks beyond me at the next person in line.

I worried this might happen, but I'm not prepared for the letdown. In my mind, the trip was over and I had already rejoined the world of solvency. I had only to touch the Atlantic Ocean, then it was going to be a straight shot to a cash machine, a motel room, a cheeseburger, and a plane ticket home. I've come penniless across America, but the journey won't end. I'm now facing two more days without money.

I ask the clerk to please take another look.

I want to jump the counter and hug him when he returns with the red, white, and blue envelope.

I place the envelope unopened in my pack and head for Cape Fear.

North Carolina has been bad for rides. I don't have the patience to wait. I also don't want to take any chances now that I'm so close. I decide to walk the last twelve miles.

I hike east on Market Street. It stretches more than fifty blocks—past fast food joints, gas stations, discount tire centers, cheap motels, and endless strip malls. It will be the last time on this trip that I'm malled by America.

The commercial area falls behind me and I continue east on Route 74. It starts to sprinkle. I tighten my shoulder straps and break into a run.

I'm flanked by a stand of pine trees. The side of the road is wide and flat. Sand appears in the grass, and I know I'm near the end.

But these last few miles become the hardest part of the journey. My thighs ache and my feet throb. I'm mentally exhausted. I have to stop. I sit atop the concrete railing of a bridge, gazing at the horizon of a place that now seems impossible to reach.

I once ran a marathon. Twenty-six point two miles. Until this trip, it was the biggest challenge of my life. What made the race especially tough was that I did not train for it. Up to that point, I had never run more than a mile. I went out and bought a new pair of shoes, and when the starter's gun fired, I simply put one foot in front of the other. After ten miles, it felt like I broke my left foot, so I started to favor it. After thirteen miles, it felt like I broke my right foot, so I favored it. I kept running. When I crossed the finish line, I was struck by two opposing thoughts: I always knew I was going to make it, yet I was amazed that I had.

It is in this fashion that I hobble into Cape Fear.

The first thing I notice is a bank. Then another, and another still. There is money everywhere. BMWs and Mercedes Benzes glide past me. White yachts cruise the intercoastal waterway. High-rise luxury condominiums tower above.

It is a funny spot to end a penniless journey.

The sky is gray but it has stopped raining. The few people on the beach are bundled up in coats. I am the only person with hiking boots and a backpack.

I walk down to the water, wind whipping sand in my face. A group of older women stroll by. I ask one if she will snap my picture, and I hand her my camera. She appears to be a tourist. From New York, if I had to guess. She wears gaudy jewelry and boasts enormous fake fingernails painted a loud purple.

The ocean is white with violence. It is a troubled surf. The waves look restless. Like me, they tossed and turned all night. It hasn't been an easy trip. But here we are at last, deposited by some unseen force onto this distant shore.

I strike a pose. There are no people in the background. No buildings. No boats. Only me and the endless sea.

"Try and capture the nothingness of it," I say to the woman taking my picture.

"The nothingness, huh? Okay."

Just as she is about to click the camera, three men appear behind her, walking down the beach. They sweep metal detectors over the sand. They are seeking treasure. I have to laugh.

It is not the last irony of the day.

A local historian tells me how Cape Fear got its name. When explorers discovered this coast in the 1500s, Latin was still the language of science. This bulge of land appeared on maps as "Cape Faire." When the maps were later transcribed into English, it became "Cape Fear." The scary name has no basis in reality, if this one explanation is to be believed. It was all a mistake.

The name is as misplaced as my own fears. I see now that I

have always been afraid of the wrong things. My great shame is not my fear of death, but my fear of life.

The final irony of the trip is also conveyed to me by the local historian:

Cape Fear does not exist. Not really.

When I spotted it on the map, I assumed it was a town. But it's not. Cape Fear is the name of a region in southeastern North Carolina. It's not one specific point. There is no such place as Cape Fear.

Cape Fear is nowhere—and everywhere.

I look to the west. Six weeks ago, I emptied my pockets of money and went looking for change. Somewhere along the way, I crossed over. I never found Cape Fear but I did find the place I was looking for: the point of no return. And though I know I will board a plane tomorrow for San Francisco, I also know I can never go back.

EPILOGUE

They called this country "Faire." It's been more than that.

On my way back into Wilmington, I tally the trip:

Four thousand two hundred twenty-three miles, fourteen states, eighty-two rides, seventy-eight meals, five loads of laundry, one round of golf—a million thanks.

I tremble before the money machine. Part of me is afraid my ATM card won't work. Another part of me is afraid it will.

I punch in the numbers and the money machine rumbles to life. It groans as it spits out a stack of twenties. I stuff the green wad in my pocket, feeling poor.

I buy a sack of fast food and check into a motel. In the morning, I fly back to San Francisco.

I know there is something wrong the second I see Anne.

I've stayed with strangers all across America. Now I feel like a stranger in my own home.

It seems that Anne has been on an inner journey of her own while I've been away. She has decided she wants to go it alone.

"I just want to be twenty-four again," she says.

I can't blame her. I'd like to be twenty-four again myself.

Life may not be too short, but it's short enough. I grab my travel alarm clock and wish Anne well.

I head for the place I feel most at home: the road.

Thanksgiving approaches. I don't know where I'll be this year, but I know I'll be grateful.

Wherever I am, I will remember my continental leap of faith—and the country that caught me.

ACKNOWLEDGMENTS

Good fortune led me to a few more kind strangers after this journey ended. I benefited greatly from the wisdom, perseverance and charm of my agent Katharine Kidde. I also was lucky to have the clever input of her associate Laura Langlie.

Many thanks to all the folks at Berkley who were willing to gamble on a proposal by an unknown author. I'm especially grateful to my editor, Elizabeth Beier, for her enthusiasm and support.

I owe a tremendous debt to Andrea Boyles, director of the Kite Street Artists Colony, who allowed me to complete the manuscript while I was still literally penniless.

Anne DeSchweinitz, Jerry Ellis and Deborah Jeanne McIntyre did not question my sanity when I chose to embark on this journey. Memories of their encouragement sustained me during the first scary days on the road to Cape Fear.

My deepest appreciation is reserved for the people who appear in these pages. I will forever be in awe of their generosity and trust. This book is a product of their efforts far more than mine.